SOUL JOURNEY TO THE EARTH

Seeds for a New Humanity

Christina Warmenbol

This book is dedicated

To all the sparks

Those that are hidden

and those that are shining bright

Those that are here

And those that are on their way

"Women hold the keys,
they are capable of transforming humanity."
- O.M. Aïvanhov

CONTENT

FOREWORD

A child coming into our world opens doors we cannot foresee. The calling from a child is the calling from a soul to put one foot into a world we forgot about. We were there ourselves, long ago. We forgot. We forgot where we came from. We forgot how we got here. We might have forgotten who we really are…

What did we come here to do? Do you remember? Would you like to remember?

What was it all about?

Stumbling into remembering, peeling off the layers, rediscovering the child within. That inner child wants to reach out to this soul that is calling you to become its parent. It knows how to do that. It wants you to trust. Let you be taken by its hand.

Maybe it leads you through a landscape of hidden memories, stacked hurts to shake off. Another layer peeled off, giving the space to one cell to change. In turn opening even more space for other cells to change.

Just as one single cell in the body changes and catalyzes change in other cells, so too can our personal choices influence the broader landscape around us.

Your change and your healing will have a ripple effect on the rest of the world. As Norton Juster expressed, "When a butterfly flaps its wings, a breeze goes round the world."

This book can give a simple but powerful idea about how to jumpstart the breeze around the world of regeneration, by welcoming the new inheritors of the earth as our children, the way we would welcome a prince or princess into our midst. A prince or princess of the soul, a divine seed from Source.

Changing humanity one child at a time.

Geoffrey Hodson said it like this:

Uplift the women of your race till all are seen as queens,
and to such queens, let every man be a king,
that each may honour each, seeing the other's royalty.
Let every home, however small, become a court,
every son a knight, every child a page.
Let all treat all with chivalry, honouring in each
their royal parentage, their kingly birth
for there is royal blood in every man
all are the children of the KING.

CHAPTER 1

INTRODUCTION

"It is easier to build strong children than to repair broken men." - Frederick Douglas

Every soul comes to the earth with the silent desire to radiate its pure essence into the world. They secretly wish to be seen as the shining diamonds they are. "Perhaps you do too?"

From the moment of conception, they hope to be cared for, connected to their parents, loved, and discovered. This new human being relies completely on their parents' benevolence, and they give themselves over in complete trust as they take form in the secluded space of the womb.

Maybe they want to bring their warmth to the world, to love all that lives. Maybe they aspire to become a healer, or to be an inventor, a musician, a teacher with a deep understanding of their students, a scientist whose discoveries help humanity evolve…

Will the doors open to them? Will they find recognition, connection, understanding and support? Will they be able to unfurl their talents, to blossom and realize their full potential? Will Mom and Dad honour the needs of their body, heart, mind, and soul?

Socrates taught that "the beginning is the most important of any work, especially in dealing with anything young and tender."

Most parents are ready to prepare on the physical level what is best for their baby and decide to eat healthier, change habits like smoking and substance abuse or eliminate alcohol consumption.

Suddenly, life changes completely for them, excited as they are to follow the growth of their unborn baby. They may wonder how they can contribute even more to be there for their baby with all its needs, wishes, and expectations. Integrating this new life into their established adult existence is not always easy; it can be challenging.

Science has affirmed what ancient cultures have always known: that the beginning of life, from pre-conception through gestation, birth, and the first year, lays the foundation for adult life. The unborn baby is an aware mini-human being. His mother's thoughts and feelings program his subconsciousness. Both parents, and particularly the mother during pregnancy, have a tremendous impact on the quality of this growing life through their lifestyle choices, feelings, and thoughts.

However, the ecology of the womb encompasses more than the physical elements the parents want to avoid: it goes beyond pollution, junk food, or noise.

Pollution can manifest in other forms: ongoing stress, concealed depression, unresolved conflicts, unhealed trauma, or fear towards the upcoming birth or this new life as a mother. Unless consciously transformed, these negative influences can leave lasting imprints on the baby.

The situation in the world today draws a picture of higher rates of suicide, addiction and drug overdose and mental health issues such as depression and anxiety, feelings of loneliness and disconnection. We see also a rise of autism, ADHD and chronic illness in children. The roots of these issues can often be found in early life and even before birth.

Science established the link between stress and difficult situations the pregnant mother goes through and the effect on the baby regarding a healthy neurological and emotional development of the baby. But if negative emotions can have such an impact, the positive emotions will also shape the life of the baby as they absorb the patterns of their mother's experiences. So, why not explore ways to prepare before conception and resolve past hurts? Transform beliefs of unworthiness into self-worth, feelings of powerlessness into empowerment? Helplessness into self-trust? Connecting with your authentic self so you can deeply connect to the soul of this radiant new human being? "Your child's first classroom is the womb," said David Chamberlain. It already learns many things: how you think, how you resolve conflict, how you love yourself and others and how you relate and engage with the world. There are countless ways for your child to learn from the authentic you, rooted in love.

Your child deserves to encounter the genuine you as their parent. Do you want to meet this authentic you beforehand, before inviting a soul into your life? This is crucial so you can avoid many complications, conflicts, misunderstandings, and failure. But even more important, it is crucial for your little one. Failure to address unresolved issues before conception risks burdening your child with your emotional baggage.

And don't worry: even if you cleared everything you encountered in yourself before conception—confronting every upheaval, every turmoil—life will still present its share of challenges during parenthood. But it will not be overwhelming. You'll know how to deal with it as you went into the habit of being present to yourself and transforming your issues.

This book leads you through the realm of our deepest essence: the soul. It is that essence that helped me grow quicker through a difficult period in my life. It is also that soul-essence that can be the efficient key for healing. So what *is* the soul? How does it incarnate and manifest in us as human being? How can we give it attention and what happens if we ignore it? How does it play a role in the regeneration of humanity?

I invite you to discover the answers as well as sources of inspiration through beauty, harmony, uplifting feelings, and creative thoughts that will affect each cell of your baby and imprint patterns of love, resilience, and integrity as the foundation for the rest of its life.

The Dream of a New Tomorrow

"It is necessary to create a new being with a maximal power of love."

- Michel Odent, OB-GYN

Humanity is waking up to the call to evolve. The dream of a new tomorrow is taking root in the hearts and minds of countless individuals. Never was the need to reinvent society so urgent and so clear. The current system is in dire need of rejuvenation. The structures are antiquated and crumbling across all facets of society— economic, political, legal, medical, and educational. New structures are what society needs.

However, these new structures need to be made by balanced people who are grounded in honesty, integrity, and nobility. People who have as much as possible healed their past and aspire to evolve towards a higher consciousness based on love, collaboration, compassion, and wisdom: there is an immense need for souls of this caliber.

In recent years, a multitude of advanced souls with elevated vibrations desire to incarnate on Earth. These souls are highly evolved and ready to bring harmony, peace, love, and wisdom to the Earth. They live in the purest truth.

However, there are not many parents adequately prepared to assume the role of parents to these souls. They wish to find parents who are aware of the impact they have on their unborn children, enabling them to nurture and cultivate the rich talents these souls possess.

They need awakened parents who have been able to free themselves from the negative aspects of their start in life and the limited perceptions they have of themselves and of the world. They need parents who live authentically. A parent who has connected to their essence and tries to manifest it consciously is best equipped to recognize and help to manifest this pure essence of their child.

Nowadays, preparations for childbirth revolve primarily around medical and financial considerations, often neglecting the inner world of the future parent. However, it is that inner you that will need to deal with life's challenges and that will need to keep up with what life wants from you: balancing work, motherhood, relationships, and navigating through a time of change can be overwhelming. We have the choice between survival mode or surfing the waves of growth. Consciously undertaking to prepare before conception puts you on the road toward inner freedom, harmony and love and so will your child.

Pregnancy under these circumstances is a celebration where both parents can cultivate the most inspiring thoughts, feelings and activities to nourish this precious soul that is taking shape as a baby.

Throughout this book, we will see how the soul that is coming from a world of light, morphs into a fetus, absorbing an abundance of information about life, the world, relationships, music, language, and more.

This prenatal education is nothing like the forced learning we had in school. Learning goes on all the time, even if the mother does nothing special. The fetus absorbs unconsciously what the mother experiences. Why not make it a *conscious* endeavor, steering this learning toward the development of a resilient, joyful, and healthy child?

Parents who invest in this prenatal education have children who are happier, calmer, and show more respect, maturity, and consciousness compared to their peers.

Have you heard the call to become that parent, that beacon of love and stability for your offspring as you orient yourself toward this bright new life? Allow yourself to align with the vibration of these beautiful souls to the best of your ability. Life may present a myriad of challenges—balancing work, family, relationships, and household responsibilities can feel overwhelming—but every small step is important.

The dream of tomorrow starts at the beginning of life: in the womb. Conscious future parents are the key. They can bring the world a step further. One baby at a time.

CHAPTER 2

MY STORY

Letting Go

At 36 years old, I had finally found the love of my life! If you had been with me in May in Western Canada, you'd have seen the earth in full bloom, with the trees dressed in subtle green and exploding with blossoms. In this gorgeous setting, we married.

Yves, with his brown piercing eyes, possessed not only a sharp intellect but also a profound humility, a loving heart, and an indomitable will. I couldn't believe it—me, feeling so insignificant and small, to be wedded to the man hailed as a hero, having conquered Mount Everest as the first alpinist of Québec.

Just half a year before, I had made the leap from Belgium, where I grew up, to settle in Canada. At 21, I had graduated as an Occupational Therapist. However, my interest went to the beginning of life, which was a promising field to work in a preventive rather than curative way. I had already understood the critical importance of the nine months before birth, when the baby's mind and body are built and programmed. I was more motivated to work in this direction and was passionate about bringing this information to the public. I read all the books I could put my hands on.

I wanted to work with pregnant mothers, but there was no training yet to be found. I embarked on a journey of self- education, exploring modalities such as sophrology (auto- hypnosis), naturopathy, prenatal singing and energy healing. After many years, I was invited to start a prenatal class. I was inventing the profession of Childbirth Educator because nobody in the 90s in Belgium was taking care of pregnant women to make them aware of the importance of the prenatal period. Midwives didn't have the time for education and physiotherapists only gave physical exercises to pregnant women. I was a pioneer as a Childbirth Educator, even more so because I dedicated half of the prenatal class to singing to uplift and energize the parents and the baby. I was very successful and gave courses in several different cities in the northern Dutch speaking part of Belgium. I was the president of the Dutch part of the Association for Prenatal Education and organized conferences and seminars.

After a few years, I felt a need for change. Canada called me because of the like-minded professionals working towards a similar goal. There I was, a few months later, married in Western Canada.

As we felt the presence of a soul wanting to incarnate, Yves and I embarked on a journey of preparation, undertaking fasting, meditation, and clearing family history. I encountered a lingering internal block rooted in feelings of unworthiness, traced back to my prenatal experiences. I knew that any uncleared limiting beliefs would affect the baby. It would unconsciously take it all over, and that was not what we wanted. Determined to address this, we travelled to Quebec, where I pursued certification as a Therapist of

Intra-Uterine Life. Through this process, I not only confronted my prenatal wounds but also supported Yves in navigating his childhood traumas.

Right after the end of the course, Yves wanted to try out a new expedition in Western Canada. Together with three other adventurers, they wanted to reach the summit of a mountain in British Columbia, Canada, which had never been climbed, Mount Hope. It was a small summit for Yves, as he was used to climbing higher mountains. Yves was the leader of the mountaineering part of the expedition. The climb was not difficult, even if they had to make a path for themselves through the dense vegetation to reach the top at 9,000 feet.

They had to come back over the river Incomapleux that serpentines at the foot of the mountain. It was a pristine jungle, and there was no road towards the foot of the mountain. They had been brought to the foot of the mountain by helicopter to start their trip, but picking them up after their mountain trip wasn't possible for the pilot, nor any pilot.

The month of July became fire season, and all the helicopter pilots were asked to stand by and help extinguish the fires. They were not allowed to make personal trips for clients. Because of that, the expedition team needed boats to come back over the river which joined a big lake at the end, Upper Arrow Lake. The river was never completely navigated. That didn't seem to frighten the leader of the second part of the expedition, Marc. They had inflatable kayaks, so they could be taken into the helicopter to the foot of the mountain.

They made it to the top as the first climbers to have reached the summit.

When the time came to return over the river with the inflatable kayaks, they were seated, two by two, in each kayak. The climbing gear, tents, sleeping bags, and food were all stowed at the back. They navigated cautiously, pausing periodically to assess the upcoming stretch of the river. However, there was a tricky section beyond the river bend they couldn't anticipate. They left off anyway.

The water was tumultuous. They capsized. Very cold glacier water chilled them to the bone within minutes.

We waited for them at the lake, camping and looking out for them.

We didn't know what had happened. We didn't know that the beaver dams had been destroyed in the mountain rivers and lakes to provide enough water for the firefighting helicopters. We didn't know that the river's water level had been going up by eight feet, making it Olympic level to navigate. We waited and hoped for the best... until we decided to seek help.

The whole story of the Search and Rescue is too long for this book. But the two weeks of searching were two weeks of miracles. The only miracle that didn't happen was to find the 3 missing adventurers. One, Martin, was rescued. The boats and the life vests were found, empty and distorted. No bodies, no survivors other than Martin.

Acceptance was out of the question, so we persisted in the search. I made a vow to myself: I would not leave until we found answers. I needed closure.

So we continued until the seventeenth day. That was the day that, in a vision, it became clear to me that Yves stood at the end of a tunnel, ready to embrace the light. We never found their bodies.

I was still numb to the fact that he was gone. But the sight of his belongings at home, waiting for his return, was a painful coming to the evidence.

WHY? WHY ME? The normal question. Why do you do this to me? Revolt, non-acceptance, grief. The world had turned inside out.

Then some elements surfaced that had prepared me subconsciously. The Chinese proverb: "There is only one constant in the universe, and that is that everything changes." I had heard it ten years before. It resonated with profound truth. Do not cling to anything in life.

An astrologer had warned me, "Always keep a sleeping bag on the foot of your bed." Life can change in an instant, making it necessary to adapt, adjust, or leave. Don't anchor yourself to the situation you are in, I understood.

And then, memories of past lives surfaced. For some people they are the collective unconscious manifesting in me. Anyways, I recalled a lifetime when I was wealthy and pregnant. My husband was a knight who left for a battle. He didn't return. I was desperate. Desperation led me to end my life when my child was barely a year old.

Half a year before the accident I revisited another past life as a young Inuit woman. My husband of that life left with a kayak on an icy river and didn't come back. He slipped under a piece of ice and I wasn't able to rescue him. The lack of emotional support from my community left me battered and depleted.

These memories haunted me during the search for Yves and his friends. I hoped that I had learned enough from these experiences this time to avoid repeating them.

I understood that there was a pattern here—a karmic cycle. After two decades of spiritual exploration, I realized there was a profound lesson to be learned. It wasn't just about understanding the past, but I also had to develop resilience and strength to deal with the loss of my husband this time.

The incessant questions WHY? WHY ME? were getting answers. They rose from the depths of my subconscious. They unsettled me and woke up resistance. I heard from my whispering inner voice: 'There is something to learn, something to develop. That is why. It calmed me down. I knew then and there that there was a purpose in this life experience. It came up again: 'Why? Why me?' I explained again: 'There is something to learn, to pay, or to develop.' It happened over and over. Again and again, it came to the surface, dealing with the revolt. And again, I explained. I taught my suffering unconscious and subconscious, my inner underworld that there was a reason, that I needed to be courageous this time and learn what my soul wanted me to learn and develop. Until the questions didn't come up anymore. Focussing on that message lifted me up. It healed and brought me to acceptance.

Pregnant!

While all this was going on, I discovered that I was pregnant. The stretching of my uterus and the absence of my periods told me I had to come to a conclusion. Yves left an incredible legacy in the form of an incarnating soul, growing within me. I welcomed this new life with open arms, but I was sad that the baby would never see his dad. Our child would never know his father's love and attention, which every child needs so much.

Not long after that, I had a dream in which I saw two baby boys each in their cradle, each holding a quartz crystal in their hands. My God, two babies! Could I handle that?

I then understood that probably one of them had left during the cramps I had felt during the search and rescue period. Cramps of my periods without a lot of blood. I had thought: 'Maybe because of the stress I don't bleed as much this time'. No, it was the twin leaving. The physician had me listen to the evidence of the heartbeat! One heartbeat: there was only one.

I knew that stress and negative circumstances, like depression or anxiety, would deeply affect the baby and program it for life. The baby could take over my depression - if I would develop that - or have developmental, learning or behavioral problems. I knew all about what the baby goes through in utero but how can I cope with that all by myself? I had some support, but this was so special.

I was dealing with numbness, non-acceptance, daunting sadness, and distress. Curiously, crying never lasted long. After a few minutes, a fountain of loving, healing energy in myself sprang up. Where did it come from? From the light beings that were helping the growing baby? From the soul of my baby? It is still a mystery.

I tried to be the best I could in the circumstances, going through the grief process, clearing all the revolt and the mourning while trying to bond with my baby, giving him all my love so he would not feel like a victim.

I had the insight that I was a soul in evolution over several lifetimes. My soul had chosen this situation so I could learn not to be a victim and to accept what life throws at me. If I go against it, I block my path.

I gave myself time to digest as I didn't want to spoil his coming into this earth through a teardrop valley. In steps, I went through the whole grief process. I didn't want to run away from confrontation with the memories of Yves. Little by little I brought myself to listen to recordings of his voice, of the many interviews he had done on radio and television. I visited all the special places where we had been together, feeling the pain of the loss, but also remembering the love, the attention, the happiness of the relationship and the closeness. I streamed tears of gratefulness.

Forgiveness. Coming to forgiveness. If everything is healed, forgiveness is the end of all suffering. I was able to forgive him from the deepest level of my soul.

Difficulties invite us to grow, just getting stronger, wiser, and more in contact with our hearts. Yves opened my heart to the feeling of deserving love during his life with me. I didn't feel I deserved to be loved. I felt small and insignificant. He has healed me from this unworthiness. He had opened the door to deserving to be loved. After his passing, I remembered what my teacher taught: that unconditional love can be found everywhere in the universe and in nature, not only in a relationship. Gradually I found that path. I am just enormously grateful that Yves had opened the door to the knowing that I deserved love. Love that I was able to find after his passing in the huge temple of nature.

We are still in contact. The line of the heart, the rainbow-coloured bridge between him and me, is still operating, sending and receiving love. There were days I couldn't feel it—too much sadness. I knew it was me closing the gateway with a curtain of self-pity and sorrow. I managed to open the curtain by receiving the sorrow and crying.

Years later, I found The Journey method developed by Brandon Bays and was able to clear further this unworthiness so I could enhance my ability to bring to the world what I have to bring. I became a Certified Journey Practitioner.

About fifteen years later, I got the message from a sensitive person that Yves and I had made a soul contract: he would leave early - he was 47 - but he would stay in contact to tell me about the other world. Well, I needed some help to be sure that this contact with him or the other world was no fantasy of mine. That led me to discover the Akashic Records and become a Certified Akashic Record Reader through the help of my teacher, Lisa Barnett.

When I look back, it all makes sense. My soul had planned to make this happen, all the suffering, learning, and transformation. My Higher Self guided me to the right people at the right moment to become who I am now, realizing my task in life and gaining and developing important qualities and skills. Without these unfortunate happenings, I wouldn't have done that.

Knowing that there was a purpose, a higher level of development to attain, an ideal that my Higher Self had in store for me was an incredible force that lifted me up. It helped me in the fight of climbing the mountain that was presented to me to come to an inner balance, to a higher form of inner harmony.

My son is now 20 years old and as a child, he had always been quite mature, intelligent and balanced. So, it is possible to find resources to make the best out of all circumstances that life offers.

Certainly, spirituality in my life has trained me to see reality beyond the veil of illusion, being ready to find the truth, even if that's hard for the ego.

Thanks to all the evolved beings who have been on my path and who have helped me tremendously, I was able to grow through it all and be of service to those who want to transform their lives, either for themselves or to be conscious parents.

Growing through my grief process

What has helped me through the grief process is a mix of elements: my inner work, together with some mitigating circumstances that supported me tremendously through the ordeal. Not that it was easy though!

1. My preparation through 20 years of spirituality was a shock breaker. It helped me to connect to the world of serenity and love through which you create a bumper that allows you to mitigate the shocks of life.

2. Spiritual teachings taught me that we, as souls, choose our own difficult passages to grow. I knew about a few past lives that had created some karmic life lessons. The knowledge that my soul had chosen this experience helped me to accept more quickly what I needed to learn and to develop the resources I needed.

3. The questions "Why?" "Why me?" and "Why do you do this to me?" came to the surface with all the emotions. I had already worked with emotions before, being open to them and learning to transform them. I informed my deep subconscious that there was something to learn, to let go. These questions found their answer in the knowing that I needed to develop resiliency, strength, hope and humble acceptation to learn what my own Higher Self had planned to learn. Every time these questions came up, I informed them. It happened over and over again until the questions didn't come up anymore.

4. I had just finished my training in Therapy of Intra-Uterine Life, where I also cleared deep sitting blocks. One great help was

working around the experience of separation we all go through when we come as souls to this earth: separation from my twin soul, the soul deeply connected with me. He was staying behind in the other realm. Because of having worked through that deep hurt, all other "separation events" are made less difficult. That helped me tremendously to heal the 'separation' with my husband. I felt that there was no real separation: it was there only on the physical level, but not on the inner plane.

Another trained Therapist of Intra-Uterine Life coached me to guide me in the healing process during the pregnancy and to alleviate the trauma my unborn son went through.

5. Cultivating gratitude was an immense help. I listened to all the audio and video recordings of the interviews with Yves to confront myself with who he was. I visited certain places where we had been together and let the emotions of sadness come up but also the gratitude for all these precious moments and the love they had generated.

6. I lived and still live in an intentional community where we meditate, sing, pray, and work together each day, which was a huge support. It would have been very different if I had lived alone and isolated in an apartment in a big city. Some special moments were organized with the women of the center to uplift, inspire, and energize this precious work of bringing a baby into this world.

CHAPTER 3

THE SOUL

'The Soul is the essence that is wearing a human form." –

Anonymous

The Soul Has Been Crushed: Archeology of the Soul

Life is an unending journey to find our essence. This essence hides behind a veil. A curtain separates us from the real world. How can we find our essence and be able to accompany another human being who wants to discover its essence also?

Look behind the curtain. Your soul is waiting. Once we look behind the curtain and find the soul, it needs to be pulled from under the rubble. It has been oppressed for so long.

It is that part of yourself that has never been taken seriously. It is not something you can grasp, smell, taste, see or hear. It is very subtle, but if we don't listen to it, we are unhappy, depressed or we become ill. So the soul is down under a mountain of rubble, disavowal and hurt. It is starving.

How do we meet it again? How do we restore it? Respect it? Honour it? By sensing the undercurrent of our life. It is in your hands. Nobody can do it for you. Staying still, coming to a halt. Getting off the hamster wheel. Listening, feeling, greeting the real you that might have another face than the one you want to show the world. Take away the armor that protected you from finding the real you.

It takes bravery to break free from the confines of societal norms and to confront the suppressed parts of your being: the ones that were silenced and controlled to avoid rejection or judgment. Enhance your self-awareness by listening to your inner voice, like you would to a distressed child. You are the adult. You are compassionate, you are in control.

Go towards the pain and meet it. Surround it with acceptance and love. It has been there long enough. It frankly wants to be seen and healed. This pain is the dust on your diamond. The diamond is hidden. It can't shine. Meet the dust, blow it away. The soul is the diamond, the one that wishes to be discovered.

Maybe a kind of help is needed to come through this process, but it is an absolute necessity if you want to be a whole person who is hiding nothing from yourself and the world. It is called 'being authentic'.

Listen to the stream
Of unbridled connection
Connection to the trees
To the flowers
To the bees
Extracting the treasures of love
Of life and bubbling energy
From all you meet
In synergy with nature

What is the Soul?

> *The soul is infinite, eternal, unbounded. Water cannot wet it, fire cannot burn it, and weapons cannot shatter it.*
>
> *Unborn, it does not die with the death of the body. It is without beginning and without ending.* - From de Bhagavad Gita

According to the Merriam-Webster Dictionary, the soul is the immaterial essence, the animating principle in a living being. In therapeutic circles, the term 'non-local consciousness' is used.

Popular language speaks about the word "soul" in many expressions: "a soulful interpretation" and "soulless actions". "He is the soul of the organization", "There wasn't a soul to be seen", "soul-searching", and "soul-stirring music."

What is the soul? It is the subtle presence that animates us, guides us and brings us higher up. It gives this feeling of being connected to our deepest self. We can compare that feeling between two situations: you have accomplished a task, a job, a paid job that doesn't really interest you. You feel ok, you've earned some money. But if you have had the chance to accomplish a task or a job that really makes you feel fulfilled, deeply happy, even if it was difficult, it is your soul that gives you this happy feeling. The soul says: " *That* was what I wanted you to do."

We are all running after happiness, don't we? So if the connection with the soul brings happiness, why not finding out what this soul essence is all about?

Somebody is 'the soul of a company'. How would it be if this person is not there anymore? It feels very empty: this person was animating the company, guiding it, knowing where to go and how to do it.

As we are immersed in a material world, we have lost contact with that presence of the soul: life feels empty.

If there are these fugitive moments of fulfillment and deep happiness, why not looking in the possibilities to make these moments more frequent, so we can at the end of our lives feel accomplished: that means that we have realized, manifested the deeper essence of ourselves: our soul. We have enriched our soul and that enrichment is what we leave the earth with.

Even more so in our task as a parent to accompany a new human fellow: how different would it be if we could see this tiny body rather as the embodiment of a soul?

During my studies in occupational therapy in the 1980s, I was intrigued by a course titled "Science of the Soul." However, to my surprise, it was later changed to "Psychology." This shift left me with a lingering question: Why did the concept of the soul seem to disappear from the academic discourse?

Soul or Psyche?

> *"What has not been linked to the soul*
> *is an illusion."* – O.M. Aïvanhov

The word "Psyche" is the Greek word for "Soul," as in Greek mythology, Psyche was the Goddess of the soul. The original meaning of "soul" has now been reduced to "mind". The soul aspect has been relegated to religion. But there also, the true reality of the soul is not portrayed.

Although the ancient Greek philosophers like Plato and Aristotle were convinced of the existence of the soul, today the world of science does not accept the existence of the soul anymore. Objective science uses observation to study a subject. It is not possible to study the soul with our five senses. It can only be perceived or experienced by an inner perception. That is why science has chosen to change the study of the soul to the study of the psyche, which means the mind. There is a world of difference between the two. Psychology studies the mind and behavior of a human being: its emotions, thoughts and motives. It is the world of conscious and unconscious behavior, which is in itself an immense and important field.

Nevertheless, the science of the soul is also a legitimate science based on very ancient knowledge received through experience and inner perception. It studies the higher states of consciousness. The science of quantum physics is now on the road to confirming this thousand years old wisdom.

Dr. Anna Yusim is a psychiatrist working at Yale University. She tells her story of searching for the science of the soul. She explains that psychiatry can be translated as either the science of the soul or the science of the mind and most people translate it as "mind." But it could also be translated as the science of the soul. She says: "As a psychiatrist, I am supposed to be treating the soul, not just the mind. But in all my schooling the word "soul" had not been mentioned once. But what is the "soul"? I travelled the world in search of the concept of the soul, how other cultures use it in healing and what exactly it means. It took me to two ashrams in India, to Buddhist meditation in Thailand, working with different shamans in South Africa and South America. My favorite definition came from Francesco Broca, a shaman. He says that the soul is comprised of two parts. The first part is our interconnectedness to all and the second part is the unique set of talents, skills, abilities and interests: your uniqueness."[1]

The psyche or the mind is the product of one lifetime. In cultures where spirituality is still very much part of life, the soul is an eternal being whose evolution stretches over many lifetimes.

Indeed, to be able to manifest this deepest essence of the soul, we need to learn so much and it is impossible to do that in one lifetime. Just as it is impossible to accomplish in one day everything a company needs to be done. You come back the next day and continue. In this way, at the end of a life when we feel tired, worn out, we leave the earth and come back to continue.

Dr. Brian Weiss, psychiatrist and Chairman Emeritus of Psychiatry at the Mount Sinai Medical Center in Miami, discovered past life memories through a spontaneous regression of his client, who through this approach was able to heal from anxiety, panic attacks and phobias. He states: "There is far too much about the human mind that is beyond our comprehension."[2]

The concept of the immortality of the soul, which comes back in cycles to the earth to continue its development, has been accepted as a reality in many ancient cultures. We have all had experiences like a "déjà-vu": such as being certain to know somebody without having seen him. Strongly being attracted or repulsed by somebody, or being very curious about having met someone, even superficially, that leaves a mark in your memory. Remembering a town where you have never been; you could navigate the roads as if you had been living there forever. My son Omael, when he was about four years old, watching a movie spoken in Hindi, exclaimed: "This is my language, Mommie!"

Dr. Ian P. Stevenson was a Canadian-born American psychiatrist, the founder and director of the Division of Perceptual Studies at the University of Virginia School of Medicine. He was a professor at this University for fifty years. His extensive research with 3,000 cases of children remembering their past lives points to the evidence of reincarnation, because of the correspondences between their memories and retrievable facts.

Let's look for occurrences where the soul plays an important role. Near Death Experiences or NDE's are one of these mysteries where a person who is clinically dead can see what physicians are doing and hear what they say while they see themselves floating to the ceiling.

Next to NDEs or remembering past lives, we can find phenomena like telepathy, intuition, prophetic dreams, premonition, empathic consciousness, communication with supernatural forces, and synchronicity. These are all phenomena and skills that testify to the sensory development of the soul and point to the soul's capacities.

> *"The intuitive mind is a sacred gift and the rational mind is a faithful servant. We have created a society that honours the servant and has forgotten the gift."* -
> Albert Einstein

Lisa Renée expresses the damaging effects of the exclusion of the soul in modern life:

'**To intentionally disconnect the existence of the mind from the existence of the soul is extremely destructive and damaging to all human beings.** This fact is what contributes to the manifestation of disconnected and chronically miserable people who intentionally create harm without moral conscience."[3]

According to the science of the soul, the soul is part of the human being: you are made of a body, a soul and a spirit.

> *You don't have a soul,*
> *you ARE a soul and you have a body.*

Human Evolution: Self-Centered or Soul-Centered?

"The world of the five senses is not the true reality. The true reality is the one of the soul and the spirit" - O.M.Aïvanhov

Gradually, over the last hundreds of years, the soul has been taken out of the equation. We have disconnected from it by more and more growing roots in the material world. We left the subtle world of the spirit behind, and we oriented only toward the outer world. The inner world dried up, and we became disconnected from it. In human evolution, we developed the intellect through the five senses. We sought satisfaction only through the external world, through these five senses.

We looked at the world asking what we could get from it, how it could serve us. It became our self-centered way of life. We became identified with the material world. Having and possessing was the goal. Ultimately, we felt very limited and stuck in a prison. It became impossible to reach lasting happiness.

With the development of the intellect, a wish was born for independence and freedom. But in that process, humanity has disconnected itself from the Source or God. That is why we struggle with separation from the world of unity we come from. We feel isolated and lonely, thinking we are alone in our struggle on earth. The wish for freedom and independence pushed human beings to disobey divine law. The next step is to reconnect and respect again Universal or Divine law.

Now humanity is rediscovering spirituality, wanting to reconnect again to a higher world, to God or Source. The only way back is through the connection with our soul. Simply by "being", instead of only "having" or "doing." We are invited to live a soul-centered life, instead of a self-centered life. Which one is most fulfilling, according to you?

Disconnected

Have you ever cried without cause? It is the deep yearning that calls us back to reconnect with our soul essence, with Source. When we find ourselves in the depths of unhappiness, feeling abandoned or isolated, it's a sign that we've lost touch with our soul. The suffering we experience is not a product of the soul, but a consequence of our disconnection from it. The illusion of separation is a significant obstacle we must overcome in our journey. This suffering is our soul's plea for attention, for reconnection, for recognition of its existence, so we can finally hear its voice. The soul, like the spirit, is unbreakable.

Our tendency to focus on the external, material world often hinders our journey to reconnect with our soul. Additionally, unresolved pain, a victim mentality, and anything that weighs us down can also act as barriers. Feelings of unworthiness, jealousy, sadness, revenge, pride, and daily concerns can cloud our connection to the higher realm of the soul.

Michael Newton states, "Fear arises when we separate ourselves from our spiritual power." Fear now dominates much of our lives: fear for survival, fear of rejection, of not being loved, etc.

If we are not conscious of the existence of the soul, we remain disconnected from life-sustaining energy. We lack support, regeneration and ways to transform life's difficulties. Without consciousness of the soul, it will be impossible to manifest the perfection of the divine world on this earth, which is the goal our soul strives for. So we need to understand its essence, its function and why Source has given us a soul.

What is the Soul all About?

A woman tells her partner: "I'd like to have a baby." Well, this baby will become a full-grown human being who carries a soul. Knowing the nature of the soul is crucial if we want to invite a soul to build a body in the womb! We cannot talk about the soul without talking about the spirit. What is the difference? Even in some spiritual traditions, these two concepts have been mixed up.

The spirit, the divine spark that created us, wishes to manifest through the body. It wishes to manifest the perfection of the divine world on the physical level. The spirit cannot do that directly because of its high frequency. It is very subtle, too far away from the density of matter to reach the body. The spirit needs a mediator, which is the soul. The soul energy is closer to earth matter. Therefore, the soul needs to be the intermediate between them. As a comparison, the sun can erode the rocks on the beach but only through the action of the wind that acts upon the water. The water waves sweep endlessly over the rocks. In this way a very subtle influence - the warmth of the sun - becomes powerful in affecting matter through its action on the air: the wind - which is less subtle – makes the water - even less subtle - sweep over the dense matter of the rocks. The water erodes it and smooths it out, sculpting its artwork in the rock. In the same way, the spirit can have a deep effect on the body, but only through an intermediary: the soul.

The soul animates the body. It is the funnel for sustaining life energy and is connected to the Divine Source of Life. At death, the soul is removed, and a lifeless body remains.

The "motor" or essence of the soul is love, unconditional love. Love is capable of elevating vibrations, thoughts, and feelings. The soul is the spring that nourishes our being, the love that bubbles up endlessly, coming from another realm than human love.

The power of the soul comes from its submission to the Spirit: it perceives, accepts, absorbs and transmits the impulses coming from higher up.

How can we Find our Soul Again?

We can discover our soul again if the need to find ourselves again is intense enough. In a profound search for deeper meaning, we are pushed to explore the path of self-discovery. It goes further than trying to understand our emotions and qualities and finding ways to cope with difficulties in life. Even when we have done all that, we can still feel that something is missing.

A need for connection to the universally present life energy puts us eventually on the path of spirituality. Wanting to look through the outside forms of beings and nature to find the subtle life beyond is what is calling us to spirituality. Observing, feeling into, peeling away the layer of appearances and the outer world to find the essence. This is the realm of the soul. Finding this realm again is eternally gratifying. What can be in the way is everything the ego brings us. We cannot find this realm if we are too conditioned by the intellect or too extinguished by heavy emotions that pull us down. Or we may become numb to the world because it is too difficult to cope with life's challenges. We first need to clear that all out. Only the inextinguishable, unquenchable yearning to find freedom and happiness deep in us can light the spark of recognition of the soul.

We can connect to the soul through mindfulness: it is a way of knowing at each moment what we feel, what we think and in which direction it brings us. Towards happiness or unhappiness? Towards harmony or disharmony? Stillness, prayer, meditation and contemplation help us on the path of connection to the soul.

How do we know that we are in contact or in harmony with the soul? When we feel we are in our element, we feel we are on the right path by doing what our soul wants from us. We feel deeply fulfilled and a profound joy, even ecstasy.

When we allow the stream of Source energy, of pure love that transcends our self-centeredness, to flow through us, we open ourselves to abundance. This is the essence of Source: a boundless, giving force.

What is Food for the Soul?

Once we find the soul, where can we find food to nurture it? The soul doesn't like to be limited; it feels constrained in the physical body or when we focus on our small personality. It needs limitlessness. It needs immense open spaces, like the prairies in the middle provinces of Canada, where the open flat space of the earth blends into the immensity of the sky. Or where you cannot find the separation, where the waters of the ocean roll into the space of the firmament.

Meditation can bring us into this state of immensity and expansion or it can be reached by cultivating uplifting thoughts, feelings and actions. You can feel your soul living intensely by nourishing noble, altruistic, generous feelings and actions. When you are ready to sacrifice something of yourself, you nourish your soul. In contemplating a higher world of unconditional love energy, we make the soul happy and expanded. Opening to the vastness of the universe is where the soul recognizes itself. It steps out of the borders of its limited, separate self and dissolves in the limitlessness of the cosmos. When we can reach ecstasy – not through drugs but through meditation – we are immersed in the realm of the soul. We then encounter the light beings of love whom we can invite through prayer to come and help us elevate our feelings, thoughts and actions daily.

By simply creating an ambiance of love, harmony, and peace, we nourish the deepest essence of our soul. Everything beautiful in music, dance, art, or inspired poetry elevates us to the splendour of this soul realm.

What is the Soul Like?

> *"The soul has such majesty that it is beyond description"* - Michael Newton

Sensitive people can perceive the soul as an oval-shaped light with two poles: one higher up, connecting to the spirit and one pole on the lower end connecting to the personality and the body.

The light of the soul is not the same as the light of the aura. The aura is to the soul what the skin is to the body: its functions are protection, sensitivity and connection to the outer world. So, the aura is the outer layer of the soul, like the skin is the outer layer of our body.

The soul is the connector in two directions: it circulates energies from the spirit to the body and from the body to the spirit.

By the first movement, from the spirit to the body, the soul is the extension of the spirit, a transformer or a translator. It is a funnel that brings life force into the body by animating it. It funnels in consciousness, inspiration and life force. It reveals itself through these revelations. 'Revelation is the disclosure of the soul," says Ralph Waldo Emerson.

In the second movement, from the body to the spirit, the soul not only elevates the body's matter by making it lighter, more subtle, and transparent but also serves as a catalyst for human evolution. It achieves this by elevating our consciousness through the rich tapestry of life experiences, enlightening and inspiring us along the way.

How Does the Soul Manifest Itself?

Natacha Kolesar, PhD and Founder of Ideal Society in Canada explains that the main functions of the soul are:

- connection: between spirit and body, to other people, to the universal soul

- circulation of energies

- evolution through experience

- acceleration of vibration

- acquiring and elevating consciousness.

The soul acts as a transistor, a transformer that translates the messages, insights, indications and guidance from the spirit to the personality, which is the mind and the heart. It brings us a higher consciousness. It contains all the divine elements you need to manifest this higher consciousness.

The soul makes sense of life's experiences. It gives us a broader view and makes us see them from a larger perspective of evolution and growth. Through contact with the soul, we can perceive and discern truth despite having been programmed to distorted views through education or religion.

Soul consciousness, a beacon of hope, aids the personality in transforming difficult human experiences, such as traumatic events, rejection, discouragement, envy, revenge, or even hate. It serves as a guiding light, healing, uplifting, and transmuting these painful experiences through the unconditional love that it is made of. It is the soul that whispers forgiveness in our hearts, empowering us to overcome conflict. It illuminates these experiences in a higher light, offering us creative ideas or innovative solutions to a problem.

We could consider the soul as the princess, filled with grace and higher values. The servant is the personality—the mind, the heart, and the body. The princess instructs the servant on how to think, feel and act. The soul makes us understand that the body needs to become a temple, a sacred dwelling where it can express itself totally and freely.

The Soul is the Memory Keeper

Everything a human being experiences, feels and thinks through the subtle matter of the soul is recorded throughout life. Lisa Renée states: "The Soul body is the threefold principle of creative imagination, receptivity and feeling perception and holds the recorded memories of the consciousness."

People with a Near Death Experience tell us about the movie that shows their memories played backwards. Everything was recorded, even the things they had forgotten for a long time.

Twin Soul and Soul Family

Our soul is both masculine and feminine. The twin soul is the other half of our being, the other pole or principle. If we were incarnated in a feminine body, the masculine part of us would stay 'on the other side'. It didn't incarnate with us but guides and protects us from this higher realm. Only twelve times in our soul evolution can we incarnate together. It is the Romeo and Juliette type of incarnation, where both are so intensely connected, like a hand in a glove. When one leaves, the other cannot stay alone.

Our stories are unconscious searches for this ultimate partner. The unconscious image of our twin soul hidden somewhere in us acts as a blueprint to compare a possible partner to whom we feel attracted. This standard explains repulsion or attraction towards other people in general. We can be over the moon when we feel attracted to 'The One and Only,' but sadly enough, we struggle with disappointment after some time.

Sometimes, we are lucky: the twin soul can manifest itself in a glimpse through a closely connected person or someone from the other gender on whom we then easily project the deep love we mean to have found. But it was only an instant that the twin soul manifested itself to encourage us.

The soul belongs to a soul family. The other members of the soul family may or may not be incarnated at the same time but evolve together and learn from each other's experiences while we are incarnated. There is a deep affinity to these members. When we leave Earth, we reconnect with these other members of our soul family. It is like coming home.

Through the soul, we can connect with other souls and human beings, understanding them through compassion and intuition, feeling the frequency of the other, and helping them to uplift themselves. The soul is also able to feel into an animal, a plant, a tree or a stone and understand which essence it carries.

Universal Soul

The soul is embedded in the Universal Soul, the cosmic level of the soul energy. It is like a drop of water connected to the ocean because it has the same essence. The soul is connected to the light that permeates and sustains everything. This light is the Universal Soul, the energy from which all matter is derived. The Cosmic Spirit or Source has created it to manifest itself into matter.

As there are laws in the physical world, like the law of gravity, the law of inertia, and the law of osmosis, there are also laws in the more subtle realms, in the Universal Soul. The universal Soul carries the knowledge of Universal or Divine Law. Everything in creation has been created based on this Divine Law.

Endowed with boundless love, the soul is not just aware of, but intimately familiar with all the laws that govern the universe. It serves as a beacon of consciousness, illuminating these laws for us, guiding us on our spiritual journey.

The soul, when we establish a connection with it, becomes our teacher, imparting the wisdom of these universal laws. It yearns not just for acceptance and obedience, but also for recognition and respect. It beckons the personality to surrender to its guidance, so that it may manifest its divine essence within a human being.

The Soul has the Blueprint

Every soul has a blueprint of specific talents, qualities, and virtues that it wants to manifest through the personality, mind, heart, and body in which it lives. It is immensely evolved, much more than we can manifest. It is like a virtuoso who wants to express its excellence through us, but it needs an instrument that is attuned to this excellence. A virtuoso violin player cannot express himself on a broken or untuned violin.

Soul Purpose

"Birth is the path on which you walk to resemble your Creator."- O.M. Aïvanhov

It is in the middle of life that we suddenly become aware that something essential is missing. The midlife crisis usually wakes us up to the question: What am I supposed to do with my life? Am I doing that or not? What needs to be adjusted to get there?

The soul has a purpose in this life, but we mostly all forget about it. We can waste a lot of time if we don't know what we should manifest, develop, or learn.

"The two most important days in your life are
the day you are born and the day you find out why"
– Mark Twain

This purpose can differ from life to life: in one life it wants to be a musician, in another a judge, in another a truck driver or a mother elevating her kids.

Michael Newton explains: "Souls evolve through many lives to manifest at the highest level the mastery of their all- knowing consciousness and steadiness in emotions of unconditional love."[4]

The wish of the soul is to connect with other souls in one big human family, in service to one another, stepping over all the illusionary divisions.

The ultimate purpose, which can only be reached after many lifetimes, is total union, oneness with the Spirit or Source.

Soul Plan

> *"The privilege of a lifetime is to become*
> *who you truly are"*- Carl Jung

With the help of spirit guides, the soul that wants to step again into another life will bring together the elements that will be important in the earth experience. The focus will be on learning lessons that were previously not learned and repairing errors made in the past. Karmic elements are taken into account to determine the plan.

The focus can also be on developing certain missing qualities, virtues or skills that turn out to be important steps in becoming the person the Divine Source has intended for us, like discernment, communication, inner strength, vulnerability, willpower or selfless love.

Together, they choose which continent, country, and family the soul needs to be born into, in order to realize its plan. The more the soul evolves, the more choices it has. The soul chooses the difficulties to go through to evolve. It can, for example, choose to plan an accident or an illness because it knows that it has the strength to deal with it; otherwise, it wouldn't choose it.

In this preparation, on the other side, we make soul contracts with other souls who will play the role of mother or father for us or will be your son or daughter, a good friend, or an influential teacher. These can be karmic soul contracts or not. These critical roles are not always hunky-dory. They can be flat-out difficult. The most challenging experiences come from contracts we made with souls with whom we feel very close and loving on the other side.

But in some cases, they accept *to play the role* of the villain, of the opposition, just like in a theatre play. In a theatrical drama, the opponent plays his role, but he meets the other actors in the local café to have a beer together after the play. Life is like this drama: the opponents in our lives accept this challenging role out of love for you! They know this is the only way to learn to overcome some draining emotions like shame, guilt, hate, anger or unworthiness. The only way to learn to grow is to be confronted with these feelings inside us so intensely that we have the choice: go under or transform and evolve.

This person giving us a hard time is helping us to get a step closer to perfection. If life were too easy, we would only stay asleep in old thought habits and never make a step forward.

But as the soul plan has been made in a world of peace, joy and love, we are not in contact with the suffering. We might be overconfident and make unrealistic plans about what we can handle, and the consequences may not be clear enough to see how hard it will be. Once here, this "laboratory of chaos we call earth," as Michael

Newton coined it, might turn out differently because we must deal with the free will of others, which makes our path more difficult.

We encounter setbacks. We are overwhelmed with emotions from which the by-products are depression and anxiety. Finding the way back then to the Source of unlimited energy is key. Soul plans can be adapted if they are too harsh. There is no judgement or rejection from the Higher Soul World, but only understanding and compassion.

Healing Through the Soul

When the heart struggles with feelings of unworthiness, discouragement, revolt, powerlessness, anger or fear, a therapy with which we just stir all these emotions from the same level as where they are formed, healing cannot take place. Just talking about what we experienced can help to some extent, but it can take a long time and the healing might not be complete.

It is only when we can look at the issue from a higher standpoint that we can see the bigger picture. Here the soul is the real answer through her unconditional love and wisdom to provide the higher energy to uncover the quintessence of the suffering.

Lisa Renée states: "For true healing to occur, the Soul is the part of us that is the most powerful in effecting mental shifts and behavioural changes and can greatly improve our self- esteem and self-confidence."[5]

The healing methods I work with are based on the input of the higher point of view of the soul. In Therapy of Intra-Uterine Life, the soul can answer deep questions about difficult events and, from that position, helps the client come to a true perspective. The profound insight, the true perspective, or the life lesson comes from the soul level. When we access this wisdom, the difficult emotions fade away, never to come back, because the quintessence of the event has been extracted.

With the method of The Journey, which treats the emotional roots of an illness, it is also through an authentic immersion in the soul essence that the hurtful events can be transcended and healed. The soul, as the transmitter of spirit, is the most essential and precious part of our being. Let's help it to grow!

> *"When the human soul blooms like a flower, it*
> *spreads an aura, a fragrance, a light around the being.*
> *To preserve this life that manifests itself around us,*
> *we must live in Harmony, Purity and Love!"* – O. M.
> Aïvanhov[6]

Loving someone, *really* loving someone, is finding this Source in him that connects you with the forgotten realm of unspoken treasure, the realm of the divine. Through the one you love, you connect with his soul, with Source that flows through him or her. This soul that wants to love simply for loving.

Break the seal of inspiration, letting it flow. You have the power to unlock this flow anytime you want, even when everyone leaves you, turns their backs on you, or when nobody fulfills your expectation of being recognized for who you are. You can celebrate this precious connection to Source any moment when you listen to the yearning of your soul. Yearning to be immersed in love, in beauty, in the secrets that silence only can bring.

Restoring the soul is the most important path for humanity to take right now. Respecting it again, nourishing it, and expanding its richness in yourself and in the people you live with…

Bringing the water of your love into this dry inner earth that we have neglected for too long. The soul has been drying out, cut off from our attention by the demands of the material world. The clumps of pain and distortion, suffering and rejection can be dissolved again and become fertile soil for an inner garden of colourful flowers and fruits.

The dry sand of an inner desert of numbness can be fertilized by planting and watering seeds of love in action.

Journey of Embodiment of the Soul

"When we are born, we come into this world under the law of blessing" - O.M. Aïvanhov

The soul has already had a whole evolution before this lifetime. It is not a blank page. It has gone through a whole labyrinth of experiences, happy and unhappy ones. But as life is limited in time, there comes a moment to rest and integrate these experiences and the soul is called home.

After the death of the body, the soul lets go of all its different parts: the different bodies that were active during life. First, of course, the physical body has died. After three days, the etheric body detaches itself from the physical body and starts deteriorating. Much later, it is the body of emotions or the astral body which needs to dissolve. The soul disconnects from the astral body, also its mental body, purifying and reviewing, clearing out thoughts and feelings that were heavy and not in harmony with divine life. The soul extracts the essence of its experiences. It has been thinning out to become only its pure essence. It ends up in the world of the causal plane, which is the superior mental plane, as a soul that carries a tiny permanent atom. This permanent atom holds the blueprint of his essence, of all his experiences in past lives, of all his unselfish accomplishments, its peace, love and the heavier elements of selfish and unmastered thoughts and feelings that were not transformed yet. The soul can rest in this world of absolute beauty and light, of divine love.

Then at a certain moment, the soul feels satiated with all the splendour it has been soaking in, in the subtle world of the light, and the earth calls again. It is a call to continue its development because there are still elements that are too personal such as personal desires, passions, cravings or compulsions that it wants to transform. The soul wants to grow through the material world and express itself in it, always more perfect, more loving, harmonious and conscious. It wants to develop other qualities, virtues, and skills that it hasn't mastered yet.

When the soul feels called again to the earth to continue its development, it still resides on a very high vibrational realm of the causal plane. The journey to be born is a passage through many different subtle worlds, always denser and denser. It is a condensing of subtle energies into physical form. We can compare it to the element of the air that can condense into water through the effect of temperature which can in turn condense even more and become ice. So the divine spirit, through the soul, starts condensing and creating bodies of different densities: from the most subtle, the mental body, into the astral body, which is denser over the etheric body, which is even denser into finally, the densest physical body.

Long before the conception of the physical body, the soul has already started to prepare for its incarnation. The soul goes to the Hall of Wisdom where, with the help of its guides, the soul chooses the country in which it wants to incarnate. This choice determines its temperament: the southern countries with their warm climate will determine rather outgoing, warm, expressive temperaments. In contrast, a northern country will be influential to an introverted, calm, thoughtful temperament. Other aspects are determined such as which profession it wants to have. Which experiences does it want to have. What does it want to learn. Which parents will be its perfect genitors or educators. Where can it find the DNA that corresponds to its essence. The more the soul is developed, the harder the program with tests and suffering. But it has several choices. Young souls who didn't have any or few incarnations will have only one possibility, no choices. Very evolved souls who don't need to come anymore to pay karma and who have finished their evolution have infinite choices. They have the free will to come or not to the earth to help the evolution of mankind.

The soul itself, together with its guides, determines the moment of conception and birth. The permanent atom is projected to the lower mental plane or concrete mental plane from the higher mental plane- also called the causal plane. In this mental plane exist very different qualities of mental matter: from cloudy or dark to light and colourful. The permanent atom, according to the frequency it carries, attracts subtle but still formless matter to build up its mental body, corresponding to the mental capacities it has developed in its previous lives. If the soul has worked only for its profit or for evil goals, if it likes deceptions and lies, it will attract the heavy, cloudy, dark matter, like raw material. This human being, once formed, will manifest selfish tendencies, only thinking about himself, being disconnected from others or he might have destructive thoughts. But if the soul has been developing qualities that were oriented towards the good of others, towards peace, life or human development, the matter it attracts will be pure, light, transparent and colourful. That will give a mental body that might become genius or capable of inventing new things.

Then the permanent atom descends lower into the astral plane of the emotions. It means that it slows down its vibrations to adapt to a denser environment. There it will attract the subtle matter that corresponds to the emotional heart qualities it had already developed in previous lifetimes. This matter will be used to love, to serve, to help. It will determine the vices that will keep the human being imprisoned in self-centeredness or express altruistic loving feelings and actions.

The next step for the soul, still before conception, is to prepare a mould that is called the etheric body. The permanent atom is sent to the etheric realm, attracting even denser matter. This mould will be the container in which the physical body will mould itself once conception has happened. It determines the size of the body, the size of the head and the finesse of the limbs. When it is ready it is placed in the body of the mother at conception. A psychic can see it as a subtle light form of the very physical body that it will become with all the features, sizes and measurements. All this preparation can happen months or even sometimes years before the actual conception.

At the moment of conception, the spirit sends its powerful energy towards the formation of this first cell through the permanent atom that is now deposited in the vestige of physical life: the first cell. A powerful current of energy sustains the start of this new life. This current of energy is channeled and attached to the growing blastula and will remain attached to the body during life in what is called the silver cord. The silver cord links the spirit and soul on one side and the physical body on the other. During sleep, the soul detaches from the body to be restored in the subtle realms but stays always connected to the body through the silver cord. It is cut off at the moment of death: the soul cannot animate the body anymore.

The choice of the kind of soul that has connected at conception has most of the time been determined for a long time. The soul contracts made before coming into this life will have determined the choices of the souls we'll have as our children. Soul contracts are based on the relationships we built before this lifetime and, eventually, on karmic aspects our super consciousness has chosen to tackle. But if we as parents start investing in a high ideal to be available for the transformation of the earth into a paradise and we act appropriately, we can change the soul contracts and attract a more evolved soul. It takes determination and sincere efforts to clear out on different levels in the field of emotions, thoughts and the physical body, to uplift the vibrations on all these levels to come to the clarity of mind, purity of heart and health of the body. Then, through prayer, a special intention can be sent out to the divine world, with the wish to serve humanity by inviting the soul that would match your higher vibration.

The Four Currents in the Silver Cord

The current of energy that comes in at conception through the silver cord carries four strands, so four different kinds of energies:

1. The first **current of life energy** is attached to the **heart** which will be the seat of the vital life energy in the **physical body**. This current of life energy is only attached to the heart at birth at the moment of the first breath. The heart of the embryo and fetus is already beating before that, but the mother gives support to the heart before birth. At the first breath, the impulse to the beating of the baby's heart becomes independent from the mother: the baby's soul has entered on the physical level and takes over the impulses to the beating of the heart until the end of life. This stream of life energy is the power behind the push to evolve from a

low vibrational, sleepy life to a more intense life connected to Source.

2. The second current of energy is the **current of consciousness** and it is attached to **the brain**. It is the seat of **the mental body**. It is attached to the first cell, but only very gradually throughout life will it become stronger and evolve through the experiences it goes through. It will bring higher thoughts to the human being according to the degree of consciousness it wants to invest in. It can be disturbed in the case of mental illness and even absent in a state of coma.

3. The third current of energy is the **current of strength of the personality** that will be attached to the **solar plexus** on the etheric level and the **liver** on the physical level. The health of the liver doesn't only depend on nutrition but also on the feelings we nourish. As discussed in a further part about the solar plexus we know that through this door enter all the subtle cosmic influences. It is the seat of the **astral body**. All the impressions coming from the immediate environment, the people we live with, and the fluidic influences coming from the universe determine how we feel nourished on a subtle level. We can receive beautiful influences of peace or harmonious ones like music or, on the contrary, more disturbing energies. We learn to deal with these influences by filtering what comes to us and transforming the negative impressions into insights, qualities and virtues.

4. The fourth current of energy is the **current of universal energy**. It is a synthesis of the earth's energy that can adapt

its vibrations to what our body needs. It is rooted in the **spleen,** which becomes the seat of the **etheric body**. The state of the etheric body will determine the state of health of the physical body depending on the level of respect we have for universal order. It will help us to connect to the earth's telluric energies and transform them to be absorbed through the spleen.

The principal currents of energy are the heart (current of life) and the brain (current of consciousness), which support our individuality or divine nature. The two other currents are secondary currents. They are located in the liver (current of force of personality) and the spleen (current of universal energy) and support our personality: our human feelings, desires, and personal thoughts.[7]

Blending the Psyche with the Soul

From the moment the first cell is created, the energies stored in the permanent atom, determining the life force, attract the physical atoms and molecules according to their vibration rate. Lower vibrations tend to attract matter of inferior quality and condense into organs that might become deficient. Higher vibrations, on the contrary, will attract matter that has resilience, strong vital forces, and health.

The soul and spirit at conception have brought in divine energies corresponding to the essence of the soul and have overseen the fusion of the two gametes into the first cell, guiding the choices of the genetic material. Some of the genetic material of both parents is not adapted to the soul and DNA coming from ancestors that can be strange to the soul essence. The genome or DNA organizes itself into the systems and organs according to the quality of the totality of the genes and determines the colour of the eyes and of the skin, the health of the bodily systems and organs.

Cell memory is active from the first moment and absorbs all imprints and information coming from its surroundings in its subconsciousness. This will become the world of the psyche. The soul and the psyche live in different worlds. The soul is active on the level of super consciousness, whereas the psyche is connected to the conscious or subconscious level.

The wish of the soul when choosing the parents was that the quality of the body of the baby would be as much as possible in harmony with the needs of the soul. The higher the soul is evolved, the better they will be adjusted to one another. A virtuoso violin player needs an instrument that is of high quality to be able to express its virtuosity. If the instrument is broken, it is impossible to do that. Compared to this, the soul needs the instrument of the body, the heart and the brain to be attuned. A soul that wants to be a musician will need a very well-developed ear. The soul of a genius needs a well-evolved brain.

The soul proceeds to influence the building of the physical, etheric, astral and mental bodies together with a whole host of light beings. The light beings are specialized in different elements: the building of the etheric, astral or mental body. Under the guidance of the Lord of Karma, these light beings build up the babies' bodies according to the lessons that need to be learned. The soul and the light beings or angels form a team of protection around the mother to keep out harmful influences. Although light energies are constantly present, the soul is not always present in the mother. It comes and goes, still needing contact with the divine realms.

When the soul perceives that the baby's psyche is suffering because of some negative imprints of sadness or fear on the mother, it tries to reach out to her to uplift her emotional state. The more evolved souls can transform the mother's tendencies. They inspire her to eat better and leave bad habits behind, such as alcohol or smoking. They project light on the body of the fetus.

When I was pregnant and still grieving, I cried. But it never lasted very long because I felt a fountain of energy and love in me that calmed me down. I am sure this was the soul together with light beings caring for me.

During the regressions under hypnosis to the time between the lives of Michael Newton's clients, they remember their existence as souls. They report how they try to interact with the body of the fetus to adapt it to their needs. Discovering these hidden experiences through hypnosis differs from the science that came to us through clear knowing, such as in the science of Theosophy. The narrative is slightly different. In his book 'Destiny of Souls' Newton brings forward the story of an advanced soul visiting the body of the baby it will incarnate in:

> *"No two brains are constructed in precisely the same way. When I initially enter the womb of my*

mother, I touch the brain gently. I flow in… seeking…probing… searching. It is like osmosis. I know immediately if this brain is "going to be smooth or rough sailing for our mutual communication. I will receive my mother's emotional feelings during pregnancy more than her clear thoughts. That's how I know if the baby is wanted or not, and this makes a difference in the baby getting a good or a bad start.

When I enter the fetus of an unwanted baby, I can make a positive difference by energy engagement with this child. When I was a young soul I would get caught up with the alienation of a parent and both the child and I felt a separation. I have been working with babies for thousands of years and I can handle whatever sort of child they give me, so we are both fulfilled by coming together. I have too much work to do in life to be slowed down by a body match which does not happen to be perfect for me."[8]

Three Trimesters of Building

According to the three trimesters, a different kind of building goes on.

- **The first trimester** lays the basis for the embryological and fetal development of the physical body. From the first cell, a myriad of cell divisions and structuring, impressive organization happens throughout the gestation of the different physical organs and systems. At the end of the first three months, after the embryo has morphed into all successive life forms, the basic development of a mini human being will be in place.

On the seventeenth day of pregnancy, a remarkable event occurs the primitive form of the heart begins to beat, a rhythm that will continue until the end of life.

While the astral body of the embryo is still in its early stages, it can sense the mother's emotional state. The mother is encouraged to establish a conscious connection with the embryo, welcoming it with love. Though not fully formed, the embryo's mental body is receptive to the mother's thoughts. It continues to gather subtle mental matter, shaping it into a formless conglomerate that will be utilized later in development.

For the mother in these first three months, the presence of the embryo is not yet very real. It feels very subtle still, so she can easily connect to the spirit world and nourish her high ideal, this intention of nobility, wisdom and love that will influence the vibratory quality of the matter that will be attracted to the mould of the etheric body into the physical body. Visualize your womb as a sacred temple, creating a healthy baby body with all its necessary systems: bones, muscles, respiratory and circulatory system, forming a resilient body in a network of vital life forces.

- **The second trimester** sees the rapid growth of the physical body, which, at the end of this trimester, will have half the baby's size at birth. Between the 16th and the 20th week, the mother starts feeling the movements of the fetus in her womb, which is a very heartfelt moment. The astral body builds up in and around the etheric and physical body. The formless matter that was attracted earlier starts organizing and expanding. The fetus is much more receptive to emotions now. It baths in paradise-like feelings, enjoying the connection to Source if undisturbed.

Also, for the mother this is the most enjoyable part of the pregnancy as she can freely connect to the fetus that she feels moving. Whenever difficult events disturb her joy, she can surround the fetus with a cocoon of light and tell it that he is not concerned by this upset. Imagining qualities and virtues will awaken the corresponding seeds in your baby's emotional energy field.

Although the brain is at a basic developmental stage, the mental body is not yet very active. However, keep your intentions and mental attitudes positive, as they will already affect the baby. Avoid chaotic and violent scenes and events on television, movies and social media.

Geoffrey Hodson in his clairvoyant observations of the activity of the light beings, building the astral body of an unborn baby saw them gather all spiritually elevated energies a mother might generate while meditating or participating in a spiritual or religious service. and add them to its construction. Suppose there are karmic elements that need to be built in. In that case, these elevated feelings of altruism or divine love will diminish the effect of the karmic elements and allow the child to deal with some hard life lessons more easily. Your power as the mother is immense at this stage! You have the power to change karma! Create as much as possible moments of deep meditation, of being immersed in sacred energies, whether in a church or in the temple of nature. Sacred music and songs can vibrate through to the growing body and add a dimension to his being through which he can always feel supported by the sacredness of divine life.

- During the third trimester, the baby gains lots of weight. All the body parts, organs and systems are perfected. The emotional perception is even more present and a warm connection between his and your heart can be cultivated even more. The very subtle substance of the mental body is now also present and brings the fetus to a form of self-identity. A chance for full-on communication and deepening of the bonding is here in the united temples of your two beings. Your thoughts are furnishing the mental house of your prenate. You can show him the wonders of the world in which he will arrive. You can tell inspiring stories and read poetry. His memory expands and he is learning from your voice, your language and how you deal with life.

The Struggles of the Incarnating Consciousness

The unborn baby is the embodiment of a soul that comes from another world, a world of absolute love. That love doesn't exist on earth. The biggest challenge for the incarnating soul is to lose the light of that higher world, that immense light of unconditional love. It can be an excruciating pain to separate from that world once it resides in the body. The soul can have difficulties adapting to that change of environment and vibration. Resistance can grow in the soul by incarnating because of this difficulty of adapting. The soul, encountering matter, remembers the pain, hardship and struggle in the earth's three-dimensional world from past lifetimes. It can be the primary difficulty to deal with on earth: anger, fear, powerlessness, desperation, revolt and separation.

From the moment the soul meets matter through the first conceived cell, cell consciousness experiences a gradual loss of connection to the higher world. Throughout pregnancy and birth, the veil gets thicker. We need forty to fifty years to understand that we lost something essential and try to find it again. What if we could avoid this time-lapse by a conscious pregnancy and birth?

The Future Mother Holds the Line

The consciousness of the future mother is as critical as giving the unborn baby the proper nutrition. Through her connection to the light of the spirit world, she provides the incoming soul with a boost of confidence and trust that it will find light here on earth too. By being consciously connected to this higher world, she can understand where the incoming soul comes from and guide the psyche of the growing fetus, comfort it and help it to stay connected to the light and to the soul world, even through the embodying process. Without a mother's beautiful connection to this world of light, the connection may break for the incarnating soul. The psyche will experience the deep pain of separation. Our main task on earth is to overcome this trauma of separation, which is an illusion.

Contact With the Parents Before Conception

Even before conception, contact between the incoming soul and the parents is already possible. Many future parents have reported stories about dreams, visions, or sensations in which their child's soul made itself known. A sensitive father could already feel a presence close to him. It can be the soul of his child that makes contact and urges him to bring it into existence through conception. The wish to have a child can also come from the future mother. It is the soul ringing the bell that it wants to come.

Both parents-to-be can connect to the incarnating soul, even before conception. In this way, they can help the incoming soul in its incarnation process by connecting to the divine world. They can welcome it with the warmth of their hearts, reassuring it and presenting themselves to the soul of their future child.

Gradual Indwelling of the Soul

It is the father who receives the permanent atom of the child- to-be. He transmits it at conception through one of his sperm cells and is transferred to the first cell. The soul is connected to the first cell but has yet to be incarnated. It comes and goes throughout the pregnancy.

At birth, the soul incarnates in the body but not totally. It descends in stages. Over the developmental years, the child gradually receives the different parts of his soul.

During the prenatal period, with the help of light beings, the soul gathers the subtle material for the different bodies through the experiences and consciousness of the mother. Her emotions and thoughts are reinforcing or dimming this build- up depending on the quality of her thoughts and feelings. The mother can help the soul of the unborn baby tremendously through her conscious way of living, noble thoughts, loving feelings, and the right actions. In a later part of this book, we will see how she can do that.

The first breath incarnates part of the soul in the baby's body. This is a very sacred moment. It imprints its essence into the body, together with the cosmic influences. The body is still like unsolidified wax that is impressionable. Once solidified, the marks are set. That is why astrology calculates the time for the birth chart on the moment of the first breath. If the baby is given the time to start breathing, the incoming breath is like a holy energy. The Spirit of Life will be much more consciously present in the life of this mini-human being. If the cord is cut too early, the body receives a shock and the intense emotion of anxiousness prints itself in the psyche of the baby. The imprint of anxiousness wakes up the fear of dying because there is not enough oxygen to be able to live. This anxiousness will constantly activate throughout life with the smallest event that can wake up fear. This anxiousness holds the soul back from manifesting itself.

During birth, the soul of the physical body incarnates, connecting to the left ventricle of the heart, where it deposits the permanent atom. During sleep, the soul can still flip out of the body and visit its celestial realms again.

At the moment of birth, only a portion of the soul, specifically the part related to the physical body, incarnates through the first breath. The remaining part of the soul, its ethereal essence, remains outside of the body, a reminder of its vast and infinite nature.

The baby's consciousness will still be connected to the world of the soul. But so much is going on with the adaptation to the physical realm and the care that goes with it. From the transcendent experiences of the soul, the baby comes now into the limited cocoon of the physical body. It is a significant adaptation not to be able to control the limbs' movements and the organs' functioning. If the caretakers of the baby can feel that compassionately and treat baby's body with respect, the transition will happen more easily. The baby can cry just because of difficulties in adapting to the new vibrations, the needs of the body and the feeling of frustration and powerlessness. It is also still integrating the journey through birth and the eventual traumatic parts that have disturbed his energy. Time and lots of empathy will help the baby restore itself.

Growing up

Gradually, the soul prepares and incarnates at different times. In the first seven years, the etheric body continues to develop. It helps in the further development of the organs and body movements, such as learning to walk and manipulating objects.

At 7 years of age, the etheric body is complete: the child 'masters' the movements of his physical body.

From 7 to 14 years old, the astral body incarnates and opens the child up to the world of emotions.

At 21 years, the mental body is now also incarnated.

From 28 years of age, higher parts of the soul, also called the divine soul, are developed, based on the evolution the soul made before this lifetime.

Once an adult, only a fraction of the soul is incarnated. The soul is immense, and the most significant part remains embedded in the universal soul.

Higher and Lower Nature

At birth two seeds are present in the baby's being: a seed of the terrestrial self or the lower self and a seed of the higher self.

What is the higher self?

Each person has a higher and a lower nature, a higher and a lower self. But what is precisely the difference?

We know the lower nature pretty well! Most humans have rooted their being in this nature. It holds all that is self-centered, whimsical, chaotic, revolted, disorganized, eternal victim, powerless, stubborn, controlling, dominating, manipulating, blaming, and convinced that this is the way to live. If we live in this lower nature, we think we are always right and don't care if we lie or abuse something or someone.

The rule is to take, which is never enough. In this lower nature, people are never satisfied. Their instinct, not their intuition, guides them, so they are easily misguided. Desires and passions are to be followed and listened to. They only perceive and recognize what is to be measured by the five senses. They feel easily excluded, and in fact, they are! They excluded themselves from a higher consciousness. On this level, they are like serfs to their lower nature and proud of it too. We can all recognize ourselves a bit or very much so in this caricature.

The higher nature tries to pull this lower nature out of the mess, but that's an arduous task, as this lower nature doesn't see any advantage in being pulled up. It doesn't even recognize that it is swimming in the swamp of this lower self.

The higher nature has many levels, but it is the synthesis of the higher heart or the soul, a higher mental plane and a powerful spirit or higher willpower. Someone who has climbed up to that level manifests that higher consciousness and is self-actualized as a selfless divine being. He is always in wonder for everything beautiful, enthusiastic and joyful, full of love. Because of their intuition, they can penetrate or merge with an object or an animal and feel and know their essence. With a plant, they know their medicinal properties; with a human being very far away, they can sense what is going on in him. They know the past and the future and live in the eternal present. No secret is hidden from them. They don't know suffering, sadness or discouragement or can transform it immediately. They are detached from possessions. They live a fulfilled life because they are always connected to Source, constantly immersed in divine consciousness, and are identified with it. They manifest all virtues.

This nature inspires everything generous, noble, excellent and spiritual. They are constantly enlightened, guided, comforted, supported and protected. This is the real human being: unlimited, omniscient and all-powerful. Their ideal is to give and to be in service to humanity. They are free human beings because they obey divine laws.

We all have this divine nature, but it stays mostly outside of us. It can't manifest itself yet through our mind, heart and body because our being is not attuned to this high frequency, but we can decide to grow in this direction by saying yes to this high ideal and by tirelessly stepping up the ladder towards this beautiful goal.

The Soul's Learning of Overcoming Obstacles

Why does it seem 'easier' to reach the summit of a mountain than to overcome a difficulty in life?

When we want to reach the summit of a mountain, we have chosen to go up this mountain. We prepared for the ascension by selecting the path, gathering all the equipment, exchanging with the team we were part of, and so on.

On the contrary, if life is difficult, we think we didn't choose it. It just falls in our lap, and we don't want it. It seemed like a mountain, but it wasn't *that* mountain we wanted to climb.

The wisdom of the elders tells us that a part of us has attracted this obstacle or this difficulty to evolve, become richer inside, develop qualities, and overcome the tricks of the ego.

Life on earth is designed for us to evolve. So why fight the path that a part of ourselves has arranged for us? Our Higher Self organized it. To meet that person at that precise moment or to have that accident or misfortune, these are the mountains we are invited to climb. We didn't consciously prepare for them. We sure wouldn't be looking for misfortune consciously, but it has been written on our life path. We even have chosen it ourselves before coming to this earth, or we have created it in some way. We are responsible for what overcomes us. But we suffer if we don't accept the program we wrote out for ourselves. Suffering is the result of resistance to what is happening. We don't want it, and we cannot adapt to it. We cannot see how we can be happy with these challenges.

Things don't happen *to* us but *for* us.

We can make sense of adversities or obstacles on the road through the connection with our deeper knowing coming from the soul. Why did we attract or create them? Maybe there is something to learn:

- How can I use my mental clarity to view this event in the right frame of mind?

- The negative emotion of anger or discouragement that came up because of the obstacle: how can I transform it? Which quality or virtue is it inviting me to develop? What do I need to let go of?

- What can I do to change the situation?

The obstacle on the road obliges us to uncover treasures deeply hidden in our souls. It allows us to react with our ego which causes suffering or choosing to understand what we are invited to learn or develop and find positive solutions.

CHAPTER 4

PRENATAL PSYCHOLOGY

"The womb is a vehicle of immense, intelligent programming" – Namgyal Rinpoche

Our history is a testament to the profound understanding many cultures had about the profound influence of the pregnant mother on her child. From the ancient Egyptians, Greeks, and Chinese to the Native Americans, these cultures revered the golden rules of pregnancy, ensuring the best conditions for the mother-to-be and the next generation. The sacred scriptures of India, such as the Upanishads, echo this wisdom, emphasizing the importance of conception and pregnancy.

However, we have gradually forgotten this ancient wisdom. In modern times, the care around pregnancy focusses only on the material and medical needs of the future mother. Neither the mother's inner needs nor the baby's needs are met.

Science rediscovered everything about 100 years ago. With Freud, we were long convinced that memory only starts after two years of age. The world believed in the myth that an unborn baby could not feel, be conscious, or have a memory about birth or the period before birth. Surgery on a newborn baby was done without anesthesia, for example.

But Freud's student Otto Rank was aware of the possibility of birth memories and, because of that, was excluded from the psychoanalysis training. Many other pioneers have included more aspects of prenatal existence in the science of psychology, neurobiology, genetics, and sociology. Dr. Thomas Verny, a psychiatrist and a pioneer in the field of pre- and perinatal psychology says: "Findings in the peer-reviewed literature over the course of decades establish, *beyond any doubt*, that parents have overwhelming influence on the mental and physical attributes of the children they raise." (2003)

The science of pre - and perinatal psychology and health has exploded in the last four decades. It became clear that the baby in the womb is a conscious human with many capacities. David Chamberlain, a psychotherapist and pioneer of this science, states that "the womb is the first classroom for the baby." In his book "Windows to the Womb" (2013), he describes how and what the unborn baby learns:

- Taste, sounds, rhythms, words and tactile experiences are the teachers

- The fetus uses not five senses of awareness but twelve

- The baby is sensitive to the mother's voice

- Secure attachment is the condition for a life of balance and independence

- Unresolved trauma of the mother will impede the attachment of the baby to her.

They discovered that what the future mother experiences as feelings and thoughts affect the baby and create life-long memories for him.

Her inner state translates into biological, hormonal and neurological reactions that are transmitted to the baby. The baby knows if he is welcome or not, if his mother is happy or not. He absorbs everything like a sponge, and this creates his basis of self-worth, self-confidence and trust for the rest of his life. The baby's emotions, intelligence, creativity and balance have their foundation in the womb.

The development of the human brain is a balance between *nature*, for example genetics, and nurture: nutrition, care, environment, interaction, stimulation and teaching. Allan Schore, a famous psychoanalyst in the US, expresses this: "Nature's potential can only be reached if it is enabled by nurture."[9]

Brain development depends on experience, but especially throughout this critical period before and immediately after birth, experience organizes the brain. Bruce Perry, an American psychiatrist, states: "Experience is the chief architect of the brain." The very state of the mother influences the development of all the physical organs of the fetus. If intense stress occurs during the formation of a specific organ, this organ might develop failures or weaknesses.

Dr. Bruce Lipton, a renowned stem cell biologist, posits that "beliefs are *the* key determinant of whether cellular activity is growth-oriented or protection-oriented. This concept is particularly relevant to prenates and babies, who learn at the level of perceptions. The early perceptions they acquire have a profound impact on their physiology and behaviour, and these perceptions eventually form hardwired synaptic pathways that shape their *subconscious beliefs. These beliefs* then serve as a lens through which all later experiences are filtered and organized."[10]

The mother shouldn't just passively "expect" a baby but can actively participate and already be a caretaker during pregnancy.

A healthy womb creates a healthy world! By giving the mother not only medical but also mental support so she can live a peaceful, happy, and inspired pregnancy, we can turn this world into a place of peace, compassion, and comprehension where collaboration and harmony thrive.

Putting the pregnant woman and the baby at the center of our attention is crucial for society if we want to escape the chaos and societal breakdown, and restoration and renewal become possible.

In the many testimonials that will follow, it is clear that the future child has been carrying many of the mother's burdens. If she doesn't feel accepted in life or feels unworthy, devalued, or easily rejected, the baby will absorb these beliefs as if they were its own. Her stress interferes with the building of the heart, the mind, and the physical body of the baby.

The same is true for the influence of the environment. In a lesser sense, if the family doesn't accept the mother's pregnancy, the baby feels he shouldn't have been there. He can create beliefs of being guilty because he is bringing his mother trouble. He feels unwelcome, which gives a blow to his self-esteem.

Crises help us dig out the deep trauma that has been undermining us. False beliefs and limiting decisions can be turned up if we know how to listen and have the support to discover where the knot is and how to transform it. Finding these situations is the treasure of life. Becoming aware of what happens and how it is related to the start of life is tremendously important.

Every little insight is a step closer to letting go of the old way and opening to a new way of being in life. It takes courage. It can be overwhelming, but in the end, it is liberating. These challenges in life can give us the biggest chances to evolve.

My Life in Utero

My entry into this life has revealed so very much to me.

My first discovery of the impact of my prenatal period was in my twenties. I wondered why I could not feel happy. Where does this numb feeling come from? I finally sat down and focused on this feeling. I knew I could go down a staircase to find answers in my subconscious. I went down and down the stairs until I saw my mother in a space to the side, who invited me to come and sit down next to her. She said: I'll tell you about when you were in my belly. I asked for guidance from some light beings to be safe during this discovery. I felt immediately supported and protected.

I realized my mother's – unconscious - ambivalence towards me: with her everyday consciousness, she wanted me. She wished to have seven children, like it was in her family. I was only the fifth. But her unconscious level said 'NO.' Her body was too depleted from having to run a household with four young boys between eighteen months and six years old. She suffered from migraines, back pain and tiredness. I missed this full YES towards me. The doctor had already, long before I came, warned her not to get pregnant again because of heavy bleeding in previous births. I concluded that I wasn't welcome.

She didn't know that I could feel all this, of course. I felt that there was love, but it didn't seem to be really for me. I decided that I wasn't good enough. I just had to become this good little girl, always quiet and happy, so I would get a bit more of this acceptance and love that I craved. I don't blame her at all; I understand the circumstances.

While learning Therapy of Intra-Uterine Life to become a certified therapist, I explored all other aspects of that prenatal period.

The moment of conception showed me how my father's and my mother's consciousness through the two gametes carried the blueprint of their essence at that precious start. The egg cell showed subordinate energy, and she could not defend her boundaries, letting it happen anyway. The sperm cell played out as an almost aggressive force, dominating the scene, crushing away all subtleties in the creation of my life. I felt like a shirt tainted in the colour bath of my parents' energies. I was the shirt, they were the colour. I was like a coloured shirt, impossible to separate the shirt from the colour.

It showed me the role I had unconsciously taken up from my mother: letting things happen without taking control or acquiescing. I was played with and easily dominated by other people.

How to clear all that? By becoming aware, understanding, forgiving and doing a Feng Shui of the first cell.

Another fascinating journey was discovering the process of the incarnation of my soul before conception. During incarnation, I already carried this emotional burden of anger and fear. Anger because I had to leave my twin soul and leave the embrace of divine love in which I felt cared for, supported and understood. I knew life on earth wouldn't bring the same. Fear of being unable to overcome all the hurdles towards my task. A crystal received from my guide and planted in my heart helped me to keep the connection to this beautiful world.

What about the egg cell trip that started from my mom's ovary? I discovered that leaving the warmth of the sisterhood between all these female egg cells was not easy. This egg cell had to be helped by an explosion to get it into the fallopian tube. The arrival in the womb after conception was one of falling into nothingness, not knowing what was happening. The egg cell experienced insecurity and freaked out. Luckily, this evolved into feeling received in a fertile place full of nutrition. The egg cell was nestling in the womb, filled with hope.

And then, after the conception I described earlier, there was the moment of discovery by my mother. She accepted and resigned, convinced that I certainly would be a boy. She had given up on the idea that it was possible to have a girl, a wish she had long let go of after four previous boys. I would have liked to tell her, "I'm a girl. Please, listen to me!" She didn't listen. She expected a boy and projected on me the image of another boy. I received it and took it all in. I changed my being to fit in, even knowing she wished for a girl.

For a long time, I have struggled to come into my body as a girl. As a child, I was seen as a boy with short hair playing the games of a boy. Luckily, I also introduced my brothers to the games of a girl.

It took me into my twenties before I started letting in the more feminine attitudes, skills and energies specific to a woman.

How was this life in utero? I saw a beautiful orange-pink glow. I felt tenderness and intense, cozy warmth. But there I discovered a big surprise: I was NOT ALONE! Another being was there next to me. Friendship, support, love. We start this journey together!

And suddenly, desperation! I was alone. She was gone!... It's only grey around me. The cozy warmth was gone. I had lost my twin sister. Sadness, loneliness, emptiness and powerlessness came up. Was I at the origin of her passing? What did I do? Was I to blame? Guilt, judgement, I felt sorry, I felt remorse. I didn't get it. Why? I believed I was not good enough for her to stay. I felt worthless. I received a complete knock-out. Numbness.

As a child, I was very attached to my niece, who was a few months older than me. We dressed in the same clothes, and people thought we were twins when we went to the park. We felt so proud. We acted as twins do. We were very close.

I also had a symbiotic relationship with my doll. I talked to her, as most girls do. This relationship lasted until I was thirteen years old. I kept her in the closet to show that I wasn't interested in her anymore, but I still talked to her, which is often the case with children who are survivors of a vanishing twin.

Later, I discovered that there was also a third twin, a brother. But I didn't have the same intense relationship with him. He was more independent, and he left early.

How did I heal? In a therapy session, I talked to the soul of this twin sister. I asked what had been happening. The answer was that she came with me to hold my hand – symbolically speaking - during the process of embodiment and the first weeks in the womb, so I would not be alone and have a more positive experience at the beginning of life. She said that we had agreed to that before I came into the womb. I had forgotten that agreement. Once the soul encounters the first cell, with matter, it forgets what she knew before. A veil falls over the soul and forgets.

What about my birth?

The emotion that came up by going back to my birth is anger. Anger because of the doctor who had said to my mom just to come in the maternity clinic on the due date if she didn't have contractions: he would jumpstart it with Pitocin (synthetic oxytocin) to start up the contractions. She obeyed. The doctor knew best. She had an immense respect for him. But she didn't know how I felt about it. The anger was there because I was supposed to ring the bell at the start of the birth. When the lungs are ripe, they produce a hormone that puts the process in motion. Starting the birth process is supposed to be the first act of the incoming soul at the moment of birth. The first act in life. This first act was denied to me. Rage against the doctor and against my mom who didn't know better. Anger has always been the quickest to come up in difficult situations. By clearing this birth experience, I have become more aware of anger when it comes up. It became easier to handle. It has transformed into the energy needed to solve a dreadful situation.

The moment of taking in the first breath was painful. I was being forced to breathe because of anxiety, out of fear of dying. The umbilical cord was snapped right after birth, and I was held upside down "to stimulate breathing." Because of this connection between breath and fear, I concluded that life is already tainted with death; life is drenched with fear. The first impression of life on earth was fear. This fear will drive us throughout life if it is not cleared. Fear in all kinds of ways, in all possible directions: fear of losing your life, fear of losing your house, fear of approaching others.

I have been going back to that precise moment until I could completely clear out the negative patterns created there.

Finally, I came to another layer of experience. It was the experience it was meant to be: an experience of sacredness, of receiving the sacred flame of life, leading me into my temple, which is my body through the first breath. I couldn't get to that awareness, to that layer on the soul level, until I had cleared out all the rubble that was in the way. I could finally consider the breath of life as a source of sacredness. It was a new start in life, much more conscious and connected to this sacred essence of the earth and the universe.

I experienced loneliness and desperation in the cradle! I had to cry my lungs out till I fell asleep, exhausted. Is there nobody around? Am I alone? That feels unsettling! No support… Insecurity comes in.

Breastfeeding was a joy! Finally, I felt connected again with my mom. I felt that my needs were met, both physically and emotionally. I felt cared for, cuddled, and loved.

But when my mom decided after a few weeks to stop breastfeeding because she couldn't keep up with the other four kids, the household and a new baby that needed her breastmilk. The breastmilk dried up through the stress. I certainly don't blame her. I'm only telling you how it affected me. She went on with formula. "It's so easy," the nurse had told her: "You can even structure the meals every two hours. So, the baby doesn't play games with you. She needs you to give her structure."

The bottles fed my body, but my heart was cut out. My mom gave me the bottle in the cradle. No warmth of the breast, no connection with her heart, with her eyes. This was too hard. From that moment on, I decided not to feel anymore. Emotions were too hard to deal with. 'I don't have the right to feel.' 'A part of me is bad; it must be occulted.'

As a child and youngster, I didn't know what I was feeling. I just repeated what my peers had to say, copied them, and didn't have an opinion.

Being cut off from my emotions changed, luckily, when I discovered the pain of the moment when my mother stopped breastfeeding. I allowed emotions in again fully. I gave myself the right to feel, accept, and listen to them. I knew again what was going on inside of me.

These experiences were the basis of my life. As long as they were not healed, they dominated my life. A feeling of unworthiness and being nobody, cut off from my inner world, made it hard to orient myself towards a professional choice. I chose a direction, becoming an Occupational Therapist, but I decided only mentally, not feeling into it. It was not really what I wanted. Never-ending the search: what am I here to do? Why am I on this earth? Feeling cut off from myself, I moved through life somewhat depressed, not touched by the beauty of nature.

But there was one thing that I was passionate about: learning more about my prenatal experiences and what the developing science had to teach me about them. Through that quest, I have developed many capacities with which I can now help other people free themselves.

Other Examples

So many people are now discovering the link between what happened before birth and difficulties in later life.

The following examples are a testimony to this knowledge. A previous owner of a bookshop told me her story: "I had already two grown-up girls when I wanted to start up the bookstore. While I was starting it up, I fell pregnant again. I was angry for months. Once I became aware that the baby could feel this negative energy, I flooded it with love. This love has certainly had a great effect, but my son bears the consequences of that painful start: he is difficult and easily jealous. The relationship with him has always been challenging."

A lady with psychic abilities blamed her struggle with worthlessness on the fact that she was conceived at the back of a bus! Her mom fell pregnant and her parents were obliged to get married because of her coming. According to her, this was the origin of her feeling of unworthiness.

After a talk about prenatal psychology, a therapist revealed her insight: "There is such a difference between my son and my daughter. During my first years with my son, I was married without problems. With the second pregnancy, the relationship became not fulfilling anymore, and I started planning on separating. Because of the pregnancy, I had to stay another few years with my husband. If I would have separated, I would have had to work. I didn't want to bring up my daughter by having her looked after by someone else, but I wanted to stay with her for the first five years or so. I gave her the best of the best, like healthy quality food. But now she is in her twenties and she has a food problem. She even tried to cut her wrists. Now I see how this first pregnancy experience could have influenced her somehow."

Some frequent feelings of everyday life have their basis in what happened prenatally. Recurring emotions in this life before birth create beliefs about oneself, life, the world, and relationships. These beliefs are the basis for what happens in later life and how we feel and behave.

Memory: How Does it Work?

Science developed the insight that memory wouldn't necessarily only reside in the brain. How can it be that we can find all the details about our conception and the first weeks of life when there is no brain? Could it be that memory resides in the cells, capable of replication through cellular multiplication?

But how does it work with memories when there is no brain and no cells, like with an NDE and in the process of incarnation before conception has taken place?

Consciousness outside the brain has been studied by people who have had a Near Death Experience or NDE. They remember the journey outside their body and can tell what had been said in the room while their body was clinically dead. So, if memory doesn't reside in the body, where does it reside?

Bruce Lipton, PhD, says: "A lot of people talk about cellular memory. It says that if you respond to something in the world, that memory is locked in your cells. That is an unfortunate belief because the memory is not in the cells. The memory is in the field of consciousness."

He further explains that stem cells, when they come in to replace dying cells during an illness, don't have previous memory because they are embryonic or stem cells. But they continue the disease. "The issue is: the memory is not in the cells but in the field. If we change the beliefs, we change the field."[11] What is this field?

He continues to explain: "An MRI scan doesn't read the matter but the energy. All parts of the body give off energy and are influenced by energy. Matter is influenced by energy, like iron dust particles on a piece of paper with a magnet under it: the magnet will attract the dust particles in an expression of the magnetic field. The invisible energy of the magnet, not the magnet itself, organizes the shape of the particles. A magnetic field is an example of the field. Einstein said: 'The field is the sole governing agency of the particle.' Energy is shaping the expression of matter. What is the field: invisible moving forces that influence the physical world."[12]

Bruce Lipton: "Inside the atom is nothing physical. There is an energy vortex, a nano tornado, a force field. It has the appearance of physicality, but it is an energy." Albert Einstein said: "Reality, as we perceive it, is an illusion. It is all based on energy." Lipton explains that every atom and molecule emits and absorbs light of characteristic wavelengths. The atom is a spinning energy. It gives off light and absorbs light. We are all interconnected with the field: we are radiating the energy and the energy is coming back, affecting us. Energy is shaping the expression of matter like a magnet will shape the iron particles around it.

In the spiritual teachings, we learn that the etheric body holds this memory. The etheric body is the energy body that pervades the physical body and holds life energy. One of its functions is holding memory.

To return to the brain's function: if the brain doesn't store memory, what function does it have? Dr. Bruce Greyson is an American

Psychiatrist and Professor Emeritus of Psychiatry and Neurobehavioral Sciences and President of the International Association for Near-Death Studies.

Dr. Greyson explains, "The brain is not the generator of, but the *filter* of consciousness. This can be illustrated with a radio analogy: you tune into the channel you wish to listen to and filter out all other channels. The brain is the organ that brings the focus, the attention to what consciousness has to say," as he states in his book: *"The brain is the organ of attention to life."*[13]

Healing

Bruce Lipton states: "The way we have been programmed by conventional medicine is that if there is some kind of disease or some negative aspect of our physiology, we have the tendency to blame the cells or the biochemistry of the genes for our problems. And it turns out that this is misplaced, that actually the cells are open to respond to our thoughts and our consciousness. The issues of disease are not primarily stemming from the cells. First, they stem from the consciousness and then go down to the cells. To bring health into the system: should I manipulate the cells or should I work on consciousness and the answer is: first work on consciousness and the cells will take care of themselves."[14]

Soul Healing: How I can Help

Next to being a Childbirth Educator, I work with modalities that can bring negative and traumatic experiences to your consciousness so that we can transform them.

My specialization lies in Prenatal work, and I am certified in **the Therapy of Intra-Uterine Life**, a modality based on the teachings of Dr. Claude Imbert. —called 'Sophro-Analyse' in French. This approach delves into the impactful moments of incarnation, conception, and the imprints of the nine prenatal months, birth, and the first year. Through this work I developed a deep understanding of our vulnerability in the start of a human being and the potential for transformation that lies within us.

As a **Certified Journey Practitioner,** I expanded the search for the emotional roots of illness and unbalance to life in general. Physical diseases and emotional suffering have roots in a past traumatic experience. Through the body, we can access these memories. My experiences with these modalities are rich and convincing. Early imprints determine how we see ourselves and relate to others and life. If these imprints are not transformed, they fester in the unconsciousness and create over and over again the same difficulties, frustrations, failures, blocks, and even illnesses. When a deep emotional hurt occurs that has not been made conscious and healed, the cells in the body that are weaker are blocked from receiving nutrition or letting out toxins, and they become ill. Just by returning to the moment that this hurt occurred, stepping into the difficult emotions, processing them and coming to forgiveness, we can heal even physically. But they can be turned around by looking into these early imprints and reprogramming them to restore wellbeing. This modality is the beautiful path taught by Brandon Bays, the founder of the method of The Journey ®.

In my development as a healer, I was put on the road to discovering the Akashic Records. I am a **Certified Akashic Record Reader** since 2020 through the Akashic Knowing School of Wisdom, founded by Lisa Barnett in the US.

Knowing that I still have a lot to discover and develop, I see myself in service to the people who want to explore more about their essence, their development with all its hurdles, problems and questions regarding themselves, relationships and choices to make.

There are three key elements in these healing modalities:

- The first one is accessing the *soul level* of information and healing. When we can look from a higher point of view, things change drastically and we see the truth, the essence of the experience. This way, we don't turn around in circles for weeks or months; the healing is quick and effective.

- Another precious key is understanding the current life issues by going into the *ancestral line*. More about this in another part of this book. The following examples illustrate such healings.

- The third key to clarifying current difficulties is searching for their roots in *past existences*. Although this doesn't come forward very much in the following examples, it is used extensively in this form of healing. The following examples show how physical and emotional aspects are connected and how even physical illnesses can be healed by addressing the emotional root of the ailment.

Testimonials of Physical and Emotional Healing

Rose is fourteen weeks pregnant for the second time. She had a miscarriage previously. Rose had some pain, but not extreme. She undergoes surgery to tie up the cervix. After the surgery, she is very much in pain. Painkillers don't work. The uterus is as hard as a ball. In the Journey session, she comes to the experience of fear of her mother while Rose was being born by c-section, and the inexperienced physician cuts her intestines. She understands that she has picked up the fear and the traumatic experience of her mom. Baby Rose thinks she is responsible for her mom's health problem and feels guilty and not loved, not wanted. By bringing the resources that the baby would have needed, Rose finally accepts that she is unconditionally loved. The pain in the uterus vanishes after one session.

Kayla had a car accident, after which her neck is constantly tense, rigid and painful. Writing on the computer is not possible for more than ten minutes. She had to stop working. The session brings her back to an experience of sexual abuse as a child. She also remembers her prenatal period when her mom was depressive. She lost contact with her mother before birth. She feels unloved, devalued, rejected and exploited. She decides that she must always be perfect to be loved. In the session, she connects with her soul essence, which makes her very happy. She can forgive the people involved with her tough experiences. We worked on other issues in subsequent sessions, and finally, the neck let go of tension and pain for a big part.

Eric comes with a complaint about pain in the spleen. He came into the world with a special gift of connection to a more subtle world. Eric was a very sensitive child and was rather introverted. He remembers that his family, especially his father, didn't understand his talent, and his parents' quarrels affected Eric: he disconnected from the invisible world. During the Journey session, he remembers himself as an unborn baby and how he picked up his mother's feelings. She lives through fear, anger, anxiety and nervousness because of the pregnancy that her parents did not accept. There is also a primordial fear of death that comes from a previous lifetime of Eric. In that lifetime, he was stuck in a cave covered by a landslide, which generated a deep fear of death. He decided not to feel his emotions anymore because it was too hard. In the session, with the right resources and processing, he turns this decision into a positive one: to allow to feel his feelings and the expression of his emotions. He also gives himself the right to be connected to the invisible world again. After the session, the spleen is completely fine.

Healing with this method works very well on physical ailments and is also very efficient in cases of emotional overwhelm or blockage. Spiritual issues can also be processed. The following two cases give examples.

Marylin feels she auto-sabotages herself. She is a competent entrepreneur but stays in her cocoon when she should undertake action to get a position she'd love to have. The session brings her to the time when she was four years old, seeing her mother unhappy and struggling with feelings of guilt. Marylin doesn't give herself the right to be happier than her mom and shuts down, feeling victim to her surroundings. She craves love from her father, but as it doesn't come, she believes she is unlovable. Marylin feels inferior and powerless and fears to take her place. She changes her beliefs to have the right to joy, happiness and love. She decides to be fully responsible for her happiness and sincerely forgives her parents. Because of the shift she felt during the session, she decided to take the position of manager she wished for and moved to the other side of the country. She writes: "*I feel more at my place. Thanks to this work, I could step into the job choices that I previously would have had difficulties accepting. I feel that the new job is what I deserve.*"

Wendy comes with the concern about feeling cut off from her intuition. When she investigates the origin as a child, fear, anger and disappointment come up in connection to her father. He overwhelms her quickly with his very authoritarian attitude and his strong voice. Wendy felt she didn't have the right to be there, to be herself. She was just in survival mode and felt worthless. Growing older, disdain towards him grew because of his sexual desires towards her. She needed to be more mature than him. Wendy can perceive how her father felt as a child: he accumulated rage and disappointment towards his mother. Through this empathic feeling, she can forgive. Wendy sees that it is the disdain for her father that obscures her cells as well as her intuition. She restructured this experience by cleansing her being and bringing light onto the cells and her subtle bodies.

Experiences From the Womb

"The prenatal cosmos is the primal ground for the postnatal cosmos"- Peter Sloterdijk

As we have seen in the previous examples of trauma, healing is possible by transforming the negative outcomes and reprograming the limiting imprints in a positive, supportive way. The following examples of womb experiences are also not written in stone. They can be reprogrammed. It is first important to become aware, and then we can reach out to a higher level in us to discover ways to turn these imprints into a fulfilling state of being.

Three trimesters of possible trauma

Before we continue with case studies from my practice, I would like to share the insights of William Emerson, a pioneer in Prenatal Psychology and Baby Therapist. The experiences through regression from his clients in his clinical practice allowed him to see a distinct difference in the effect of trauma depending on the trimester in which the trauma had occurred. In his co-authored book "Remembering Our Home," (1999)[15] Emerson explains the different stages of psychological development of the embryo and fetus according to the trimesters.

If there were a memory of trauma in the **first** trimester, when all the body systems and organs are formed, the trauma would result in physical malformation of organs or bodily systems.

During the **second** trimester, a spiritual connection is very present. In remembering, the adults find memories of bliss, being cared for in unity with spirit and developing trust in a higher source. Interrupting this experience by a sudden difficulty or trauma can result in the unborn baby feeling disconnected from spirit for the rest of his life, having an aversion to spirituality, or a fixation on one narrow form of spirituality. The child, later in life, can revolt against anything related to God. Feeling God's presence may trigger terror or rage. They may have difficulty connecting to their inner self. However, as we have seen in the previous examples of trauma, healing is possible by transforming the negative outcomes and reprograming the limiting imprints in a positive, supportive way. The following examples of womb experiences are also not written in stone. They can be reprogrammed. It is first important to empower ourselves with awareness, and then we can reach out to a higher level in us to discover ways to turn these imprints into a fulfilling state of being.

The **third** trimester introduces a gradual individuation process in the baby's psyche; he develops a separate sense of self. The ego or sense of self unfolds out of connection with the spirit, which continues throughout life. Trauma in this trimester is like a sudden disconnection with spirit and is felt as a sense of loss, being separated too early from the stream of trust and grace. Some situations that are very common in this third trimester for the parents are having to move or renovate their home to make a place for the baby, which can be stressful for the mother. So many women are working till the end with a big belly, not being able to sleep properly or developing anxiety towards the birth. For the baby, being in too tight a space at the end of pregnancy can be traumatizing.

Different Stages of Development

The prenatal period, a significant chapter in constructing our being, holds the key to understanding the challenges we face in life. In the following sections, we delve into the various stages of prenatal life, each with its unique influence on the development of the psyche. Drawing from my own experiences with clients, I will illustrate how trauma can originate in this period and, more importantly, how it can be healed.

The soul's journey starts in the world where the soul is at home, which means in the realm of unlimited love, eternal light, and pure Divine essence. The all-pervading love, unity, harmony, and beauty a soul experiences there are the expressions of this divine light that created everything, including the soul. It is there where we are surrounded by light beings who guide and assist us. We as a soul are also embedded in a soul family, whose members evolve together and support each other's process of evolution.

Our twin soul also exists there: our other half with whom we form one soul, each bringing forth the masculine or feminine aspect of the soul. We form one unity through the purest love possible. Imagine leaving this home to incarnate! Leaving that atmosphere of divine light to leave our soul family and, on top of that, the most profound love connection possible: leaving our twin soul! That is when our strongest trauma of separation starts. The journey to the earth is mainly described as the same for all souls. Only the attitude can be very different.

> *"You cannot gain meaningful liberation unless you*
> *fully work through or come in contact with the*
> *womb."*
>
> - Namghyal Rinpoche

Incarnation

According to William Emerson (1999), three groups of souls manifest specific reactions to this journey to the earth. Only 10 percent of souls who are very well connected to the divine remember to have wholeheartedly accepted leaving this realm and going on their mission to the earth. They live happy, loving lives and have mainly simple life purposes to which they are intensely connected. They often achieve great things.

A second group, between 60 and 70 percent, knows they have a specific task on earth that will help them to evolve. Only they are reluctant to leave their paradise. They fear they will not make it. They will feel this separation from the divine world when on earth and long to find it again. Emerson calls this "Divine Homesickness." If this feeling is not brought to consciousness, they may find life tasteless, overcast and grey and be prone to depression. Once they heal these emotions and feel their connection again to Source and know they can find it again at any moment, they see how their longing for money, power and romantic love are merely longing to reconnect with Source or God.

The third group of souls – about 20 to 30 percent – feel exiled from heaven. They feel they have been cast out against their will. A range of sharp emotions turn their hearts upside down, like anger or rage, resistance, revolt, revenge or injustice. Sometimes, they disconnect entirely from God and eventually turn against Him. They think of themselves as innately bad or wrong and deal with shame and guilt. They might become fanatic warriors against 'evil' or, on the contrary, cave into ritual abuse.

So, the soul's preparation before conception already carries a blueprint of the core emotions it must deal with during life after birth. During this time, the soul makes her choices for the next life. With their guides, they explore options and make choices regarding the country and culture to come into. Contracts are made with important players in life, such as parents, siblings, friends, and teachers. The main goals are set about what to develop, what to overcome, and what to manifest.

Let's look into the notion of karma. Much needs to be developed as all souls evolve to match the divine template of perfection. In previous lifetimes, we could not manifest that perfection yet. We made errors and karma was created. Some traditions explain karma as paying or restoring what was not right, which creates the notion of guilt. We can also understand it as learning the lesson in the best way this time. However, Kevin Todeschi in his book "Edgar Cayce on the Akashic Records" wrote that Cayce saw karma as nothing more than "memory." Cayce stated that there is no karma between people; there is only karma with oneself. To adjust our behaviour, we "meet ourselves" through our interactions with others. "It is this interesting dynamic of meeting oneself through relationships with others that often causes individuals to perceive them as the basis of one's frustrations and challenges, rather than accepting personal responsibility."

In this process of determining the critical relationships we'll cultivate on earth, we make choices and soul contracts with the motive of learning lessons, this time in a better way, or if you will, based on karma. With the help of guides and light beings, the soul can determine the best choices to make to evolve. In his book: "Courageous Souls, Do We Determine Our Challenges Before Birth?" Robert Schwarz describes ten cases in which people consciously choose their difficulties to guarantee learning and evolution. The more challenges, the quicker we evolve.

When that is all determined, the time comes to leave this divine place of unconditional love and the soul feels attracted to the earth and the family that welcomes it. The emotions coming up in this process are the concentrated essence of what to deal with in the coming life. It can become the first wound, which is the most important because it will repeat itself endlessly, attracting the situations that reinforce that wound until we connect consciously to that first moment and heal it. For example, the trauma of separation in the period before conception eventually repeats during birth or through any separation experience in life: death of a loved one, divorce, or losing your job. It will bring excruciating pain because it unconsciously wakes up the primal wound of separation from Source.

Sabina felt intense pressure on the thorax and the lungs. The memory of her incarnation came up: the time just before conception when she felt attracted to the earth. She feels frozen. "I don't want to move," she says, "I want to stay in heaven. What they ask from me is too heavy; it is enormous. I am not capable. Everything will be taken away from me, everything I know. I already lost my memory about how it was." Injustice, revolt and sadness come up. She continues: "I was obliged to go, I was forced. It is too hard. They don't understand me, they didn't explain." And: "It's as if I didn't understand something, and I have to incarnate again to understand it better." She feels insecure and her belly hurts. While leaving heaven, she feels like she is sliding into a fall and into nothingness. Emptiness, loneliness, separated from her soul. Although her twin soul reassures her: "The goal is to learn to cope alone, to have confidence in yourself and your intuition." Her guide plants a cherry seed in her heart that represents her intuition. She feels more confident stepping into this next lifetime. The pressure on her thorax decreases.

Hannah sees yellow and blue light when she decided to start her journey toward the Earth. Approaching planet Earth and the house where she will arrive, she feels a contraction in her heart. The house is rather gloomy and cold, not welcoming. "I don't feel like coming in," she says, "I want to return. There is no freedom, only confinement and sadness. There is no space. I'll not be able to flourish." She remembers the blue tunnel from before her jump to the earth. She was told: "You'll have a long way to go. There will be lots of obstacles. They are there to reinforce you. You'll want to find the light, but you'll be prevented. You'll pass through the obstacles and you'll advance nevertheless. Now, you have the chance to develop love, patience and strength. It will take a lot of courage. There will be a danger of losing your light and your inner strength. But all together, it will be worth it." These words help her to accept. She'd like to advance. She finds confidence in herself. A small flame stays ahead of her and pulls her towards advancing. This spark helps her to feel more freedom. Another message comes: 'Find refuge in your heart and try to find again this little flame. Clear out the darkness around you. Love will be the strongest. It will be larger, more powerful and stronger than anything else." She feels more secure and confident in her inner strength. Her connection with the light neutralizes all dangers.

Claire is a very spiritually developed woman, determined to listen to her intuition. When she explores her incarnation process, she remembers: "I was told to leave. I don't accept it completely. I feel abandoned and lonely." But something tells her she must sacrifice her desires because something more important must happen.

Nevertheless, she feels resentment and sadness because she doesn't feel ready. This loneliness, having to leave her soul family, is not what she wants. "I'll not be able to manage it. The job is too big. There are no tools. I'll have to fight to survive," she thinks. An angel tells her: "You're able. You can do it. You looked for it yourself, but you don't believe in yourself now. The goal of all the trouble is to get stronger and more experienced." She realized that "I am part of the puzzle of something bigger.' She gains confidence knowing she can stay connected to her higher self. The angel gives her a symbol in the form of a lotus. It feels like a key to remember her as one with them.

In my own story of saying goodbye to my husband after his nature accident, I have been helped tremendously by the work I had done previously on my prenatal roots, especially the part of the incarnation when I said goodbye to my twin soul. This was a very intense moment, as the sadness of leaving this inspiring true love was profound. The trauma of separation starts there if it is not healed. Every departure of a loved one, a dear friend or a family member can be heartbreaking because we wake up again to the trauma of this first separation. If that is healed, the grief process will be much less difficult.

Conception

We can also remember the experience of the creation of the first cell that was at the origin of our body. Vital elements of both gametes, the energy they each bring and the ambiance in which they merge constitute the basic fabric of our body and psyche. The Australian psychotherapist Graham Farrant (1988) stated that conception is not a duality but a triune constellation: the sperm, the egg and the soul meet. The whole journey of each gamete, from its creation to the union with the other gender, is registered in our being. They can be remembered while in the alpha state. It can be wonderful. Like this description by one of my clients:

"I see the colour pink... There is a dance going on: The totality of life wants to penetrate the ovum...The force of life in all its gentleness...several sperm cells surround the ovum...the egg cell waits in pink...she feels honoured and caressed... fluid movements.... The sperm cell, conscious that he will be the one penetrating, sure of himself... takes his time... The ovum also knows it is him...they recognize each other..."

People exploring the whereabouts of eggs or sperm tend to follow only the journey related to their gender. A man would identify with the experience of the sperm cells, and a woman would choose to follow the path of an egg cell.

The sperm's journey is often reported as a struggle between life and death. In their multitude, they organize into an intelligent system in which the chances of survival are enhanced. They form a team. But even with this fraternal cooperation, this journey is exhausting and dangerous for their survival; indeed, many can't reach the ovum or the egg. Finally, the egg is in sight for some of them and the penetration stage is prepared. If the couple's relationship is not the best, the sperm feels overwhelmed by the enormous size of the egg, which is thousands of times larger than a sperm cell; it feels that the egg is all-powerful and annihilating. If the parent's relationship is harmonious, the sperm still feels the powerfulness of the egg but is not overwhelmed by it. Once the chosen sperm enters the egg's body, the tail falls off and the egg consumes the head. It feels like a loss of identity, a loss of self, a sacrifice for another's purpose.

The life story of the eggs is a long one. It started in the womb of the grandmother when your mother, as a fetus, was growing her egg cells in her mother's womb. This egg cell sorority has absorbed grandmother's experiences, beliefs and hardships. When the time comes for a ripe egg cell to start on the road toward the uterus, she must leave this close-knit sisterhood and experiences loss and grief. The new experience of falling into the fallopian tube brings fear of loss of control. Later, fear of initiative or risks or being alone can start here. The egg cell is nourished and propelled by the milky liquid in the tube until the sperm cells finally meet her.

The egg cell chooses the sperm, contrary to what was previously thought. If the relationship between both partners is not harmonious, the egg can undergo the penetration of the sperm as rape or violent and overpowering. If the relationship is good, it can take a sacral aspect, in which both gametes re- enact the creation of the universe in a play of two powerful forces that create life out of love. That will give a basis for self-respect to the child and the ability to give and receive love.

The soul is aware of the experiences of the egg and sperm, as well as the relationship between their parents. If the act of conception manifests abuse, violence or dominance of one partner, it affects the basic feeling of the human being that is created. It can push the child to violent behaviour, wanting to dominate or even to an aversion against the other gender. A violent conception can be the origin of impotence. If drugs are used, the experience of the child will be one of diffuseness, loss of orientation and loss of vitality. In the case of aversion against sexual intercourse and shame, the memory of conception will be transfused with shame and guilt. The child knows if it is wanted or not, an accident or not.

These tiny cells can undergo negative experiences. Luckily though, once a person becomes conscious, they can be restructured in a positive, life-supporting way.

Cara wishes to discover this first journey to understand and free herself. She hopes to do a feng shui of the first cell that created her body if needed. She starts at the very beginning in the ovary of her mom. She feels into the cell in the ovary. It is introverted. It fears the consequences of not having all the elements she'd need for the big journey into life. The other cells of the sorority push her out. After this jump, she feels lonely; she doesn't want to go. "It will be difficult to leave a beautiful place to go to the unknown," she musters. "The place I go to is like a complicated hell. It is cold there and not welcoming." The fallopian tube feels funny with the tiny hairs that push the egg cell further. It helps her to let go of the fear.

Then, her mother comes to her awareness. She knows that her mother wishes to conceive a child that corresponds to her soul's ideal. Cara feels good about that because her mother's love is real love. However, the man with whom she conceives is not the father who brought her up. He has a higher Christ energy than the latter. Her mom feels guilty, though. Cara's egg cell absorbs this guilt.

She tunes into the sperm cells. They seem like men without heads who don't know where they are going. One has a head and resembles a proud noble knight. It is this sperm cell that meets the egg cell—an ambiance of solemnity, like a wedding. The sperm cell is dazzled by the sacredness of the moment. The egg cell opens itself, welcomes, and lets itself penetrate. Everything is respectful, cosmic and plenitude.

The first cell is created, and the DNA is established. The soul feels she can deal with all the influences of the father, the mother, the ancestors and all the subtle presences. Only, from Cara's incarnated point of view, she doesn't like the hidden real identity of her father. She never knew who her biological father was. Anger, sadness, disappointment, obliged renouncement. A shadow stays hidden, a hidden family secret. A somber veil falls over her. Resentment of the masculine and feminine principle, powerlessness, endless despair. "The paradise I hoped for isn't there," she moans. The soul comes in with healing energies of warmth, Christ energy and humility. A guide asks the Divine Mother to protect the first cell with a starry blue cloak that will help her remember the divine world. Now there is life force, total joy, zest for life, wanting to flourish, to do. "Being in doing, doing in being."

With **Vivian,** we see how the gametes carry the energy of the mother or the father. Vivian discovers fear in the egg cell. Why this fear? She'll have to change and leave behind the security of what she knew. She is afraid of being destroyed. She is afraid of leaving home and going into the unknown.

The sperm cell is perceived as the attacker. The egg cell feels threatened. But at the same time, she feels drawn to it, as the sperm cell shows a bigger force. She brings up a parallel to her feminine energy as an adult which she describes as manipulative, using her sexual force to entrap or manipulate. This brings up the wish to accept herself in all aspects. A connection to the energy of the Divine Mother helps her to do that. She steps into the child in her mother and uncovers her loneliness, and a disconnection to the divine world, she doesn't feel protected. The child in her mom saw her parents fighting and took over the fear of her mom of the other gender. A healing is done on the grandmother. Now the egg cell is shinier, much more willing and ready to embrace.

The sperm cell is aggressive from fear, an overcompensating feeling from insecurity. It wants to explore the egg cell but doesn't know how to join without destroying the other. It needs to know what love is. As a child, the father is a lonely boy with older parents that can't stand the noise. He didn't know how to connect. Love is brought into him, and a deep connection. Now he is more able to give and take and connect. He loves to be embraced by the egg cell instead of destroying it. There is more openness and acceptance. In the first cell, there is now respect for the other principle, the freedom to be, and acceptance of the roles of each gender.

Implantation

After the conception in the fallopian tube has been successful, the zygote that has evolved into a blastocyst continues its journey toward the uterus, where it arrives after about 6 or 7 days. The next stage is the implanting in the uterus, which is a very important moment and seemingly a dangerous one.

Karlton Terry explains: "Along the early human journey and within the entire prenatal realm with all its perils, the most deadly transition is implantation. It is well known that prenatal mortality is a more likely outcome than birth. The big business of In Vitro Fertilization is booming in our era, not just because it is hard to conceive but mostly because it is hard to implant. During the prenatal stage of implantation alone, the biological dangers are real and in fact only about 55% to 60% of implantations are successful."[16] The uterus is like a wild terrain with hostile, barren places that cannot supply everywhere for the incoming blastocyst.

William Emerson states: "Ideally, the psychological journey of implantation is experienced as finding one's home, a place to put down one's roots and belong. The gift of this journey in later life is the ability to find and make a home for oneself and others."[17]

My own implantation experience came to my consciousness at a moment when I went through a liver crisis. It was undoubtedly related to a financial crisis I went through because of my illusion of lack. When I explored this implantation moment, I felt the free fall of the blastocyst (fertilized egg): endless falling without being able to connect to the uterine wall. Frustration and anger of not being received by my mother. Finally, I started to adhere to the wall, but the massive uterus changed position, and I fell again. Disorientation, paralysis. For a long time, nothing had moved, and I had the impression that I was imposing myself on this place. The connection to the wall established itself, and when the uterus finally changed position again, I terribly feared falling again, but this time, I adhered well enough. I tensed up and I was afraid to lack nourishment or to die. In the restructuring, I saw how my mother brought me everything I needed. The connections on all levels were made: physically, nutritionally, emotionally and spiritually. I let myself be invaded by her warmth and love and by the love of the universe that said yes to my development. I let myself be carried in the arms of the universe through my mother. I was confident that everything comes to me for my unfolding and that I have access to all resources. My liver stopped hurting!

Discovery

Discovery is the pivotal moment when the mother becomes aware of the pregnancy. This moment, ideally filled with celebration and joy, holds immense power. The fetus, highly attuned to this moment, begins to form his self-image and perception of the world based on the mother's reaction. Whether it's a warm welcome, hesitation, or refusal, the mother's response shapes the beliefs and images the fetus constructs about himself and the world around him.

A baby who is warmly welcomed into the world not only thrives but also feels confident. This little one believes in his right to exist, to take up space, to be seen, and to impact the world. The love he received is abundant, and during life, he can easily find this love everywhere: in nature, in people, and in the spiritual world, fostering a sense of hope and anticipation for his future.

- When a baby comes as an unhappy surprise, or there is ambivalence, which is the case in half of the pregnancies in Western cultures, the baby might struggle with issues ranging from shyness and insecurity to even deep shame. Receiving attention and compliments is hard for them. Or just the opposite might be true: a compulsory seeking of attention and recognition.

- A radical non-acceptance of the pregnancy - if the pregnancy continues - might cause the child to repeat the parent's behaviour by rejecting other kids and becoming a bully. This non-acceptance in the first trimester creates a non-acceptance towards Source or God. They will reject the spiritual world.

Eva is a midwife and during the exploration of her prenatal life, she discovered that she comes in as a surprise. Nevertheless her dad rejoices. For her mother, this news creates stress, confusion and mixed emotions. They were not married yet, but they started making plans immediately to do so. They plan on moving too. An element of stress is added when her dad, coming from abroad, is not accepted to enter the United States where they want to live. Even if these plans don't affect the unborn baby, she has received the reaction of her mom as a belief that "Life is stressful" and made this belief her own. Her self-esteem dives. There, Eva decides - unconsciously, of course - that she is the one who needs to take care of her mom. "I have to accept that to thrive, to be loved," she explains. That means that she is not allowed to be just a baby. The restructuring changes the decision to have the right to feel comfortable, calm, and loved as a baby. Later, as an adult, she decides to become a midwife. Was this a substitute for taking care of her mother?

After an overwhelming quarrel, **Joseph** feels not respected, diminished, dirty and exterminated. He feels like he does not have the right to exist. To the question: when he has felt like that before, he remembers the moment his mother discovered her pregnancy. She is not married to her boyfriend. She is so disturbed, and anger comes up. She feels guilty and rejects the baby. The tiny fetus now feels guilty too and thinks he shouldn't have been there. He feels he doesn't have the right to be there and he doesn't have the right to be alive. He rejects himself.

The restructuring helps him to let go of his mom's perception and change his limiting beliefs and self-worth.

Pregnancy

The nine months of the prenatal period are rich in experiences for the unborn baby. The general belief about this period is that it is like being in paradise: the warmth of the surrounding amniotic fluid, being carried everywhere, nutrition that comes constantly. This idyllic image might be true for some unborn beings. However, many aspects can disturb the peaceful ambiance. Some of them are:

- The mother experiences a lot of stress or is emotionally unconnected to her baby.

- Financial trouble, for example, when the parents are still studying

- The parents are not married – 40 years ago, this was an issue that brought judgment, shame and rejection to the parents

- A previous miscarriage: the next child feels that the space in the uterus is not free from grief

- An adverse reaction from the family to the pregnancy

- A disharmonious relationship between the parents

- The death of a loved one

- Health problems of other children in the family

Trauma and the three trimesters

We can divide pregnancy into three trimesters. Each has its specific development and effect on the growing human being.

In Appendix 2 you can find more information about the connection between the different intensities of stress, the mother's consciousness and the effect on the physiology and psychology of the baby.

The first trimester of the prenatal period allows for the basic development of the physical body. At the end of that term, all the organs are in place and only need to develop more. William Emerson reports that trauma or stress harms the physiological systems or organs; according to the moment this stress happens during pregnancy, the organ in a critical development period will be very vulnerable and will be weaker and not optimally functioning. For instance, if a significant trauma occurs between the third and the sixth week, it can have a devastating effect on the development of the heart. The body might be healthy and strong if the first trimester went well.

The second trimester has a specific spiritual importance. It is a period of quietness, like in a yoga practice, when you get silent before meditation, as the big rush of physical development is behind and the fetus's survival is secured. Then, there is an openness to a subtle world and a bodily felt connection to the Source. Stillness is favourable for becoming aware of the natural presence of love, and the true self emerges. When adults are regressing to this second trimester, they describe it as an awareness of their spiritual essence of oneness, being part of paradise again. The mother often feels this second trimester as the period where she feels best and connects easily with the fetus as she starts to feel its movements. If there is trauma during this stage, it will be this sensitivity for spiritual connection that can be damaged. When the adult has experienced trauma during this stage and he tries to connect to Source, these traumas will be unconsciously activated also. This can create an aversion to spirituality or the opposite: a fixation on one narrow form of spirituality.

The third trimester is the beginning of a sense of self. The baby starts to feel a separate, individual being. If the first two trimesters went well, the baby begins to form a sense of self out of its connection to spirit. He is and stays connected to Source and forms a fertile open basis for the experience of union, love, peace, intuition and creativity. If trauma has been happening in the first two trimesters, the development of this sense of self happens too soon. A disconnect from openness happens, a disconnect from Source, a pervasive sense of loss. Instead of trust and faith in grace, what forms is a struggle to defend against pain. But also, anything that causes stress for the mother will be felt even more by the fetus. A myriad of origins of stress are possible: fear of the upcoming birth, moving to a bigger house, renovating or stress at work or in the relationship. It's crucial to prioritize the mother's well- being, as her stressors can significantly impact the fetus. Invoking empathy and concern are helpful in the accompaniment of the mother.

Here are a few examples of how adults in Therapy of Intra- Uterine Life experienced their prenatal period.

Patricia came to a session of Intra-Uterine Life with a deep wish to transform her prenatal and post-natal experiences. Her father wanted a boy, so he was disappointed for her being a girl. Patricia felt rejected for being a girl. The rejection continued by sexual abuse as a child. At twelve years old, she left the house. She was on her own on the street. She survived. During the session, she saw that in her prenatal existence, she felt severed from her mom. There was no emotional connection to her mom. Her mom was not even present to herself emotionally. If she is not present to herself, how can she be present to her unborn baby? Patricia felt like a stranger and would always be a stranger to her mom. She developed a belief that she will always have a life of separation. Being disconnected from others, she decided: "I'll have to do it all by myself." She did: she survived. Her prenatal belief created the situation that confirmed her belief. She felt alienated from herself to such an extent that she believed that "the human element is not important." The disconnection with her mother made her also feel disconnected from the universe, as the mother is the bridge between the unborn baby and nature. If she is disconnected from mom, the link to the universe is broken.

A reconnection to her guides made her feel part of something larger; she felt she belonged somewhere. She came to the feeling of peace, in the hands of God, to universal wisdom, plugged into Source.

Now, she is happily married and a successful healing professional. Because of her hardship, she feels her clients' pain and developed empathy.

Niki is the fifth child growing up in the womb of a depressed mother. The pregnancy wasn't planned. Her mom's relationship with her husband is emotionally distant, and also, towards her unborn child, she has no connection. No bonding is taking place with the baby. As a three-month-old fetus, she feels her mom's sadness and fear. Everything falls apart. The father is always gone and doesn't bring in any money. Niki is hopeless and finds she is a burden on top of the heaviness of the situation. She feels guilty and takes over the depression of her mother. Later in life, Niki starts drinking to become numb to it all. Finally, she frees herself with eight years of recovery through different types of therapy. She turns her old beliefs of being a burden, being a bad girl, and being scared to follow her dreams into positive ones that bring worthiness, light, and the courage to follow her passion.

The mother of **Diane** is okay with the fourth pregnancy in six years. Her father is happy and wishes for a son. As small as she is, Diane knows her father who is quite dominant, wishes to have a boy. She pretends to give him what he wants so she will be loved. Later, as a child, she is as boyish as can be. She has more fun playing with boys than being with girls. In the womb, the conflict inside grows. Even in the belly, Diane feels she doesn't exist because there is no connection. 'I'm just a bump, a part of my mother,' she says. She is unprehensive, ignored, swept aside, frustrated and angry. She doesn't feel valued and feels she is only taking up space. "I make things awkward in the womb. I'm in the way," is what she experiences. She feels terrible about herself, ashamed and guilty. Diane thinks she is responsible for things going wrong. She decides to take as little place as possible in the womb. During the restructuring part of the session, her father receives the necessary resources and accepts her as a girl. A guide gives her a star to remind her of her most profound essence. She finally feels accepted, having entirely the right to exist the way she is and take up the space she needs.

"Why do I always need to be perfect and feel guilty if I'm not?" **Lisa** asks herself. When she looks for the root of this fixation, she ends up in the womb.

There she is, motionless, "I shouldn't move in order not to displease. I shouldn't disturb my mom. It's as if I would die. I'm afraid to die, to disappear." Finally, she sees through her trouble that *her mother* has this fixation on perfection: SHE cannot displease and needs to be perfect to compensate for her unworthiness. It is suffocating and paralyzing. Lisa has taken over this pattern of her mother. "It's as if I am nothing for my mother; I don't have any value for her." She feels abandoned and lonely. "I don't have the right to exist" is her conviction. Looking from higher up, she is guided to see how layers of protection and warmth surround her. She receives nourishment from her mother constantly. Little by little, she opens up to the love surrounding her: the love coming from her mother's body. She feels loved for the first time. She can finally feel recognition of herself and the right to be herself. This is a new step on the path of healing.

Vanishing Twins

A vanishing twin is the phenomenon of the death in utero of one of the set of twins. Embryologists estimate that 30 to 80 percent of us were conceived with a twin. But not so many twins make it to the finishing line of birth. This is a big hurdle for the psyche of the surviving twin as it changes the surroundings drastically. Often, it is the first relationship that the embryo or the fetus is aware of before the mother knows that she is pregnant and can start a relationship with her unborn child. When the other dies, the surviving twin goes through deep hurts and intense emotions because it is like leaving a friend behind. Emotions of sadness, hopelessness, loneliness, disorientation and guilt are felt profoundly and, if not consciously restructured, are reactivated easily after birth during life. Limiting beliefs about relationships can originate there, which withholds the surviving adult from finding a suitable partner.

Iris studied anthropology and is passionate about listening to people's life stories. Her own life story is very unique. Her family history on the maternal side shows that every first-born baby died. Iris's mom, too: Iris was born as part of a twin. Her twin sister died just before birth. In the uterus, everything was fine: she felt the unity and connection with her twin sister as if they had always been like that. Then, before the birth process, Iris felt an undefined feeling of danger and confusion. Suddenly, there was silence and tightness. She was alone! Anxiety fell over her. All strength flew out of her body, "I can't stay here. I don't want to live." She felt guilty; something was broken and not finished. She disconnected from life to survive. She could not accept the welcome of her family because she felt responsible for her mother's sadness. Before birth, her sister and Iris were there for each other. Iris was there to help her sister, who held Iris's hand. They were equal, a two-way link. "It doesn't seem right that one left. Now I have to do everything alone. I can't count on someone else," she brought up. When during the session, Iris reached out to her sister to express how hard it was, her sister answered from her soul essence: "This was my path. This is how it needed to be." Iris accepted. She received precious resources to heal the old imprints, freeing her from guilt and changing her limiting beliefs, opening to the world and having the right to ask for help. Iris became a death doula, a doula who accompanies people who are passing on, using her experience of having processed and healed her grief.

"Points of light are dancing above me" discovers **Tony** during an exploration in the womb when he was a fetus of two months old. "There is a presence above me." He discovered the presence of a girl in the same womb space with him. This was so exciting and comforting! When we went forward in time, at five months, Tony moved around to connect with her again but couldn't find her. He perceived a dark form. She was gone... Sadness, and more profoundly, anger and confusion. He could not accept this. "Maybe it's because of me! I was too big and took too much of the food. There wasn't enough room for her... I am guilty of her passing!" During the session, Tony contacted the soul of this twin sister, who showed herself as a distant light. She explained: 'It wasn't my time to be born. I was there for you to help in the transition and the passage to this new life. I must go back. Please remember me as 'Lumina'. Tony could accept it now. With the love he received from this connection and healing, he understood the essence of this experience: to develop the ability to let go. And he knows he can continue to connect with Lumina anytime he wants.

Abortion attempt

"No! You're going to ruin my life," exclaims the mother when she discovers she is pregnant with **Bridget.** Her husband is not her true love. Her first love was impossible. If she accepts this pregnancy, she feels like she is sacrificing her life for this baby and it will prevent her from realizing something important. Already, Bridget feels she has no right to live, and she makes herself seem tiny. She tries to escape, going up as a spiral of light, high into the airy space, where there is more warmth and freedom. "I was fooled. I'm not accepted. I don't belong here," Bridget understands. The next moment, a nasty liquid enters the uterus. This threat is so brutal and incomprehensible.

Bridget fears for her life. This hostility makes her feel cold and insecure. How to escape this? Terrified, she tries to press herself up against the wall, higher up, sheltered. The storm calms down. Bridget creates the belief that "I brought a stain to my mom's sacred space." Should I leave? Should I stay? Bridget decides: "I'll stay because I came to bring something for my mother. I know I bring her joy and life energy." Nevertheless, she feels rejected and not seen for who she is. She decides to build up walls around herself where she feels safer. She needs to hide; she cannot show herself. "So be quiet, don't move, don't grow up," she tells herself. It's frustrating because she'd like to discover, explore and travel, but she doesn't give herself the right.

During the healing, she asks her soul essence to bring in life force, a big YES to life, to warmth, and gradually, she starts to accept. A beautiful rainbow bridge connects her mother's heart with Bridget's.

A healing is done on the inner child of her mother too, who was not desired either. Finally, the higher self of the mother says a convincing YES to the soul of Bridget and admits: "You have given me so much love. You have helped me above all hope. You gave my life meaning. Without you, life would have been unbearable." This makes her feel so much loved. The limiting space of the embryo becomes infinite space with endless possibilities. Now she feels that she has the right to live, grow and explore.

Assisted Reproduction Techniques (ART)

Infertility has been rising in the last decades and in 2023 it affected 17.5% of couples. The reasons can be multiple.

- The physical state of health regarding hormonal imbalance.

- The pollution of the air, the soil and food can be a contributing factor.

- The psychological level can often be the origin of an unconscious wish not to become pregnant. Psycho-genealogy can shed light on the negative experiences of the ancestors regarding war, miscarriages or death during pregnancy.

- On a spiritual level, it can be that before your conception, no soul contract was made with the soul of a future child. You choose to have a life without becoming a parent.

Science has made it possible, though, through the development of assisted reproductive technology (ART) to bridge the physical obstacles and the wish to have a baby.

ART, like In Vitro Fertilization, has been increasingly used because of this rising rate of infertility. ART is an artificial way for the child to be conceived. This intervention is invaluable for parents struggling with infertility and realizing their wishes for a child. Although the effect on the baby itself is mostly overlooked. It can have many implications for its psychic well-being.

No love energy is directly involved; it is all done in a cold laboratory environment. Karlton Terry (2004) stated that "IVF (In Vitro Fertilization) babies need help finding structure, need help 'finding their bodies' and need support in feeling safe with their emotions. Most IVF babies seem to have some disconnection from their bodies. They seem to have difficulty being grounded, organized and relaxed in their bodies."[18] The soul finds it difficult to connect to the body.

Rien Verdult (2015), a psychotherapist in Belgium, states that "psychological problems can come out of the use of anonymous sperm donors, as is mostly preferred by single mothers and lesbian couples. More donor-conceived children seem to seek their missing identity. Sharing motherhood can lead to maternal jealousy among lesbian co-mothers. Surrogate mothering, as can be the case in homosexual couples, implicates a problematic prenatal attachment development for the baby."[19] The manipulation of both the sperm cells and the egg cells in the process of fertilization can be traumatizing, depending on the method used. If the sperm is injected into the egg cell, as in the technique of ISCI, we can speak of a feeling of rape on the level of the egg cell. The freezing of the fertilized embryos affects these children, struggling with feeling cold. The loss of twins in the process can have the effects of the vanishing twin syndrome. The stress of the mother and fear of miscarriage can be present during the pregnancy and cause a delay in bonding. This does not give a positive experience for the growing fetus.

Being Born

How we pass through this entry into the big world is strongly related to previous experiences in the womb. Birth is the exam after the learning experience of nine months. What the baby goes through here is a reactivation of what happened before. Depending on the acceptance of the baby, the acceptance of its gender, the genealogical imprints of the death of the mother or baby in the ancestry, the fear of the mother towards birth, and if there is an emotional connection, the outcome will be different.

Medical interventions can be very important and lifesaving, but they can unwillingly bring in complications and make the birth experience worse. Unfortunately, the psychological implications for the baby are not taken into consideration. They can be life-programming if they are not consciously addressed.

Birth is shocking for most babies; it is even the most shocking experience in life. Is that the case for everybody? Only 5 percent experience little or no lasting trauma. About 50 percent go through trauma from mild to severe and 45 percent experience shock.

There are three main parts to a baby's experience of being born:

- The start of the birth process is the decision of the baby to initiate the birth process. The tightness of his space, the toxic environment of the womb, or a need for change can be the decision factors to the start. Physiologically it coincides with the ripeness of the lungs to have the ability to breathe once born. A protein produced substance is then secreted into the amniotic fluid that creates inflammation in the uterus, which creates the sign to start the contractions. Confidence about himself and about the welcome of the family and of the world will be helpful factors in the unfolding of the birth. If there are oppositions to him, the birth may be experienced as difficult. From this way of initiating the birth process the baby has programmed his way of initiating action in later life, the easiness of making decisions. If labour is induced by Pitocin, this ability to be confident in decision-making will be disturbed and an imprint of being invaded, intruded on, interfered or controlled is created. They feel incapable and anger can be the result in stressful situations.

- The stage of contractions, in the beginning, feels for the baby like a slight massage contrary to a sense of crushing or oppression later during birth. This stage is felt as dangerous, and fear of death is generated when the space is getting tighter and tighter and the pressure mounts, but there is no escape possible because the door is closed. Powerlessness or aggressiveness can come up. If Pitocin has been in the process, the contractions are even wilder and constant without any rest. They report a feeling of loss of control. Claustrophobia and panic can be activated. Here, the emotional connection and collaboration of the mother and father with the baby will be highly supportive to him. If there is no connection, the baby develops the belief of having to do everything alone; there is no help. This belief can be the start of loneliness in life. If the process goes too quickly or takes too long, they are both traumatizing. Suppose it takes long hours because of the inefficiency of contractions or the position of the baby in the birth canal. In that case, both mother and baby are exhausted, and the baby can suffer a lack of oxygen and heart rate decelerations. If it proceeds very quickly, the transition for the baby is overwhelming, having to process such a tremendous change in a very short time. Later in life, action might unfold too quickly, skipping important stages. Feeling stuck during birth can be reactivated in later life as failing to progress or feeling stuck in the unfolding of a desired action.

- The expulsion stage or the birth itself is again the result of many aspects that have originated earlier in the prenatal period. The ideal situation for the baby at birth is that he experiences success and completion through his efforts and buckles his hero's journey. Unfortunately, a "natural and unmedicated" birth is becoming very rare. But the babies lucky enough to have had this kind of birth have many advantages over other babies. They have more self-confidence, are energetic and trust their strength. They know for sure that the world is a safe place and feel connected to it.

Anesthesia during birth creates more difficulties in bonding after birth because these babies are too drugged to focus, make eye contact and connect. The adults who had anesthesia reported having problems with needing to be in control or surrendering control when it is not appropriate. A study found that in the case of suicide, there was a link between the kind of birth and the way the person ended his life. Drugs used during birth would correspond to a suicide through drugs or drugs overdose.

Forceps and vacuum deliveries are experienced as painful, intrusive and violent, even if anesthesia is used. These babies can be defensive when touched, cuddled, or stroked. They feel easily manipulated, forced or obliged to act. Recurring headaches or migraines can be the result in later life.

Cesarian section, especially the elective kind, when the baby is not engaged in vaginal delivery, can create a need for physical touch. They are cuddle-hungry. They tend to put themselves in dangerous situations and expect to be rescued. They might lack the confidence to solve a problem on their own. A cesarian birth takes away the experience of power to push yourself out of the body, which is essential for self- esteem. The babies already engaged in a vaginal delivery but didn't progress describe a feeling of being stuck, not having the ability to succeed or finish a task. Some feel the intervention of cesarian birth is like rape, or they can generate fear of knives. They often think they have killed their mother or feel guilty to have caused her harm. The bonding with the mother can be difficult after cesarian. If the mother were unconscious, like in an emergency cesarian, the separation from the mother during the time she remains unconscious can be devastating for the baby. If the transition from the uterus to the cold world in the operating room proceeds too quickly, the baby feels overwhelmed and confused.

Breech babies

Dr. Akira Ikegawa, OB-GYN in Japan, explains that babies can be in a breech position for two reasons. First, they want to be with their head upright like their mother. If the mother or the birth assistant talks to the baby, they will turn in 90% of the cases.

The other 10 % have a will on their own. They don't feel ready to come to earth. They don't want to be born.

There is resistance because of some scenarios that have built up in utero. They greet life backwards. They might not feel secure in the confrontation with their parents. They don't come at the right moment, or they think they are not of the proper sex in the eyes of the parents. A feeling of unworthiness can be the result. That can happen in the case of a vanishing twin, says Dr. Claude Imbert. The surviving part of the twin that is to be born is convinced of being guilty of having killed his twin and refers to the birth as appearing before a judge. It is hard work to be born like that; it can harm the mother, which generates guilt again. The baby can come in the beech position to reactivate his belief that was generated earlier in the pregnancy that "life is a battle." If the birth attendant forcefully turns the baby, they may feel they did something wrong. The importance is the connection with the baby and in the communication with him, to understand what he goes through so he might turn around on his own and accept to be born in the normal position.

Sheryl is an osteopath, writing her thesis about the spiral the baby makes during the birth process. She wants to explore her own experience of birth. Her exploration focuses both on her performance of following the natural way to turn as a spiral during the birth process and how she felt. Sheryl's mother felt embarrassed when she learned she was pregnant; she didn't particularly want to be a mother. The pregnancy was not planned, but the baby was not unwanted. Her father suffered from depression. Sheryl describes her parents as very self-centred.

Once the birth process is well on its way, Sheryl feels the tightness in front of her. But there are no contractions and labor has stalled. Sheryl feels very alone. She tries to get ahead by pushing with her feet. 'I have to do it all by myself,' she decides. She is confused and doesn't know what to do. There is no fear, but Sheryl doesn't feel supported because her mother is unaware of her presence. She is not allowed to feel what she goes through. Previously in the pregnancy, she had cut herself off from her emotions. By asking: "What would you feel if you were allowed to feel?" she uncovers powerlessness, loneliness and sadness. In her study about how she makes the spiral, she discovers that the movement her body should naturally produce is not a distinct spiral. There is a disconnect in the neck-body axe.

She is disappointed that her birth is not a creative process but a mechanical one, without any connection nor a spiritual connection.

She exclaims: "I want to feel engaged, inspired, curious. But I feel loneliness, sadness, depression. What a crap way to come into the world."

When asked how she feels about the birth itself, she responds: 'I feel security and comfort, but there is a disconnect, I'm not recognized, there is no emotional experience, no joy but logical analyzing.'

Her decision at that moment is limiting: "I will not allow myself to be emotionally attached." This limiting decision has changed into a positive one: "I am free to be fully alive, fully embodied, fully emotional, fully love, free to feel emotions, and express them." After this session, she received more information from her mother about what had happened the days before the delivery. A neighbour's child had died a few days before. Sheryl's mother had cried incessantly and wanted to shield her baby from the sadness, hence her emotional disconnectedness.

Sheryl cannot forgive her mom immediately. We have to dive into the pregnancy, where she explores how there was love coming from her mother, but Sheryl pushed it away and filtered it out. There was a conviction of unworthiness and self-hatred. Love couldn't get in. After healing her relationship with her mother, she can wholeheartedly forgive her and let go of all the hardship. She anchors new positive supporting truths about herself.

The session with **Anja** was not easy: she couldn't go into her emotions or memories. It was tough to express herself. The reason came forward after a while: during birth, the *umbilical cord was wrapped around her neck*. When she felt immersed enough in the situation of birth, her body remembered the tightness and the restrictive breathing. It was terrifying, and she was fighting for survival. Anja was stuck, and nobody knew what was happening. The cord was very tight around her neck. She immediately decided: "I cut myself off of emotions in order to survive." This was why she couldn't access her emotions from the past. She felt very determined and stubborn in the situation but not at all powerless. A new decision is consciously made when Anja perceived a bright light going up into the sky: "I am completely free to feel whatever there is to feel, both physically and emotionally." A bar has been lifted. She felt free, powerful, strong and free like a bird.

Giving Birth and Birth Trauma

The experience of delivery may not be what you expected as a mother giving birth. When birth turns out differently than what you would have liked, you suffer birth trauma, or when what happened affects the baby, it is life-changing to address these issues and transform them. It is no exception that children will suffer the same patterns as their parents if they are not redressed. Also, to prepare for the next birth, you will be much better off if you have cleared what you were not happy with, transforming the anxiety or the anger that it generated in order not to repeat it during the next birth.

- Like the situation of **Suzanne**. She is a psychiatric nurse and teaches psychiatry. Her son Pier-Luc is eighteen years old and is her second child. Between the ages of three and sixteen, he signaled regularly that he didn't want to live anymore. During the pregnancy, Suzanne was harassed by her superior; she was not accepted, and on top of that, there was a lot of tension at home with a narcissistic husband. The baby was born at home and had a low birth weight. He was able to build up weight quickly thanks to successful breastfeeding. At birth, two placentas showed up: Pier-Luc had lost a twin. His double name can already signal a double pregnancy. After an intense conflict with her husband, Suzanne found the root of her unhappiness in the period when she was a baby herself. She was emotionally neglected and felt unsafe and abandoned: "I am too much, I'd be better off dead." She delves deeper into her past and changes the old beliefs of unworthiness and the inability to count on anyone to supportive truths like "I have the right to live. I am wished for" and other positive resources.

When she connects through visualization with her baby son, taking him in her arms, flooding him with love, and letting go of her guilt, he can forgive her. Then she turns to the twin brother who passed on and learns that he was there only to help Pier-Luc feel comfortable in his new life but that his purpose was not to be born. Finally, it is clear that Pier-Luc, through his struggle with loss, had picked up on the limiting beliefs of his mother. Once she let go of them, he was also released and free.

- **Angie** is pregnant for a second time, and the memory of the first one that was stressful comes up again. Releasing these tensions is the best that can be done to prepare for the next birth. In the first birth, she had pre-eclampsia and needed an emergency delivery. For the second birth, she wishes to have a VBAC (Vaginal Delivery After Cesarian), but there is so much anxiety that it will turn out like the first one.

She explains that her parents divorced when she was three years old after lots of struggle, abuse and fighting. In the session, while going through all the emotions of the previous birth, she accesses her soul energy of love and peace. That gives her a higher consciousness to release what was lying at the origin: the difficult experience of her three-year-old self. The abuse, fighting and blaming had given her the belief that relationships always end in hate, failure and disappointment. Once these emotions are expressed and healed, her new truth is that she believes in love as the motor to a relationship. Later, she testifies: *"Thank you so much for your guidance today, I feel very positive moving forward! Our session was very beneficial, and I am feeling confident going 'into this new journey'" :)*

Cutting the Umbilical Cord

Transitioning from being dependent on mom's body to becoming independent is a huge step at the start of life. The moment the umbilical cord is cut, the baby has to breathe and feed on his own. The first breath should be the solemn, sacred moment when the soul enters the body. If this cord is cut too early, a huge shock and deep anxiety can be generated because the body is still transitioning and learning to breathe. If there is not enough oxygen coming to the lungs, the fear of dying is very present. This fear or anxiety will be the fundamental belief about life: Life is fearful and unsafe. Life carries death in it. These beliefs will then be reactivated at the slightest occasion, waking up anxiety over and over, blocking the sacred life energy that a human being is made for.

James remembers how overwhelming the moment of cord- cutting was. He was looking for the emotional root of stiffness in his left shoulder, blocks in his left hips and upper leg, with his left side holding all emotions. James came to the memory of cutting the umbilical cord. It was a massive shock because he wasn't ready to breathe on his own. He felt taken away from safety, from home. He was overwhelmed with loneliness, separation and anger, although being independent felt much freer. He needed trust, support and reassurance. Baby James found warmth and safety in his mother's arms during the healing visualization. After having healed other issues, he attested that a lot of tension in his body had been released.

Breastfeeding and Bottle Feeding

Although everybody knows that breastfeeding is the best source of nutrition for the baby, situations can arise where bottle feeding is the only solution. In the baby's mind, breastfeeding brings up total feeding on physical and emotional levels. The deep connection that was—ideally— happening during pregnancy can still go on during this precious moment at the breast.

Bottle feeding doesn't need to be an unhappy second choice. While being present to the baby's emotional need for connection, a bottle can also totally feed the baby.

The theme in **Sylvia**'s life is disconnection. There are lots of situations through which she can experience that. She often feels alienated and unsocialized. She feels even a stranger in her own body. She can feel attracted and, at the same time, pushed back by people. She craves connection and wishes to find a place where she feels at home. The people around her were unhappy and disconnected. Her mother struggled with anxiety. While looking for the origin of all this, it brings her to the bottle feeding as a baby. Her mother was unable to breastfeed because of mastitis. What she experienced with this way of feeding was neglect and anger. Deep in herself, she didn't trust life; she had cut herself off from her emotions and from life. That is how she came to neglect herself in life. In the restructuring, she decides to keep the door open to giving and receiving. She decided to be connected to her deepest self, to life and to whatever emotion came up. Sylvia testified that she was astounded and felt a whole new beginning in her life.

Baby's First Months

Finally, being on earth! Breathing, feeding, being cuddled, sleeping, crying: there is so much to learn and to take in. Adapting to being in this tiny body as an experienced soul is not an easy task. Adapting to the parents, the family, the environment, the temperature, and the day and night schedule requires lots of support, care, patience, and love. When a baby cries when everything has possibly been done, he might just express how hard it is to adapt. How frustrating it is not being able to master your movements, to be dependent on your caregiver. These first weeks and months are also crucial because how the baby is treated, understood and cared for determines how he thinks about himself.

Joseph was conceived before his parents were married, they did marry during the pregnancy, but once he was born, he was taken to a wet nurse until nine months had passed after marriage. He felt lost in this unfamiliar environment. The tension and stress built up, and he felt paralyzed and lonely. "What did I do to be abandoned?" he asked himself. "I'm not good enough, that's why!" he mustered. Devaluation became the emotional undertone of his life.

Daniella can't find a suitable partner. Her grandma brought her up. She only saw her parents during the weekend, and every time they left, she was torn apart. She felt neglected and abandoned. She was hungry both physically and emotionally, starved for affection, for attention and for food. The belief of lack made her resist and reject the love that came to her, even from her loving parents. "Love is not for me" and "Love takes my joy away" were the unconscious drivers for not finding a partner. Anger and self-pity were very present, as well as sadness that was enhanced by unconsciously picking up the unresolved sadness of her grandma, who had lost a child. During the restructuring, Daniella could step into her mother's heart and perceive the love there for her. Only then could she receive the warmth and love from her mom. She changed her beliefs into openness to love, to abundance, to trust.

Psycho-Genealogical Imprints:

"We are the fruit of a long chain"
- Chantal Rialland

A baby entering the world is the last shackle in a chain of imprints. In addition to the influences during the nine months of gestation, coming from the mother, the father, the family, and the memories from past lives we unconsciously take with us in a new life, there is also a download coming from the ancestral lines.

In the first cell created at conception, both parents' DNA determines the colour of the eyes and skin and receives the whole genealogical heritage. This transfer happens on the physical level but also on the psychological unconscious level.

Just as the parents received a 'download' from their own parents, this biological and psychological heritage was then passed on to the next generation. With each new human being in the family, a multitude of data from previous generations is transferred, creating a unique blend of ancestral lineage.

Next to biological markers that can determine the new human being, there are the weaknesses of organs or illnesses or frequent miscarriages, but also unconsciously transferred failures, accidents, tendencies for suicide, addiction or abuse. This transgenerational junk will continue to be transferred unless someone in the chain of the generations is strong enough to halt it.

As children, we naturally identify with those present to us, especially our mother and father. In the eyes of a small child, they represent the truth, the benchmark for our beliefs and our view of the world. We take over their views, beliefs, and behaviours as children. We are like little apes and unconsciously copy everything. If we don't process our childhood experiences with both our parents, we have a lot of chances to repeat the same choices. The dominant father you have will make you choose a dominant husband, and the cycle will repeat itself. The absent father – which leads to lots of trauma – will create the same situation in the next generation if it is not transmuted. One of my clients related a pattern of absent fathers over five generations.

But there is also something as an unconscious fidelity with those who passed away. Suppose there is a recurrent tendency in the previous generations to a particular illness or personality trait like gambling or alcohol abuse, miscarriage, or feelings of unworthiness of which the ancestors cannot free themselves. In that case, they hope that someone in the generation after them will have the insight and the power to change that imprint. You have the choice: you carry the heavy burden and repeat it all over again, or you wake up and free yourself. In doing so, you free the whole ancestral line, even into the future generations.

A link to them can be powerful, especially in the case of namesakes in the family. We have a special link with family members who carry the same name. We more easily inherit their problems as we unconsciously identify with them. The same is true for dates: numbers that frequently show up: the same day in the month for birth, marriage and death are also strong markers for recognition of similarities and influences.

Gerard Athias in "Tarot et Trâme Énergétique"[20] explains that we inherit mostly programming on

- the physical level from the great grandparents.

- the emotion level from the grandparents

- the mental level from the parents

Of course, this unconscious transfer can also be very positive. The ancestors have also conveyed their strengths, the qualities they developed, and their success. In the core of the parents' cells, they carry all possible life scenarios of the members of their family: achievement or failure, love or solitude, joy or sadness, security or fear, confidence or devaluation, health or illness, longevity or early death.

Three generations ago in Europe, a six-year-old boy walked to school on the first day. At that time, it was October 1st, and he was accompanied by his father. An accident occurred on that trip. The boy ended up in the hospital. The next generation, a little boy, accompanied by his father, went to the first day of school, this time on September 1st, and had an accident. He ended up in the hospital. In the next generation, exactly the same situation happened again on September 1st!

The following story finds several origins for my client's problem. The experience in the womb, past lives, and transgenerational heritage reinforces the same problem.

Marianne wanted to look into her asthma problem. It deeply tired her out. She needed strong medication throughout the day to be able to work adequately. She was born to a fearful mother of 45 years old who didn't wish to become a mother. The birth took 36 hours, during which the nurse sat on her mom's legs to withhold the baby from being born because the doctor wasn't there yet. Marianne's mom blamed her as the origin of her suffering, which Marianne took over as guilt. Her name was suggested by her grandfather, who died when Marianne was one year old. He called her 'My little Marianne' after his little sister, who died very young. She often had the feeling of oppression in her chest, and she didn't like rigid, tight clothes. She often had nightmares in which she felt pressed, crushed, and it was impossible to cry out or move, to the extent of being intolerable.

She often struggles with sadness, shyness, isolation and solitude.

She looks into the embryo that her mother had been and discovers she wasn't recognized fully and was suffering. Love and welcome were brought into her, and Marianne feels that her mom now loves her. As an embryo, Marianne was insecure and thought she shouldn't have been there. The moment of discovery by her mom and her rejection of Marianne, she already felt this oppression in her chest. She felt she shouldn't breathe in; the space was restricted. "I don't deserve to live," "I'm too much." There is a conflict between two parts of her: one part wants to live, and the other wants to die. "I have to fight to have space, to breathe."

In a past life, she discovers a situation as a soldier where she could not breathe; there was no air. The thorax was restrained.

Her father in this life was a smoker, and his lungs were not healthy. Marianne's brother and his sons also had asthma.

In the genealogical tree, she connects with her paternal grandfather, whose lungs were irritated and who was coughing constantly. He worked on the railway in a filthy environment. He died there in an accident. His father - Marianne's great- grandfather - worked also on the railway. He was a very strong man but was killed in an accident with a wagon on top of him that crushed his thorax.

Through the whole genealogical tree, the unresolved trauma of great grandfather was transferred through the downline. It reinforced Marianne's propensity to feel pressure on the thorax and a restriction to breathing. Once all this was restructured through several Therapy of Intra-Uterine Life sessions, Marianne was able to diminish almost completely her medication for asthma. She only had some at hand for rare, mild occasions of breathing difficulty.

Being Born is Distancing From the Soul World

You only see a child Tiny by its body
But do you know that at the same moment
It is a giant by his spirit?
Who do you give birth to?
The dwarf or the giant?
- Bernard Montaud

We have seen how each part of the start of life has its challenges, depending on the situation and how it creates limiting beliefs and can be restored. In birth, we can also discover in another way how these profound experiences of being born are written in the big book of evolution. What does it tell us regarding our task on earth?

The soul, in all its subtlety and beauty, has an immense power. Only, it cannot manifest this power because it remains veiled. Yes, a veil, a screen, is put between the soul and the human being. The veil that obliges us to live in a lower vibration: the lower nature. That nature is programmed in a human being to feel separate, small, powerless, anxious, numb and to judge, to lie and to hate. It brings people to save themselves only, see the outside of things, and become empty vessels without any inspiration. Unless we fight to pierce through the veil and, after a long road of searching, find the soul again.

"Lifting the veil of Isis" was the essence of the study in ancient wisdom schools. Lifting the veil of what is hidden behind the surface. Finding truth. Discovering our inner lies, throwing them out and daring to stand in the truth, knowing how to manifest this truth in everyday gestures of love. This is the only path to happiness. I am still in the process of uncovering the lies I tell myself. It is a daily discovery, a daily freeing of the shackles that bind me.

Bernard Montaud, a French Osteopath, woke up to this truth through profound soul revelations and explained them through his workshops and book "Accompagnement de la Naissance" (Accompaniment of Birth)[21]. He discovered that a veil, or a screen, is installed throughout the whole birth process, distorting our view during the rest of life. Just like an NDE (Near-Death Experience) reveals life in an undistorted view because the screen has been lifted, during an NBE (Near-Birth Experience), we experience the opposite: real life is hidden by the installation of the screen during the process of being born.

By bringing hundreds of people back to their birth, he could discern seven stages in the installation of the screen. A gradual dimming of the light perceived in life before birth happens and a shrinking of consciousness. Four of these stages occur in the womb and three right after birth. Everyone goes through these stages but only two or three are really traumatic, which are different for each person. The other stages happen almost unnoticed. Nobody has a free pass, and nobody is stuck at every stage.

The gradual dimming corresponds to the historic line found in sacred texts according to Bernard Montaud: "*In the beginning was the time of the <u>Gods</u>, followed by the time of the <u>Giants</u>. Later came the time of the <u>Heros</u>. After that followed the time of the <u>Sages</u>, which gave birth to the time of the <u>Kings</u>. Followed the time of <u>Humans</u> and finally the time of the <u>Slaves</u>.*" It is all coming forward in the story of each human birth.

- The first stage is the decision to be born. As the fetus is still totally in the arms of God, he feels himself part of God, **one with God**, with this extraordinary light and unconditional love. Identified as this divine consciousness, he brings himself to decide to start the process of birth.

- The second stage is when the contractions start. After a long period in the womb of interiorization, the baby is confronted with an exterior side: his body. He has to submit his body to this treatment of contractions beyond his control. He exteriorizes himself from God and becomes the **son of God**. Now God becomes his mother, who calls him with love. The warmth of his interiorized life is lost, but now he pursues the warmth outside of him, towards the call of love.

  Then, he must actively engage in the passage through the long corridor. It is exhausting and eternally long, and the effort is gigantic to pass through. Gigantic: like **a Giant**. The faculty to deal with suffering was created here and even recreated throughout life. Events needing engagement, stamina and faith will revive this first experience of birth. We are programmed to support or not the suffering that life offers us.

- The third stage brings the baby to a blockage: the door is closed. He is before a dilemma, or he dies, or he forces through the closed door: he must kill his mother by making an opening or having her tear her perineum. He steps into the role of **the Hero** who must 'kill' to survive.

- The fourth stage is the birth itself and the first moment on earth, but still connected with the umbilical cord: suddenly, he is drunk with the feeling of being 'outside' but still one in an embrace of the earth. When the cord is cut, this embrace falls away and the cold distance, separation, emptiness and loneliness set in. He has created how he will look at everything in life: separated. He perceives the imperfection of life, the disharmony. It is comparable to **the Sage,** who is confronted with two opposing levels of consciousness: spirit and body.

- In the fifth stage, he is washed, examined and dressed. It all happens without the love he knew before. He becomes aware of the coldness of humanity and feels abandoned. Through his hands and eyes, he perceives the hurts and inner life of those who care for him, but they are oblivious to his sensitivity and awareness. He is like **the King** on his throne, who perceives the odd behaviour of his subjects without love. He became the Judge who must come to harsh judgments regarding humanity.

- In the sixth stage, he is put in his mother's arms. With his Big Open Eyes that perceive things that we don't perceive anymore, he is confronted with the limits of love and the distortions of family life, relationships, and the ancestors who have left him with their unresolved tragedies. He faces the lies in poor humanity. People describe this stage as 'burning'. He risks madness: it is impossible to face all this. Inner death is the only solution: psychic death. But he discovers a way out, through the faculty to think and being creative. He becomes a **Human Being,** with the possibility of becoming a genius and cultivating love and forgiveness by himself.

- In the last or the seventh stage, as he must renounce madness to survive, the screen comes down: his view must be veiled, his Big Eyes close, because it is too much to bear. He becomes a **Slave** and steps into the imperfection of a lower nature of separation, smallness and loneliness, repeating the same traumatic scenarios again and again. But much later in life, he will yearn for the sacred silence inside, looking for the lost paradise again.

- This is an appeal to future parents and staff around birth, to change the way a baby is received. Respect, empathy, gentleness and genuine love are what the baby deserves. A honest talk to baby recognizing his sensitivity but also asking forgiveness of our imperfect being that tries to love sincerely. This can certainly heal a big part of the trauma and reduce the harsh entrance into this world.

Akashic Records

*"The soul has been given its own ears to hear things
that the mind does not understand."* - Rumi

The energy vibration of imprints is held in memory through a subtle field of information comparable to the quantum field or a computer's hard drive.

While the information inside the body is mainly related to the subconscious mind, there is an energy field that stretches out farther than that limited field. Higher consciousness can give answers and insights into how to overcome all the hurdles and deep hurts stored in the subconscious mind. With its overflowing boundless awareness of unconditional love, it can pull us up to these higher regions to heal the hurts with the help of Source or Grace.

The higher you go into these fields of higher consciousness, the more you start touching on the universal information fields present everywhere in the cosmos. This universal field of information has been known throughout the ages and cultures as "The Akashic Records" or "God's Book of Remembrance," as Edgar Cayce expressed it.[22]

In the Bible, it is called "The Book of Life." The Akashic Records contain all the experiences, thoughts, emotions, and actions that a living being manifested from the creation of its soul to the present moment. Everything that is alive has an Akashic Record: stones, plants, trees, animals, humans, planets and solar systems. The realm is infinitely large, and there are many levels of comprehension of this information.

A soul's eternal question is: "Who am I?"

The soul has been created in 'the image of God.' On its individual journey, it is only through personal experiences that a soul can learn to perfectly manifest its divine essence, becoming a co-creator to Source. The soul evolves through making choices and experiencing the consequences of its choices, and through that, ever learning and evolving by making better, more informed choices. This acquired knowledge leads to wisdom. Wisdom brings us to compassion, which brings us to love.

The Akashic Records are not only a gathering place of information, but they are also interactive: they influence our everyday lives by drawing elements to us in the form of events, relationships, feelings and belief systems, as well as by drawing in potential and probabilities. According to Kevin Todeschi, the Akashic Records are: "The unbiased judge and jury that attempts to guide, educate and transform every individual to become the very best that she or he can be."[23]

Some people ask profound questions such as: "What is my purpose in life?" "What does my soul want to learn in this relationship?" They want help in looking at certain aspects from the point of view of their history through many lifetimes. They are looking for clarity and healing where they cannot find it themselves. To address the Akashic Records, I connect with the Akashic Record Keepers, who give me the information.

In my development as a healer, I was put on the road to discovering the Akashic Records. I became a Certified Akashic Record Reader 2020 through the Akashic Knowing School of Wisdom, founded by Lisa Barnett in the US. Knowing that I still have a lot to discover and develop, I see myself in service to the people who want to explore more about their essence, their development with all its hurdles, problems and questions regarding themselves, relationships and choices to make. "The Akashic Records," says Lisa Barnett, (2023)[24] "are a path to self-realization. One of many ways."

My special wish is to be available to future parents who would like to be as free as possible to incarnate the child that is meant to be theirs and to be able to guide it to express its potential. The incoming soul can be followed in his journey to the earth and given the most optimal circumstances for his coming into being.

Learning which talents and qualities the soul brings with it and which ones it wishes to develop can be a source of information for parents to orient them in how they organize their lives. The soul may ask to be steeped in music, nature, poetry, or reading. It might indicate which activities he wishes his parents to engage in or what type of food to eat. For the parents, the Akashic Records can also help to discover and clear disharmonious energies and blocks on their path and bring in Source energy in support of the growing baby and the mother. Here is an example of an Akashic Record session.

Lidy contacted me for an Akashic Record Reading and suffered emotionally. She had an incredibly low self-esteem. She was pregnant but wanted to kill herself once the baby was there because she thought the baby would be better off without her. When Lidy herself was incarnating, her mom didn't know that her baby was already aware. She was in emotional turmoil and didn't acknowledge Lidy's presence or welcome her. The relationship with her husband was not a peaceful one. Emotions were intense — no time for the baby. Lidy felt the chaos; she felt alienated, and a dark cloud fell over her. But a part of her could fight and stay connected to the light, although limiting beliefs about herself were already formed: "I'm not worthy," "I'm not good enough." In previous lives, she has been experiencing extreme alienation and once even experienced almost extermination of her soul. A deep trauma stayed with her.

After the birth of Lidy, the situation didn't improve, and as a child, she became a victim of emotional neglect. To this day, after lots of counselling and therapies, she still believes that she has no self-worth. Lidy is a highly sensitive and empathic person. She knows from her intuition that her baby is aware and programmed by her states of consciousness. She sometimes receives messages from her baby that "everything's fine" and "not to worry". But as she couldn't clear the deep trauma before being pregnant, she thought her baby would be better off without her. Clearing old energies and beliefs helped her reach a higher frequency and deeper contact with her authentic self.

Her unborn baby showed me to be shy, needing acknowledgment and confirmation to come out of her cocoon. The inner work Lidy does will heal herself, and while doing that, she teaches her unborn child an important lesson: that it is possible to change, evolve, and heal the blocks on the road.

Knowing that her baby's learning depends on hers, Lidy is motivated to heal her trauma and be a living model for her daughter.

At the beginning of the pregnancy, **Beatrice** agreed to a monthly accompaniment of her pregnancy through Akashic Record Readings. In the first session, it was communicated to me that the baby's soul came from a realm where harmony is very present, and it asked me to bring about this same harmony during these nine months.

The pregnancy is a blessing for Beatrice and her partner, after a long road of trying to get pregnant, miscarriages, and finally having to resort to IVF or In Vitro Fertilization. There is still a fear of losing the baby again.

In the third month, I asked permission to contact the Akashic Records of the incarnating soul and opened the mother's records, too. The aura of the mother was more extended than in the previous session, showing a silver-green, bluish colour as protection. The fetus felt safe, warm and comfortable. It is only a tiny bit withheld by his mother's worries at work: she is unhappy there. The sensitivity and the rejection she experiences there are neutralized by working on her heart chakra. After a special meditation, the fetus feels better.

What is the soul purpose of the child? His task is to become a scientist but in balance with his spiritual side. Beatrice is happy because she is also active in both worlds. The soul expresses its wishes: "to be in nature and tell it about everything that is alive." The nutritional needs are to have lots of fruits and bananas. Beatrice confirms that she is more attracted to fruits and bananas than before.

Beatrice hasn't felt any contact with her baby yet. We did a visualization with colours and contact. It moved Beatrice dearly when she heard the baby reply, "I love you so much." Beatrice's feedback after the visualization was that the soul is very sensitive to colours and doesn't want black at all.

The fourth month. As the baby was conceived through IVF, the soul expresses its disappointment that it didn't receive any love at the moment of conception because of the cold laboratory environment. This cold affects the physical level: it was a cold invitation. The way the sperm is injected was perceived as violent: it was injected forcefully, against its will. This was painful. This experience is healed and harmonized. The embryo now accepts the start of life. The need for care is enormous.

Contrary to that, the way Beatrice warmly welcomed the pregnancy once the embryo was transferred diminished the initial shock. It influenced the psyche. Opposition and tearing are the felt emotions; disconnection from emotions, difficulty accepting the physical body, and less security and safety are prevalent. The connection between the embryo and Beatrice has not penetrated on a physical level, but the embryo feels a very deep connection now to Daddy.

The fifth month. The pelvis seemed quite dark at the beginning of the session. The baby still shows a need for adjustment towards life in a body. We work on a better connection of the first chakra by the mother so that the earth's energy can flow stronger. From past lives, there has been a resistance to incarnation, to connection to the earth and matter, both with the baby and the mother. The Akashic Record Keepers heal that part. Beatrice learned to stream the colour pink through the pelvis and legs. A visualization of a soft nest with fluffy down feathers full of rose petals helps the baby settle.

There is no fear anymore of losing the baby. The baby itself needed some clearing about having to leave. It had always been the same soul trying to come back. The remaining fear of death was cleared.

Beatrice is super sensitive to lack of respect towards the feminine on a sexual level and other exchanges. She revealed that disrespect for feminine energy was prevalent in her own prenatal period, where her dad was often irritated towards her mom. She recognized this disrespect in both ancestral lines. It was also very present in previous lives where she had been raped over several lives. All these imprints on prenatal, ancestral and previous lives were neutralized. I taught her an energy exercise to stream colours through the grounding connection with the earth.

The pelvis is much lighter at the end of the session.

Beatrice accepts the idea of consecrating the soul to the light. A beautiful image came up that made me cry: a lotus flower bud manifesting the essence of feminine energy, receiving a royal reception in the body. The soul is very grateful for all this healing and transformation.

The sixth month. The reason for IVF was that Beatrice's egg cells didn't fully mature. This was a genetic inheritance from the ancestors. Several ancestors had lost babies and didn't recover from that loss. One couple in the family tree stayed without children because of that. Heavy emotions are neutralized, so the following generations no longer carry that burden.

Through the IVF, two embryos were implanted in the womb. One of them died after three days. So there was a vanishing twin. However, the bonding time with each other was not very long, although there was some sadness, guilt, and disappointment. Source energy healed all this. Beatrice was also part of a twin. Through the information from her mom that she lost blood at the beginning of the pregnancy, she knew she lost a twin.

We work on the connection between Beatrice and the baby by visualizing the blending of the two souls together in a warm embrace, forming a deep connection. We visualize the feeling of security through the umbilical cord and especially through the heart chakra. This intensifies the heart chakra and connects it to its higher part, which expresses unconditional love. It shows itself as a spinning golden ball that engulfs the baby's body.

We know from the scientific literature about the outcome of birth after IVF that there is a heightened chance of premature birth and a higher prevalence of cesarian birth. However, through good childbirth preparation, she can prepare and look for alternatives. She chose hypnobirthing.

The seventh month. The connection to the parents can still improve. The parents are asked to explicitly welcome the baby and explain what didn't work out regarding the conception and the miscarriages. The soul of the baby informs about some negative beliefs that were present in the psyche: "Things cannot be easy and natural: they need to be complicated," "I believe that I am not worthy," "Mommy needs to work hard to come to me: I pull back," and "I don't feel secure." After the healing, the baby feels freer, more relaxed and open.

How does Beatrice feel about motherhood? The heart chakra contains some doubt, which is restored through healing. We look into the downloads from our ancestors regarding birth experiences. There are no problematic outcomes, only fear of pain. We visualize and learn to relax in preparation for labour and birth.

The eighth-month session was not possible. The baby came a week earlier than the calculated due date in the ninth month. But it wasn't a premature one! The birth was vaginal and worked out fine. The first week was a considerable adaptation for both mother and baby. The baby gained weight through breastfeeding and was very relaxed.

Three weeks later, I received this message:

> *'I want to thank you very sincerely for your guidance during my pregnancy. I found it very valuable and could also use your tips very well. I am grateful that I was able to meet you at exactly the right time.'*
> Beatrice, May 13, 2020

Mei is three months pregnant. She had a miscarriage previously but has not recovered properly. Before this series of Akashic record Readings, we worked with The Journey healing method several times. Mei is working at the university as a researcher in the faculty of philosophy.

Her grandmother brought her up for three years in early life and gave her a lovely motherly presence. Mei's mother was a philosopher too but very unhappy, depressive and anxious. She tried to take her life when Mei was about seven years old. Mei wasn't seen as complete by her mom. Mei feels responsible for her mom's difficulties. She feels unworthy and unwanted. Her mom suffered from bipolar illness but recovered partly. Mei hadn't had contact with her for two years.

The 16-year relationship with Mei's husband, David, is not easy. After all these years of being confronted with depression and his difficulty expressing himself with a normal tone of voice – he is shy and speaks very softly – Mei is frustrated and exhausted. It is a source of stress and conflict over the coming months.

During this session of the Akashic Records, we cleanse the uterus from the red energetic debris of anxiousness and sadness of the previous miscarriage. Mei believes she is not a good mother. Her mom's rejection creates a reduced space for the incoming soul. The healing fills her up with Source energy. A protection layer is installed around Mei, which is even five times stronger around the baby. In this way, the soul is disconnected from the ancestor's inheritance, leaving a homeopathic presence that the soul can use as a "compost" in its growth process.

The soul is very wise and is linked through the lineage of philosophy. He will use the philosophy connection but quickly drop the intellectual part to evolve toward wisdom.

The soul is from the same soul family; they have often incarnated together. In the past, he was Mei's brother. She will recognize him at birth.

There is a soul contract between the baby and Mei and between the father and the baby.

Once the child has grown up, they will evolve together. The baby will want to be independent but need the chance, freedom and space to be just that. That might be a learning process for Mei: she must learn to let go and give space and unconditional love.

The baby needs to feel loved and welcome despite difficulties: this is its life lesson. Nevertheless, the fetus doesn't feel guilty or responsible for his mom's difficulties. The soul needs a connection to the world of light and selfless love. Mei is the link to nourish that connection. She is asked to nourish all the soul's qualities and virtues with love, harmony and beauty.

As we enter the fourth month, the Akashic Record Keepers reveal a fascinating insight: Mei's baby carries a soul that is inherently free, having experienced numerous lifetimes as a priest. This soul has chosen to grace our world with the wisdom accumulated from these past lives, making it a profoundly evolved entity. Together with Mei, it sought me out, yearning to liberate itself from the shackles of old manifestations.

David, despite his Jewish heritage, does not actively practice the faith. He is a direct descendant of Aaron, a lineage blessed with the role of priests. However, the soul harbours a deeper calling - it refuses to confine itself to the role of a priest in a single religion. Its true aspiration is to serve all of humanity, transcending religious boundaries.

I asked the Akashic Record Keepers if the hindrances for the incoming soul come from a karmic situation that has its reason to be there. The answer is that it is like that in some situations, but not here. The soul wanted to be of service to the world, and it accepted the wounding in utero. The best for this soul is to be free of harm and will be able to absorb the healing energy that is offered. The soul is joyous about this aspect.

There is still some fear of losing the baby at the bottom of the uterus, a dark spot deeper than in the previous session.

I felt the soul much more present than last month. It is delighted with these sessions and wants to reach out to the world. He shows an image of open hands to give his talents and love.

The soul contract with David is one of recognition: they have spent many lifetimes together and are big friends. He has been the father of the baby several times. The contract is about evolving together even more, growing deeper and wider. The soul needs to be independent and develop in this direction through education, allowing him to discover on his own, even sometimes learning the hard way and helping him find the lesson from the experience. The baby is bringing the couple closer together. It feels already like a family. It helps to deepen the relationship between the parents and overcome the frustration more easily.

The baby will help David discover a part of himself he didn't know, helping him expand. He will learn to fill the role of the father that he himself didn't have.

Mei feels that her interest in work has evolved toward metaphysics. The baby's soul brings in this thirst to know on a deeper level.

The soul is aware of invisible realms. It wishes to come in deep contact with nature: stones, animals, plants. It wants to develop a deep knowing through compassion. It asks to be encouraged to keep this capacity of intuition by reading books to the child about gnomes and fairies, even when he is older than seven when the interest in this subject often diminishes in other children.

Mei was encouraged to read about philosophy to give mental elements to the growing subtle mental body.

We worked on the fear on the bottom of the uterus because Mei felt physical contractions. Now the baby feels more connected to the realm of matter and physical life.

Mei has felt anxious the last few days due to tiredness and difficulty sleeping. In that state, she is more open to the

subconscious suffering from her childhood but also more open to the surrounding atmosphere in the city of Paris, where they live. Angels come when asked to protect and surround her with a blue angel colour.

The fifth month. This time, we work around the relationship between Mei and David. It has been very tense the last weeks between them. It makes the baby nervous about life. He knows what happens between his parents. He dreaded coming in between them. He needs to feel a warm welcome towards the soul and as a web woven between the masculine and the feminine energies as a safety net for the soul. He needs warmth, understanding, and acceptance without separation, which brings blame, criticism, and control.

David pulls out of life because of the traumas he experienced with his father. The soul resonates with that and pulls towards David's shyness. But it wants to overcome that: it wants to be open to the world without shyness. Here, Mei's work can be to visualize the baby daring to discover and being open to reinforce that quality in his life. She can ask for the collaboration of light beings in that task to bring in various spiritual elements through meditation. She understands that she is the link for the baby to the invisible world that souls crave so much.

The soul's experience of the earth produces less anxiety. It is still present but in a subtle way. Through the healing, there is now more connection with planet Earth, and the incarnation process is eased.

The sixth month. Around the soul, I perceive a dark energy holding back the readiness towards the world. The soul needs reassurance. The message to the baby is: "You have a beautiful soul with lots of treasures and gifts; just bring it to the earth." A message to Mei: "You are an extension of the Divine Mother. She counts on you. You are in Her service to give particular care to your baby. Try to look through Her eyes at David and the world. In this way, you'll see with the eyes of compassion and you'll see a different David." The Divine Mother has many blankets that protect and bring in tender, warm, soft energies of love, courage and faith.

Divine protection and guidance exist, but we can strengthen or weaken them through our emotions, thoughts, and actions! Confidence, trust, safety, and security are brought in.

The seventh month. This time, we did a Journey session. Mei asked for it to work around her emotions towards David. It has been extremely difficult for her the last few weeks. Mei has a hard time dealing with the relationship struggle while being pregnant. His depression tends to tear her and her baby down. She believes she has to carry the burden of other people; otherwise, they'll collapse. She needs to take a distance from their suffering. She integrates the new healthy beliefs that she is free and strong, even when people around her are suffering.

It was not possible to organize a session in the eighth month.

> *Asher was born in December. Six months later, Mei wrote: "I thought about our sessions a lot. They gave me strength even when I went through the darkest tunnels. (…) I still don't understand how exactly that works, but Asher seems to show some of the qualities that you told me about during our sessions. He is a lovely baby by the way. Sometimes I feel like he sees through me. He is patient and very attentive, cautious but also very kind. We visited family in the month of May and it was amazing to see how he was dealing with people. He was very sick there by the way, he had pneumonia and a very bad ear infection and a skin infection on the spot where he had gotten a vaccine shot, he was very tired and he struggled with all these diseases at the same time, but he was so kind to my father and my grandmother, they both are sick. When he met somebody old, fragile, and sick, he was so kind*

to them even on the day when he was so sick that he could barely lift up his head. I could see that he was trying to be nice with those, particularly, the weak ones. I was hurt and bitter with my hurts and traumas, I was hurt and sensitive, especially with those that are weak now but were strong back then and abused me, but Asher showed so much love to them. I learned."

In these stories, we can discover that early experiences determine the next phase of life after birth. The beliefs that grew out of these experiences unconsciously program our choices and outcomes later in life. We change feelings and behaviour patterns only when we become aware of all this. More than awareness is needed, though. We need to extract the essence of the lesson and restructure the experience or the beliefs to create a positive change. Once that is done, the difficult experiences are neutralized. The undesired emotions or situations fade away. In the end, we have evolved; we have learned something essential to help us become the real person we are.

These deep dives bring us to vulnerable places inside of us. It is utterly essential to work with it ethically, not by repeatedly churning old emotions in a never-ending anger, revolt, or anxiousness. We have to break the cycle of frequently returning emotions. Not swimming in them for eternity as it is done with some modalities like, e.g., rebirthing. Only by bringing in the part of us that knows from a higher standpoint: you can call it the soul or your higher self. This part has an entirely other understanding of difficulties. It knows that some harsh experiences will bring us to understand some essential truths about life through which we can evolve, become stronger, and unfold as the real person we are, more in line with this essential part of us, the "soul."

Nobody is Perfect

These stories and science about the impact on the baby by the mother are not intended to make you feel guilty or a not-good- enough-mother or father. If we know all this through decades of scientific evidence, it is more about the responsibility to make the best of this gigantic project of bringing a child into the world. We aren't perfect and it is better just to accept our limits.

So many flaws have been woven in us throughout our life's history. They create obstructions, conflicts, pain and suffering. Even if we scrub hard to undo the past to be a conscious parent, countless elements will escape. We cannot control everything. We shouldn't control anything anyways. We are just who we are: not perfect. Accepting all incompleteness and failures in ourselves helps us to accept them in others too.

The regeneration of humanity through this prenatal education will take several generations to accomplish because we can only do that much to clear out our ancestral inheritance.

The practice of the science of prenatal education is now only in its first generation and we see improvement, but there is still a long way to go. We only have to start somewhere and trust that we have planted seeds that will grow as consciousness awakens.

THE EMBRYO

When the time comes
for the embryo
to receive the spirit of life,
at that time the sun begins to help.
This embryo is brought into movement,
for the sun quickens it with spirit.

From the other stars this embryo
received only an impression,
until the sun shone upon it.
How did it become connected
With the shining sun in the womb?

By ways hidden from our senses:
the way whereby gold is nourished,
the way a common stone becomes a garnet
and the ruby red,
the way fruit is ripened, and the way courage
comes to one distraught with fear.

Rumi

MATHNAWI I, 3775-3782
(Translated by Kabir Helminski and Camille Helminski)

CHAPTER 5

SCIENCE INTO THE FUTURE

"Thought creates our world and then
says: 'I didn't do it.'"– David Boehm

Science is ever-evolving, with more and more surprising discoveries unfolding. These discoveries launch us into new findings that can uncover mysteries that might be very promising for future development. Even if we don't yet understand the complete basis for the following sciences, let's have a sneak peek into these exciting possibilities that can be useful in improving the mother-baby dyad.

How Energy Can Heal

Bruce Lipton states that cell healing comes from changing the beliefs present in the field of consciousness. He continues that by changing our beliefs, we change the field. Then, the cells can restore the body because they are no longer stuck in that old belief pattern. We don't need to focus as much on the cells anymore, but we can look at the field that shapes matter—that means our beliefs and our minds.

Candace Perth, in her book "Molecules of Emotion" (1999)[25] described first how our emotions determine which peptides - which are proteins - and hormones are secreted in the body. These hormones and peptides influence the cells and create health or disease. In his book "Biology of Belief," (2016)[26] Bruce Lipton explains that the receptors on the membrane of the cell are like little antennas that react to vibratory energy like light, sound, and radio frequencies. These influences determine which proteins are attracted and will connect to the receptors. The receptors can read energy fields. Invisible forces like thoughts, as well as physical molecules like penicillin, can control biological behaviour.

Epigenetic Science

Epigenetics is a relatively new branch in genetic science that sheds an entirely new light on the functioning of genes in the body. The generally accepted idea in genetics is that genes are all-powerful; they determine every function and generate health or illness. The new insights from quantum physics revealed that genes, without changing the DNA sequence, can be switched on or off by environmental aspects. Michael Meany from McGill University states: "At no point in life is the operation of the genome independent of the context in which it functions." This influence from outside on the genes is called epigenetics (epi = above).

Laurel Wilson compares the genome (the complete set of genes in an organism) to the "hard drive" in the computer world. The epigenome could be compared to the "software" that can be changed. Together, they create the phenotype: the program that is running, such as personality, the colour of the eyes and diseases. You can change the program that is running by changing the software.

Three possible influences regulate gene activity.

1. The intracellular environment

2. The extracellular environment, such as hormones, neurotransmitters and nutrients

3. The environment of the individual: neurotransmitters and hormones are affected by social interactions. The influences from outside the organism can be environmental: e.g., exposure to chemicals. Nutrition, stress, and emotions are essential elements.

Bruce Lipton (2001) expresses:

"The activation of the programs of the genes is controlled by the atmosphere of the environment. More precisely by the perception the organism has of this atmosphere... Maternal emotions such as anxiety or anger or, on the contrary, love and hope influence biochemically the selection and the rewriting of the genetic code of the child in utero with very profound evolutionary consequences on future generations. Parents-to- be are real 'genetic engineers.' It is urgent for them to be informed."[27]

So, it is not the events happening in our lives that determine our reactions to our genes but the way we perceive them. Simply stated, genes are switched on and off, but we should speak about dimming, as there is more variety in gene expression. The methylation of the DNA does this dimming reaction in the genes: methyl groups attach themselves to strands of DNA, silencing them.

This is a very important discovery to understand our power over our body's functioning. We are not "victims" of our genetic inheritance, but we can influence the expression of our genes by choosing our environment, or better: how we respond to our environment.

This invites us to ignite the power waiting to be tapped into in our DNA to express the health, vitality, and well-being within us.

Epigenetics has an extreme impact on the unborn baby until two years of age. Experts argue that the most critical period of human development is the 1000 days from pregnancy to a child's second birthday, a period known as the 1000-day window.

This is emphasized through the discovery that the in-utero environment that a fetus is exposed to can cause direct negative epigenetic effects in the fetus, resulting in the offspring being predisposed to several conditions including autism and the child's cognitive performance and ability for memory and learning. Decades later it can start cardiovascular disease, diabetes, obesity, schizophrenia and reduced lifespan.

The genome we inherit from our parents only counts for 5% of "uncontrollable genetic inheritance": only a small percentage of genes are unchangeable by epigenetics. But it is encouraging to know that 95% of our genes can be turned 'on' or 'off' through epigenetic effects. The epigenome will be inherited by the next generations. Some changes are long- term, whereas others are open to change.

Many circumstances and choices of the mother-to-be can have epigenetic effects on the baby, including:

- **A toxic environment**, smoking and alcohol intake

- **Nutrition**: an unbalanced, high-fat, low-protein or energy-restricted diet can modify epigenetic marks. It is recommended to take methyl-rich foods before and during pregnancy, such as dark leafy greens, legumes, seeds etc.

Wealth or the absence of wealth in the family is another aspect that shows a difference in the intensity of gene methylation.

- **The activities of the parents-to-be** have their influence, such as the music they listen to and the interactions with others and themselves.

- **The mothers' emotions, moods, surroundings and state of mind** significantly impact the developing baby.

- **Emotions** of fear, anxiety and how the parents perceive themselves.

The quality of the parental relationship and the communication with the baby all have a crucial importance in affecting the genes.

- **Intense stressful events** or long-term stressful situations, if not addressed, will change the epigenome.

- **Abusive behaviour** like physical, emotional, or verbal abuse.

- **The kind of birth** of the baby: either vaginal or c-section will have its epigenetic effect.

- **And the way a mother cares for her baby** in the very first period after birth: if she is involved or indifferent to her baby leaves its marks on the epigenome of the baby.

There are so many ways to impede a baby's natural development, but life just happens. We cannot always control what life throws our way.

But it is as important to know that the epigenetic effect of these adverse circumstances can be neutralized if the mother, during these difficulties like stress, financial struggle, conflicts, and loss of a loved one, can talk to the baby and tell him that he is loved, that he is not responsible for these circumstances – because babies often unconsciously feel guilty for the adverse events of the parents. Communicating that he is loved is the most important message he needs to hear. By your conscious way of living, the negative effects will be neutralized.

Obviously, epigenetics can have also a positive effect and can improve the expression of the genome by healthy life choices like nutrition, pure air and water, emotional balance and conscious positive thoughts. Even if the father has transmitted less quality DNA the mother can improve the effect on the baby through these principles.

Changing DNA in a New Way

Western scientists working with classical genetics saw only a way to change DNA by splicing and editing the DNA like in the CRISPR technology (Clustered Regularly Interspaced Short Palindromic Repeats), for which the implications are not fully understood yet.

Russian scientists developed another route of investigation of DNA.

In 1925, AA Lubishchev recognized that our DNA and genes are not the code for the living organism in themselves but are the link to our bio-informational field where this information resides and operates at the quantum level as waves and fields.

DNA turns out to be able to store incredible amounts of information. According to Science.org 215 petabytes (215 million gigabytes) can be found in a single gram of DNA. This information can even be transferred to other species using electromagnetic and acoustic waves.

According to the Russian scientist Dr. Peter Garyaev, genes function at a quantum level, contrary to the theory and practice of classical genetics, which led to modified viruses, bacteria, plants, animals, and finally humans, causing a gradual genetic collapse and total degradation of life.

Garyaev discovered the function of the so-called junk DNA. He found that the codes in this junk DNA were written based on linguistic and grammatical syntax that gives context to this DNA. Gariaev continued his research into the function of DNA and concluded that due to its wave and particle basis and in line with its linguistic characteristics, DNA functions on an electromagnetic and acoustic level and can thus be reprogrammed using frequency as sound and words.

He then did a remarkable experiment in which he shone a low-power laser through some Salamander embryos in one container onto some frog embryos in a separate container. The frog embryos developed into adult salamanders thus overwriting the frog's codes & turning it into a salamander. All DNA is editable!

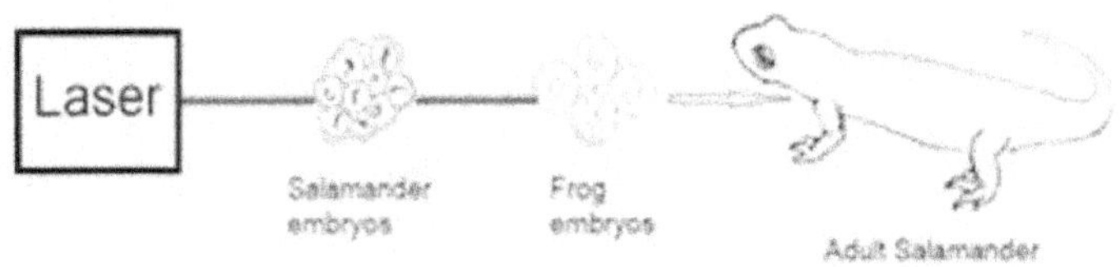

His theory, "Linguistic-Wave Genetics," is an answer to healing any illness and could prolong life indefinitely by quantum programming human stem cells. Linguistic-Wave Genetics provides the basis for the creation of quantum biocomputers. Also, long distance communication without electronics is possible: a bio-internet based on telepathy. It would help students with fairly rapid learning. Linguistic- Wave Genetics will provide a breakthrough for humanity to the highest level of development. Garyaev was a candidate for the Nobel Prize in 2022 but passed away in 2020.[28] Imagine the implications of these discoveries: we now have the power to alter the expression of our DNA using light, sound, and words.

Water Holds Memory

Water is the very element we need to understand if we want to upgrade our bodies to be a high-quality receptacle for building the body of your child's soul.

What have Jacques Benveniste, Dr. Masaru Emoto, Nobelprize winner Luc Montagnier and the Aerospace Institute in Stuttgard in common? They uncovered the best- kept secret of water. They all researched the capacity of water to hold information. Conventional scientific models cannot explain the experiments they did. However, the results show that there is such a phenomenon of the capacity of water to hold information.

Jacques Benveniste was a scientist in the '80s who discovered in his specific way how homeopathy might work, as it leaves an energetic imprint in water even when after many dilutions no plant molecule is present anymore.

The scientific investigations of Luc Montaignier concluded that DNA in water emits low electromagnetic frequencies and even when the water is heavily diluted, it is altered by the DNA in a way that retains some properties of the molecules.

The Aerospace Institute in Stuttgart studied how water drops show a unique image of every drop under the microscope. An experiment was done where several participants took water from the same recipient and made several drops at the same time. When the drops were collected and dried, the result was that every participant's drops showed the same image for that particular person. From person to person, they were all different. In another experiment, a flower was put in water, and drops under the microscope showed the same forms, referring to the shape of the flower. All the drops from a different flower showed the same shape, different from the previous flower. The informational content changes after it has been irradiated with electromagnetic energy. The images of the drops change compared to the original water source.[29]

Dr. Masaru Emoto (2005)[30] has shown the world how water crystals can be geometrically very different from each other according to intentions given to the water container. These waterdrops are then frozen and examined under the microscope. The words "I love you," "thank you," "truth" or "eternal" created the most harmonious hexagonal shapes of the water crystals. Whereas "hate" and "you fool" created asymmetric, misshaped forms. The same difference is to be seen with polluted water versus spring water. Also, music has its different effects: Mozart's music shows very beautiful shapes, whereas heavy metal music influences the shape of water crystals in a disharmonious way.

Dr. Emoto explains the Japanese word "hado," which literally means "life vibration." His expanded definition of hado is "the inherent energy in all things," and "all the subtle energy that exists in the Universe." Hado is a technique where water is used for healing by charging the water molecules with positive thoughts or positive music.

Dr. Masaru's experiments proved that the molecular structure of water can be altered. This is based on water's ability to retain the memory of everything it comes across. Positive words and good thoughts can bring positive changes to water. Drinking clean water with positive energy can have a beneficial impact on our well-being. Water with a negatively altered molecular structure is unsuitable for the human body.

Wikisbios.com

Water is the source of life on earth, and our bodies contain 90% of it. This information about the memory of water underlines the importance of the structure of water molecules for our body and the body of an unborn child. The unborn baby is surrounded with amniotic fluid which contains 98% water! It indicates the need for drinking the purest, alive water possible and for conscious and constructive thoughts and feelings all along the pregnancy and beyond as well as keeping us away from the source of electromagnetic influences through computers, cell phones and microwave ovens. The body's functions and well-being depend on our consideration of this sacred source of life, which is water.

Brain Waves in Pregnancy and Birth

When we want to consciously dive into ourselves, explore, and experience different aspects of ourselves that we didn't know before, we create states of consciousness that are very different from the 'normal everyday' consciousness. Every state of consciousness creates different brainwaves, measurable by EEG. Let's just discover these different brain waves to bring more insight into developing and realizing our potential. Science tells us that we only use 5% of our brain capacity. Let's see how that relates to pregnancy, childbirth, unborn babies and growing infants.

Think about your brain waves as a spectrum ranging from very fast to very slow. When we go through the day working, driving or running errands, we are in Beta (38-14 Hz), which brings attentiveness, alertness and focus. It orients us towards the outside world and helps us function in the world.

Our world is beta-dominant, full of activity and information. Too many beta frequencies, though, correlate with overwhelm, anxiety, frustration, and stress. Pregnant women should avoid these states. That is why they need to stop regularly and find the realm of alpha.

Alpha (14-08 Hz) state is the slower brain wave that brings a relaxed awareness that helps to shift from the external to the internal world. That means that by daydreaming, using imagination or doing a visualization, you turn your attention more inward, and you're able to find that much-needed peace and calm. Alpha is the frequency bridge between the conscious and the subconscious mind.

This is - or should be - the natural state of a pregnant woman. It is also the heart space. It should be her natural state, but life doesn't let her be there. If she allows it, she can connect deeper to her surroundings through this natural state and appreciate its beauty. Coming to gratefulness and appreciation of what is, finding what moves her in her life is like coming home to yourself and watering the flowers in the garden of your heart.

This state needs to be solidly present for the mother to give birth, especially during the labour process. Distractions during labour will take her out of that alpha state and into the beta frequencies, where anxiety can come up easily, and the contractions will reduce or stop. A labouring woman needs to be left to her own inward realm, her cocoon. Communication needs to be done only by whispering to her or talking through eye contact to respect the state she is in.

Theta (8-4 Hz) is even a slower brain wave that we access when we're drifting off to sleep or suspended in that light phase of sleep just before waking up. You can also access the subconscious mind of long-term memory through Theta while awake or in meditation. It is where emotional healing, spiritual insight, and intuition take place. It is the place where you can connect to your essential being, your soul, your core self. It is also the frequency of trance or hypnosis. Theta can enhance creativity, giving you suddenly new ideas and insights. Theta can reduce pain, stimulate even euphoria and the release of endorphins.

Theta is such an important frequency for a pregnant mom to be in so that she can access her soul essence. It is the state in which she can deeply connect with herself. This theta state helps her build the bridge to the unborn baby, to a deep emotional connection.

From that state, you can work with affirmations like "I am in harmony," "I am peace," "I am powerful," "I can do this," etc., which can be very helpful in preparing for birth. These affirmations program the subconscious mind toward a resourceful, positive birth experience.

It is also the state where you can focus on qualities you wish your child would develop. Do you wish him or her to manifest gentleness, tolerance, love or intelligence? We'll come back to this later.

From that soul space, we can also heal the difficult experiences that happened in our past, preferably before conception. Here is the place where the mother can also access what happens in her body and what happens with the baby during pregnancy and birth. This inner knowing helps her restore emotional disturbances and even physical ailments. During labour and birth, accessing theta can help reduce pain and release endorphins, which is a very desirable place to be during delivery!

The **Delta** State (4-0.5 Hz) produces the slowest waves and is a deep, dreamless sleep. This deep sleep helps restore the body and build a healthy immune system. Through meditation, we can enter the unconscious mind, which can lead us to Universal Consciousness and empathy. The Delta state is a kind of instinctual radar that scans the environment and psychically picks up information and energy.

The unborn baby is in this Delta state until two years after birth. This means that they receive unconsciously deeply penetrating imprints because they are continuously scanning for information that is then stored in the unconscious mind. All the states of mind and emotions of the mother and the environment are very precisely received. Babies live in altered states of deep suggestibility and learning. That is why it is so important to filter out and transform all limiting beliefs and expectations as parents or caregivers.

Children begin developing the theta state between three and six years of age. In this state, children spend much of their time mixing the imaginary world with the real world.

Theta is the very impressionable state used in hypnosis. In these early stages, the child is literally hypnotized by everything that happens around him. In other words, the first six years of a child's life are spent in a hypnotic trance! The levels of delta and theta that a child experiences until six years of age indicate that their brains are operating below consciousness. That means that they are very impressionable, like sponges, absorbing everything they perceive, see and hear in terms of beliefs, thoughts, emotions and behaviours that they will repeat throughout life and will constitute their character.

Wendy Anne McCarty, PhD is the founding chair of the Pre- and Perinatal Psychology Program in Santa Barbara, California. She writes about the journey of birth during which the baby receives indelible imprints because of his heightened state of consciousness during birth. She states:

"From a Pre- and Perinatal perspective, this journey serves as the inner blueprint for nearly every aspect of human life. If traversed well, it provides a positive foundation for core elements in the person's life. For example, birth and bonding is the spiritual journey in human form. It holds that archetypal journey of separation and reunion with Source and when supported and undisturbed, it can instill the innate confidence that 'I can find my way home.' It is also the map of what it means to move forward in life, to change, and to move through challenges and "tight spots." It etches in whether we feel we can 'meet the challenge', whether the journey of life feels like a lonely or a loving one, and whether we look forward optimistically to future outcomes or not. How we are treated and valued for our gender, appearance, and the person we are, lays the foundation for self-worth and self-image."[31]

Gamma (30-100 Hz) is experienced when in a hyper-focused state, finding solutions, for example. It is also accessed in meditation when you come to superconscious awareness. It brings peace, transcendence, and super-lucidity, giving instantaneous insights and answers to deep questions. Deep love, altruism, and compassion evoke it. It is associated with mystical union and spiritual ecstasy. This state can restore the neurological system and repair DNA.

Imagine intensifying your meditation so you can access this splendid realm of higher consciousness. Where love is evident and solutions just flow out of that state you can imprint this high frequency in your unborn child so it can learn that this is possible for him later, too. The matter he'll attract to build up his body will be of better quality, through its purity, incorruptibility and resilience.

Physical Matter is a Condensation of Subtle Matter

> *"I regard consciousness as fundamental.*
> *All matter is a derivative of consciousness"*
> - Max Plank

In a traditional objective scientific way of looking at matter, only three stages exist: gas, liquid, and solid matter. What about the subtle matter? We know that inner states of mind, like thoughts, intentions, expectations, and emotions, influence matter. Although this subjective aspect is real—we are sure to feel love or pain—how it changes matter is still open for debate.

A relatively new science has been developed in the last decades: Noetic Sciences study the connection between mind and matter. Noetic means inner wisdom or direct knowing. The Institute of Noetic Sciences (IONS) was founded by the Apollo 14 Astronaut Dr. Edgar Mitchell. The institute aims to study and experience everything related to the interconnectedness between the inner and outer worlds, bridging science and spirituality and better understanding reality's true nature.

Since 1973, IONS has been at the forefront of the scientific investigation of consciousness and its role in our lives and the physical world.

It reiterates millennium-old knowledge that now finds it a scientific acknowledgment that our mind influences the body and vice versa: the body can also have an effect on the mind.

Max Planck, who was at the basis of the development of quantum physics, states: *"In all my research, I have never come across matter. To me, the term matter implies a bundle of energy which is given form by an intelligent spirit." "There is no matter as such. Mind is the matrix of all matter."*

Science has not yet revealed *everything* about how reality works, but we can already acknowledge the inner knowing and intuition and at least be open to its manifestations in our lives. And especially to put into practice what is described in this book. A woman in contact with her intuition knows this is the truth. Even when your partner, your friends or your family don't acknowledge your intuition, please listen to it and conduct your life according to it; your children will benefit from it. Science will follow one day and confirm your intuition.

The castle of your soul

I dwell in the castle of your soul
It is not you who is my guest
It is me who is yours

You invite me to your palace of crystal
of lace and incorruptible gemstones

You make me discover
Your vasty gardens
Savour your perfume
Extremely precious and rare

I am your lady-in-waiting
Cared for, elevated
In your dream of pure beauty
Such a King that invites me!

Such a profound and conscious breath
I'll need to receive, to give
You a proper body

What a sacrifice to show
You the right path that you deserve…

I love you more than Life
Be blessed

And may the bridge between our souls
Be always more pure and light
By love

MCW

Your soul

Sparkles of diamonds

Has heard

The screams of this

Unsettling world

You offer yourself

In the hands

Of the One who

Will shape you and lead you

In becoming

A servant of the light

You'll impregnate

The earth

With diamond rays

You'll plant

The coloured seeds

Of your heavenly

Love

- MCW

CHAPTER 6

AN ENLIGHTENED START IN LIFE

"It is easier to build strong children than to repair broken men." – Frederick Douglas

The new paradigm is to give our children a start in harmony, in a strong connection with nature and with the divine nature in all of us. Evolution can only happen if we start from the beginning.

There is a higher world that is mostly invisible to us. This higher world of unconditional love and harmony wants to manifest and incarnate in the physical world.

We have both worlds in us: a higher self and a lower self. The higher self wants to manifest itself and transmute the lower self. The reason for life on earth is only this: to become an expression of this higher self. Each birth of a child is an attempt to evolve in this direction. Each life is a step further. You have the reins in your hands for your child to help it in that attempt.

Indeed, a simple step inside can bring with it a non-stoppable stream of changes, a cascade of never-ending evolution. Undo the first button and the rest opens up.

The need to grow the seed of a new humanity, a humanity 2.0—not through artificial intelligence—is getting more and more intense. The new consciousness, however, is germinating, and we are coming closer to the hatching of the seeds. To create this new humanity, parents-to-be are an intrinsic part of this evolution. They have the keys in their hands. They can determine by their own willpower to turn things around.

First, for themselves, they can take the bull by the horns and start clearing themselves from past blocks, traumas, and misconceptions. That will greatly influence their children, who are the basis for an evolving society based on higher principles.

Resurrection

> *"When I let go of what I am, I become what I might be."*
>
> - Lao Tzu

Our world is crumbling on all levels: economically, politically, and environmentally. Everything was based on a lower consciousness of greed, selfishness, and ignorance.

We are cut off from the divine with its wisdom and cosmic laws. We are on the verge of a new way of understanding, with a wish to wake up to who we really are, out of the slavery of our lower nature that dictated way too long its egotistic inferior way of feeling, thinking and acting or rather staying put, hardly evolving towards a higher spirit. Now we are breaking the shackles of apathy. We suffered enough. Our eyes are opened to the world's suffering that was created through our inability to act appropriately and end this suffering.

> *"We must be willing to get rid of the life we've*
> *planned to have the life that is waiting for us. The old*
> *skin has to be shed before the new one can come."* -
> Joseph Campbell

We wanted to stay asleep because facing the truth and waking up from ignorance takes courage and honesty.

There is only one way out: waking up to a higher consciousness that will inspire us to act in the right way.

Mothers are the channels through which this new humanity will become by incarnating an awake human being, able to take a step further in realizing this new humanity.

Future parents will be the portals to the world of unconditional love, purity, and light. They will bring in the highest vibrational matter to clothe the awakened souls who were entrusted to them.

What is an awakened soul?

It is a soul that has elevated its vibration by being drenched in the essence of the Spirit. They are in touch with their Wise- Self. All they want is to put that wise Self in service to the Great All.

They have overcome their ego and old programming from past lives. They are in contact with their higher self, who has all the wisdom and capacity to love. They can live according to their divine blueprint.

It is possible to attract these awakened souls as your future child by living a life connected to your soul and cultivating its qualities and virtues. Let yourself be guided by a high ideal and yearn to live a life of harmony, love, wisdom, and truth— a life connected to the divine. By prayer and meditation, you can free yourself as much as possible from old patterns and blocks that no longer help you on your path.

This work requires a long preparation: it can be weeks or months, but we better speak about years. The more you can prepare, the better. The nine months of pregnancy will be just a period of intensification of this life of dedication to health, enlightened thoughts and feelings, and the divine and spiritual elements that you will attract through your lifestyle.

As we have seen before, during pregnancy, your thoughts and feelings are the magnet that attracts the corresponding mental, astral, etheric, and physical matter to your baby. In this way, you can bring your child the purest material to build up his psyche and body.

Being steeped in love, compassion, and gratitude and having enlightened, inspired thoughts attract the purest, resilient elements of matter. Emotional struggles, feelings of vengeance, ongoing stress, thoughts of judgement, rejection, or egotism will attract physical building blocks of lower quality and build up weaker organs prone to illness.

The divine feminine, in harmony with the divine masculine, will be able to break through the matrix of the old world and gather the building blocks of this free humanity.

This new paradigm will come slowly but surely for those who choose to go ahead, for those who want to step into their dignity, the dignity of the divine in them. It wants to show its wonders in our world through you.

The Call of the Parents

"Parenting needs to be entirely redesigned"
- David Chamberlain, PhD

The wish to become a parent is a call to step up the ladder of responsibility: wanting to share your inner riches of love with another soul to help it develop. It is a beautiful inner call to complete oneself, to unfold further. 'Parenting, it turns out, is humbling in the way it exposes your insecurities and personality flaws.' says David Allan. There is no better way to learn patience, empathy, flexibility, creativity and authenticity than becoming a parent…

So, as a future parent, what is it that brings you to conceive a child? What about your personal desires, history, influences and beliefs that led to such a major life decision? Why spend so much time and money and take on all that additional stress and responsibility?

For many parents, it has been simply an unconscious evolutionary drive to propagate, to carry on their DNA to the next generation, to meet society's expectations, or to give in to a biological urge…Maybe you want to give what you have received. To share in the abundance of love generated by the love between you and your partner?

Maybe it is to bring in an awakened soul who can guide humanity on the path of a new consciousness of harmony and light.

According to your conscious or unconscious call, you attract a soul that matches your vibrational energy and inner nature. It will respond to what your higher self wants you to develop, let go of, or clear from the past. There might be ties that bind you from long ago, wishing to be together finally or to work out some hurdles from the past.

Look honestly in your heart what is the deep reason for wanting to be a parent.

- Why do I want a child?

- What do I have to offer?

- What do I leave behind when having a child?

- What are my fears about becoming a parent?

- Can I invest enough time to elevate this child?

- Do I have what it takes to support the soul-purpose of this child?

The Call of the Soul

"The meaning of life lies in perfecting the human soul."
- P.Deunov

On the other end of the veil is a soul that has a wish for his next life experience. If it is a young, inexperienced soul, it might roam on this earth without discovering its real essence, its divine being. It can become an endless game of making errors and creating karma, then paying karma and creating new karma to be paid in the next life.

An older soul wishes to manifest its divine essence and their inner power. It wishes to test its insights and share its experiences with humanity. Their body needs to become the finetuned instrument to this soul so that it can manifest the higher powers of the soul and spirit, overgrowing the ego through gaining wisdom through experience, insight and transparency.

The soul's goal is to freely express its divine nature through the human personality without the traps of the ego.

As a pregnant woman, you are the architect of your child's body. Are you ready as parents to sign a contract with your future child that ensures their accomplishment of that goal?

Of course, your role is a small part of your child's total evolution. The soul's development goes beyond the borders of one lifetime. The soul comes into your family to pick up a specific experience that will push him in a certain direction, to bring it a step further. The soul has picked you as a parent to give him just that. But the deepest wish of any soul is to discover his real essence, just as it is for you.

If you are oriented towards this higher point of consciousness, this sublime love in which the universe is bathed, if that consciousness is a living light in you, you will have all the power within to live on this frequency, this high vibration.

The world needs evolved souls to incarnate. To show us the way, to help us organize society based on divine love and light. A society functioning harmoniously is based on divine laws, not human laws that are mostly corrupt. These souls have been evolving over uncountable lives. They have been preparing for this crucial time in the history of humanity. They are highly evolved and they are connected to the divine. They are the teachers, the saints, the initiates, and the masters who have been helping humanity in the past. They are ready to come over. They are impatient to jump in.

Only they lack parents who are ready to welcome them. Humanity needs parents who have really gone through a deep clearing of all that is in the way of being a fully awake and aware soul. The awakened souls are looking to find the genetic material that matches their own qualities. They need conscious, harmonious, compassionate parents devoted to the light. They need unconditionally loving arms and wise, guiding hands. Are you a candidate?

Thinking this way and realizing the steps that need to be taken, you can be a strong pillar in the birth of this new humanity. There is no need to be perfect! Just be who you are, growing one step at a time. The soul you will attract will be the right soul, connected to you, to learn from each other and evolve together.

Life Begins at Conception, or is it Before?

Primal Health

The "primal period," coined by the French former obstetrician Dr. Michel Odent, is the period from conception to the first year. Dr. Michel Odent, was the leading pioneer for natural childbirth. He indicates that the period between conception and a child's first birthday is critical to life-long health. Out of the scientific synthesis of correlations between early life conditions and the state of health in adult life, he distilled the "primal adaptive system." Different parts of this system develop, regulate, and adjust during fetal life and the time around birth and infancy. He states: "Everything that happens during this period of dependency on the mother has an influence on this basic state of health, this primal health."

He suggests that the later well-being of adults, their ability to withstand the "diseases of civilization" such as hypertension, cancer, alcoholism and failures of the immune system resulting in Aids, allergies and viral diseases, can all be traced back to society's ignorance of the vital importance of the primal period.

Michel Odent founded the Primal Health Research Centre in London and designed a database (primalhealthhresearch.org) that gathers all the scientific material that supports his concept of primal health.

These 21 months - nine months of prenatal life and twelve months of the first year - are crucial in the start of human life.

Meanwhile, there is evidence that the period *before* conception is also part of that crucial health basis for the formation of a balanced and healthy person. Jean-Philippe Brébion considers 27 months: nine months before conception, nine months of prenatal life and nine months after birth. In his first book: "L'Empreinte de Naissance" (Brébion, 2004) or translated: The Imprint of Birth, he brings the nine months prior to conception in connection with "the plan," the nine months of pregnancy with the "execution of the plan, the fabrication" and the first nine months after birth with the "manifestation."[32]

Conception is the moment that downloads lots of information into the first cell. What does this information look like? It is the synthesis of mom and dad's physical health as well as their emotional and mental functioning. It is the synthesis of their experiences, unresolved traumas, healthy or unhealthy beliefs, struggles with unworthiness, unmanifested desires, state of physical balance or unbalance, and genetic blueprint. A lot of information is downloaded in this first cell.

This first created cell will then carry the information into the next generations of cells into the future. That's why the first conceived cell holds the blueprint of the new human life. Elisabeth Nobel calls it "The Primal Life Script." If we know that this magical moment will transfer the synthesis of their life until then, plus the dynamics of the moment to the first cell, we need to see the broader picture; we need to prepare before conception to give the best inheritance to the incoming soul.

Bruce Lipton states: "Research reveals that in the months prior to conception, future parents play the role of engineers for their future children. In the final maturation state of an ovum and a sperm cell, a process called 'genomic imprint', regulates the activity of specific gene groups which will form the character of the child before conception (Surani, 2001; Reik & Walter, 2001). According to research, what happens in the parents' life during the process of genomic imprint profoundly affects the mind and body of the future child." (2006)

This statement of Bruce Lipton implicates that preparing consciously to become a parent starts long before conception!

The spermatogenesis cycle of a man is 64 days. It takes roughly two months to create new sperm cells. That means that the way this man lives, eats, thinks, feels and acts will be reflected in the quality of his sperm cells. It is not because a man knows this and tries to overturn bad habits in his way of life that he can suddenly be a new man in two months' time. It takes more than two months to be able to finally in this period prior to conception, create these healthy, dynamic carriers of life energy that will transmit his real essence to the next generation. Six months would be the best time before conception to detox and change habits.

A woman carries egg cells that have been formed in her mother's belly: her eggs have already been forming during the future mom's own prenatal period. They were exposed to the experiences of her mother – grandmother to the future baby - during these nine months. As this grandmother is also a product of her female lineage, she transmits all the past imprints of this lineage to these eggs that will be the start of life. As we know, the previous generations were not very strong in respect for female life. Was there physical or sexual abuse? Were there abortions or miscarriages in the ancestry? Deaths during childbirth? Secrets? Unwanted pregnancies? They can be activated again if they are not cleared, disturbing the wish for a harmonious and natural childbearing year.

Ancient wisdom tells us that the father is responsible for the vitality of the baby's respiratory, nervous, and glandular systems. The mother brings in the energy for the development of the baby's circulatory, digestive, bone, and muscular systems, the connective tissue present almost everywhere in the body.

This 'genomic imprint' offered by both parents will be the matching point for the quality of the soul they will attract. As everything has a frequency, a vibration, and attracts everything that matches that frequency, the vibration of the gametes attracts a soul whose life purpose corresponds to that vibration. The higher our inner freedom on all levels and the higher the ideal we focus on, the more chance we will bring a child into our life who will be free to shine.

PREPARATION BEFORE CONCEPTION

Wanting to become pregnant is an invitation to clear out the body so it can be a radiant healthy vessel to become the clear foundation for building a healthy child inside of you. Through the quality of the physical material you offer, as well as the pure heart surrounding your little one and the transparent thoughts you weave in and around the beginning life of your baby, you will create the best possible conditions for the beautiful soul you will attract.

A deep transformation needs to take place to give this sacred soul you'll bring into the world its rightful envelope of healthy, sacred matter. A spiritual awakening and becoming conscious are necessary if you are not on that path yet. Because living unconsciously means staying stuck in old programming. Do you still cling to your 'pain' identity of how you were starving in childhood, your cultural conditioning, your beliefs, your memories, your thoughts about what's wrong with you, about not having any value. Eckhart Tolle says it like this:

> *"Suffering is not caused by the circumstances but by the narrative in your mind about the circumstance. A very heavy identity builds up and that becomes your sense of Self. You're so identified with it, that you don't exist outside of the story. It is the mind-made sense of Self. At the moment of realization, another consciousness is risen in you, which is not your mind. We could call it 'awareness' or 'presence'. You experience your 'Essence'. The essence of who you are is pure consciousness."*

This pure consciousness is your soul essence.

Piercing the veil of suffering reveals the spark of the spirit and joy and sets in motion a motor of higher consciousness and insights. Lightness is the result, and it promises many extraordinary discoveries.

Being Mentally Prepared

Your thoughts have an incredible power to create your reality. You always create your reality, but mostly unconsciously: your world is your creation. For example, the beliefs we nourish attract the elements that will condense these beliefs in our lives. If that belief is limiting or unsupportive, like "I am not good enough," or "I am unlovable," your life will become the exact reality matching your beliefs. Once you become aware of this, you can change that by consciously only creating supportive truths.

We only use a part of our brain capacities. So, we have a huge program to become aware of this powerhouse of thought and mental capacities and use it creatively to support ourselves and our offspring.

As a psychological preparation, it is important to take a closer look at the intentions you had before conception and the circumstances around the period of conception because they weave the child's unconsciousness.

Before conceiving the couple is invited to answer these questions:

1. *What is the Intention Behind Having Your Child?*

The intention you consciously or unconsciously might have for your future child is crucial to bring to light. It gives direction to his life; he will unconsciously be directed to work out the intended program in his life. We can call it a '*project intent*'.

What are your hopes, wishes, challenges, doubts, and the basis on which you want to start this endeavor?

Are there some strings attached to the soul of the baby? If there is a conscious or unconscious personal wish for the child that serves you but not the child, it will get caught in that goal and cannot be free.

Understanding your real motivation for bringing this child into the world is important. Be very thorough and honest about it.

Are you calling this child to meet your needs:

- A need for companionship for yourself, to fill up the emptiness?

- To have a brother or sister to play with the older sibling?

- Will it fulfill your need for someone to look after you when you're old?

- Do you want to glue the relationship together by having this child?

- Or maybe to ensure an inheritor of your wealth?

- The expectation that your offspring will accomplish the goals you were not able to achieve?

These intentions or expectations with which you invite the soul, this project intent, will tremendously affect him. It is *your* wish that will stay glued to the child. He is bound by it. Unconsciously he needs to abide by it to be accepted or recognized. It blocks out his own soul's purpose. He will not be able to find his own essence, because it will be hidden behind your unconscious intention for him. That only brings unhappiness, blockages, limitation and failure. A child needs to be able to come in, not for the sake of the parent but for his own purpose.

<u>Crystal</u> is a doula in training and wants to understand her prenatal experiences. Her mother was in constant conflict with her own mother and her sisters. She conceived Crystal with the wish that she would bring peace and reconciliation. This was Crystal's project intent. During a session about birth, Crystal remembers that she didn't want to emerge because there was so much expectation towards her. She feels she had to perform heavily to be accepted. Unconsciously, she wanted to help her mother and believed it was up to her to help her mother: "I came to protect my mother," is what she tells herself. She believes: "I have to control everything," and "I

am only here to make others feel good." She is quite a perfectionist towards herself. Her mother is very demanding but finally doesn't want to be helped. Crystal leaves home at 17 because she had enough. And finally, here she is, wanting to help other mothers than her own mom as a doula. Is it a free choice, or is it her unconscious programming that says, "I am only here to make others feel good?" She turned the beliefs around and stated consciously: "I have the right to be who I am," and "I love myself as I am." Now she feels freer to give support out of the freedom to do so, not out of programming.

2. Are there Gender Preferences?

Not being of the right gender in the eyes of the parents sure pulls the child away from what his soul wants to manifest. The gender confusion we see nowadays can have its origin there, although many other origins are playing too.

Let go of all expectations, consciously and unconsciously. The choice of gender is already made on a subtle level before conception. Your higher self has agreed to the gender the child has chosen. Respect the divine choice that has been made. Maybe the soul of the baby will show you in a vision or a dream which gender it will have.

Psychically the baby can feel disappointed and unsettled if it knows that the gender it has is not the preferred gender for mom or dad. The child will try to play the role of the other gender, just to be loved and accepted.

My own experience before conception regarding the gender of my child: 'I always had the idea that a girl would be easier to educate because I know what it is all about. So I had a tendency to wish for a girl before conception. But a few months before I conceived, I was resting and in a state of deep relaxation, and I saw in a vision a cute little boy of about two years old smiling at me. He was so charming and resembled Yves, my husband. I was sold! I was so happy that I had the time to adjust to this choice, to accept it and to look out for the little boy that wanted to come. A year later I gave birth to a boy.

3. Do you Know Your Genealogical Tree?

We are the product, not only of the two gametes of the parents but of a line of ancestors who have shaped the DNA we carry. This DNA of the ancestors, too, will influence the outcome of the baby. It is a study on its own that can be done by delving into the family history through official sources and also by investigating our subconscious in deep relaxation.

Psycho-genealogy has been described in a previous chapter of Psycho-Genealogical Imprints.

Undertake an in-depth look at your genealogical tree to detect any tendencies you might have picked up. Check the people in the tree who are namesakes or were born or died on the same dates in the month. Through Therapy of Intra-Uterine Life in deep relaxation, it is possible to visualize the family tree and ask questions about whom you need to connect with in your ancestry to free yourself.

Total Biology is the science of the development of illnesses on a psycho-energetic level and studies, among other subjects, the connection we have with our ancestors. Gérard Athias (2018) casts a light on how previous generations affect us on different levels:

- Our physical body has a strong connection to our Great- grandparents' lives.

- Our emotional functioning is linked to what our Grandparents experienced.

- Our mental capacities are, for a big part, the expression of our parents' way of thinking.

Naturally, we also inherited their qualities and strengths, for which we can only be thankful.

Remember the epigenetic science that explains how genes don't determine the next generation's health; their activation depends on your way of life, thinking and feeling.

4. Astrology

It is very important to know in which astrological sign you want to conceive your child. The parents can project their child's future by choosing a specific birth date, based on the best aspects they have themselves for the conception.

Comparing family charts between parents, children and grandparents helps us become aware of limiting unconscious ancestral memories.

A child is unconsciously conceived to heal some family patterns. For example, a family that had difficulties gaining wealth and failing to keep money conceived in Leo and had the child born in Taurus, a sign of stability on the level of material possessions. The child healed the family.

The Emotional Preparation

'People who trigger us to feel negative emotions are messengers. They are messengers for the unhealed part of our being.' - Anonymous

Emotional preparation is a huge key to clearing your inner world. We are emotional beings, and emotions play a big role in our lives, whether we are aware of them or not.

How is your emotional well-being? Do you feel fulfilled and happy? Or is there any story of depression, of unworthiness, of the feeling of disconnection to your emotions? Sometimes we are so overwhelmed that we simply disconnect from emotions to survive. Or we are so involved in tensions and conflicts in our daily lives that we need to stop ruminating about the hurt.

Take a step back and step off the hamster wheel of doing, of telling yourself stories of how difficult it is. Just detach from the story and be present to what you feel. Welcoming all feelings, calming down into mindfulness. Slowly an element of peace wakes up and brings insight into what you go through. Mindfulness helps in releasing pressure and stress. It can help in fighting depression.

Emotional suffering represents the dust on our inner diamond, our higher self that is pure love, insight, intuition. Suffering can bring the motivation to detect who we really are. Self- awareness brings you to discover the thoughts of self-sabotage and control or the deep emotions we feel in contact with the big world from conception on. This hurt created beliefs and unconscious decisions that conditioned us to live small, unfulfilled and never really happy. Uncovering and neutralizing these blocks to happiness is as important as stopping smoking or changing unhealthy eating patterns before getting pregnant.

The baby will pick up on your depression, your anxiety or your beliefs of unworthiness and simply copy them. The unborn baby has no sense of distinction between the mother and itself. It has no self-identity yet. It just "copies" and "pastes" the emotional environment it lives in for nine months. After birth, he will unconsciously struggle with this emotional inheritance. Until a big crisis 40 or 50 years later, he discovers that the feelings he struggled with originated in utero and that these were just taken over from his mother.

Feel whatever emotion is present at any moment. Do not bury difficult experiences in the sand of forgetting, but look them in the eye. Healing them by going back to the first time you felt them.

Many of our recurrent emotions can be traced back to prenatal life.

Learn to forgive people who've hurt you. No lip service but honestly, from the deepest part of your heart. You are not forgiving them because they deserve forgiveness, but you are forgiving them because you deserve not to carry that burden with you anymore.

Once you are pregnant, the experiences you had throughout the period before and after birth might wake up and throw your emotions upside down, which is to be avoided. Before being pregnant, you can dig out the earliest experiences you had as an unborn baby to know what was playing out there. Therapy of Intra-Uterine Life can be helpful in supporting you in restoring the integrity of your being.

Daily events can so easily trigger emotions that want to come to the surface to be seen and to be healed. Let's be open to them in all honesty so they can be transformed into your inner beauty.

> *'Life is not about waiting for the storm to pass,*
> *it's about learning to dance in the rain.'*
> – Viviane Green

There are many methods for clearing these traumas, pain, misinterpretations, and old beliefs about ourselves and the world.

Previously, I described the method of The Journey, which I practice. You can learn it yourself and be helped by people who are on the road of healing, too.

Akashic Records can even more quicker relieve us from these burdens, as the Akashic Record Keepers are not only giving information but also healers and can efficiently lighten your burden.

Take time to look into your present and past

- Are there still traumas to release?

- Are there beliefs you took on or unconscious decisions you took?

- Make a list of everybody who has wronged you and forgive them. Don't forgive them from a place of reluctance or lip service but from a true place of forgiveness.

1. How was Your Childhood?

'The shape of the past is the mold that holds you back'

- Nimka

Starting with your very start in life: clearing out your own prenatal period is crucial so as not to convey to your children the same patterns as you have unconsciously absorbed. Taking time out to go visit again your own conception, prenatal period and birth gives a precious experience to understand what your unborn baby goes through. Clearing the hurdles and transforming the negative imprints into positive ones guarantees that your unborn child will not repeat the same suffering. You will be able to guide it effectively and restore any disturbance immediately because you have been sensitized to this early world.

If you don't want to repeat the same patterns of your own upbringing, you cannot escape a deeper look into the family dynamics of your childhood. How our relationships play out often shows us what we have been programmed to do in our own childhood by picking up the patterns of communication and behaviour of our parents.

Overcoming the fear of becoming a mother – or father is the most important element of your preparation. Changing your stance on your capacity to grow into your role as a mother or father will be necessary to become one. Strong ideas of lacking value, anxiousness or being held back by your moods are blocks that will withhold you from getting there. They need to be overcome, cleaned up.

Start with how your own mom treated you: Were you belittled, unworthy, or not perfect enough? Did she see your capacities, talents, and qualities? Did she praise you honestly? Was there jealousy because you became more beautiful and successful than she was?

Never stay in that sphere of negativity to keep burdening yourself with her voice and her lack of value. Drain it all into the earth. See how it leaves you, all these little dark spots blocking your light, never to come back…

The same with your father: how did he see you, understand you, acknowledge you? Did he see the strong tree in your deepest being, full of potential fruits you could bring into the world? Was he able to see beyond his own problems and responsibilities, finding the time to connect? Or was he never home, always achieving, running after this or that opportunity? Maybe he was home but not really present.

Write down:

- What was the intention, the wish of your parents for conceiving you?

- What did you experience or lack in terms of a warm welcome, acceptance, recognition and acknowledgment?

- Were you welcomed just for being you, or were there strings attached?

- What were the deep hurts or maybe traumas?

- What were the beliefs that circulated consciously or under the surface?

- How was the relationship between your parents?

- How was your relationship with your mother?

- How was your relationship with your father?

- Were your parents emotionally present to you?

- How was the communication with you?

- What were the values that played a big role in the family?

- What did you learn in this family in both positive and negative aspects?

Take some time to write these all down. Then, consciously change the beliefs and heal the hurts.

2. What are Your Wishes?

Your attitude has a huge effect on the attitude of the other. In a relationship, some qualities help to reflect a harmonious way of interacting, like patience, compassion, respect, commitment, and responsibility. Which ones are dear to you?

Together with your partner, write down clearly

- What do you wish as values in the family you want to form?

- What are the positive truths you'd like to bring in?

- What qualities do you feel you lack and want to develop to parent your child in the best way?

- What are the qualities, virtues and skills you want to develop in your child?

3. How is your Couple's Ambiance?

How is the relationship? Is it harmonious? Is there any stress between the couple?

Relationships quickly show us "where the shoe pinches." The dynamics between two people are the building blocks for this project of a coming baby. As the baby is totally dependent on the ambiance in your home, it makes sense that we need to look into that element.

The parent's relationship forms the house of the greater nest in which the child forms itself. Unconsciously, it perfectly knows the couple's dynamics. The baby doesn't look at the outside of people. He can look inside! He is aware of all the subtle exchanges and the games that are played. He unconsciously picks it up and copies it.

Ideally, in a relationship, we nourish each other's soul. You cannot successfully do that if you are just giving from yourself. You'll get exhausted and you'll dry up. To be constantly inspired and able to nourish the other, you first need to connect to Source for each of you. Source really knows your needs and can fulfill them. Then you can gradually learn to become a source of joy, love and inspiration to others, a spring that constantly bubbles and clears out all debris.

If you have not investigated your upbringing, there is a great chance that you chose your husband who resembles your father's energy or your wife as a reminder of your mother.

Compassion is the most precious investment in family life. It is an absolute necessity to shape this new culture. Knowing that the other isn't perfect will help a lot. Having no expectations is the best way not to be disappointed.

"Love is a verb." It is hard work to come back to that basis of love again, to find it anew, time and time again. Building bridges when they have blown up. Going inside immediately when we are hurt to see what is needed to be healed, what we need to practice more, or let go.

Is there a dominant partner who determines mostly everything, or is their decision-making based on open communication and equality? Is there profound support and investment in each other's evolution, or do you go each your own way? Life together can be difficult because we trigger each other's weak points so often. But that can be worked out and transformed so we can understand and accept each other unconditionally.

If there is a pattern of *co-dependency*, you are not free in the relationship. You need the other to survive. You are vulnerable because you depend on your partner's acknowledgement, love and attention. Only *inter-dependency* comes from a free you, where you are a sovereign being who is able to give and shine. Knowing that love will come back to you, but without being dependent on it. That is giving freely. Of course, this will only be possible if you choose a partner who has these same values. In this way, you invest in each other by being a free and loving human being.

The basis of stability for a couple is how you consider the other. To keep it simple, we can state that there are two ways of considering each other. One is limiting and doesn't last. The second is based on freedom and can make the couple endure any struggle:

1. **You consider the other with expectations**: Do you expect the other to be the one who will give you physical gratification, who will work for you, who is obliged to love you no matter how you behave, who should make you happy, who should be able to know what you need even when you are a closed book, who must give back in return to what you gave him. This is based on **self-centeredness, dependency, control and possession.**

There will always be a need for balance, of course, and if nothing or very little comes back in return to what you freely gave, you didn't make the right choice as a life partner.

2. **You consider the other in freedom to love and, in turn, be loved.** From the abundance of love for yourself, you pour this love into the soul of the other so the seeds he carries inside can grow. Here you are NOT dependent on the other but dependent on the sacred cosmic Source of love, opening the connection daily and from where you receive the energy, the love and insight to share with the other. **This relationship is soul-centered and based on freedom.**

Make time for meditation and connection to this sacred energy of love, joy, clarity, and light from Source so it can pour into you. Share it with the other and uplift him or her. Your appreciation and gratitude will open the heart of the other, and he'll be inspired out of freedom to do the same.

Investing time in and nurturing the relationship is an important pillar of the relationship. Be transparent about yourself to the other and transform disharmony, as this is crucial to creating a warm nest for the soul to be born into.

You can start working on your relationship long before conception: learning to listen and comprehend the other, respect the other and appreciate and admire all his or her qualities.

An excellent way to learn to communicate in a relationship is explained in the book "Non-Violent Communication, A Language of Life" by Marshall Rosenberg. It is a way of verbally expressing your feelings and emotions, while taking responsibility for your own inner state, without blaming the other for how you feel. It is a number one condition to keep a relationship healthy.

To bring it all together:

- Healing the difficult experiences in your prenatal period, your childhood, and your education.

- Healing the relationship.

- Working at new ways to transform everyday experiences by putting them in a higher perspective.

- Developing qualities and virtues that reflect a harmonious way of interacting.

- Knowing how to create joy, happiness and contentment are jewels in your treasure chest as a future parent.

Preparing the Body

A farmer uses winter to prepare seeds for the next season. Why wouldn't we do the same to prepare for conception? Gametes are the condensation of our state of health. Harmonizing the body becomes a necessary step in the preparation. In natural medicine, a choice of several methods is possible to harmonize the body.

1. Cleansing the body

Naturopathy, osteopathy, homeopathy, touch for health, bodywork, acupuncture or reflexology, just to name a few, are all great ways to balance and strengthen fragile systems in the body. They all prepare the body for optimal conditions at conception by harmonizing nervous and hormonal dysfunctions.

Body energy work consists of working on the body's energy fields. It benefits the body, its energy, the mind, and the spirit of the future parents.

Fasting and curing can detox the body. We all gather so many pollutants through the air, water, and food. The cleaner your system, the better the quality of the material that you can give to the baby before and after birth. Consult a health professional to be guided in this detox.

2. Nutrition

Nutrition is an obvious way to enhance health in the body. Many books indicate what future parents would need regarding specific foods. I leave that to the experts. The essence is to nourish yourself as much as possible with organically grown fruits and vegetables as well as superfoods. Food that is not processed nor has chemicals or artificial colours is the best because anything artificial will start inflammation in the body, which can trigger illnesses.

What I would add is the way you take your meals: eating in an atmosphere of quiet and peace helps to digest better and absorb the subtle elements in the food. Why not receive these nutrients as a sacred gift from nature, with reverence and gratitude? Try it out and feel how different it is from taking a meal in chaos, loud noise and heavy discussions.

3. Breathwork

Another way of caring for your physical well-being is yoga and breathwork. Deep breathing is an excellent exercise that brings you back into the body. We are so easily focused on what goes on outside of us. It helps you to relax and shift your focus inside. Making a habit of taking a moment several times a day to fill your body up with oxygen and letting go of stress is so precious. It fills you up with new energy. Holding your breath after breathing in slowly can even reach further than just the physical oxygen. This way, the energetic essence that the air holds, called 'prana', enters your system, which helps cleanse and energize your whole being. It opens the pathways to connect with your deepest self. Concentrating on the breath during pregnancy is a powerful way to prepare your organs for optimal functioning during birth. It just takes some discipline.

Father's Time

Growing into fatherhood in this gigantic enterprise is as important as the journey to motherhood. It is more difficult in a sense because you feel so much out of the story. You are the main support for the mother. He is the cloak, embracing and protecting both.

A North American Native wisdom says: "Mothers carry the baby in their womb, as fathers carry them both in their heart."

You are the cloak, embracing and protecting both. Your involvement before conception, during pregnancy, birth and beyond also marks the baby's body and soul. Preparation is as much a deep process internally for you as it is for the mother. Dive in your own upbringing and look at the role model you had as your father. Take time to release any pain, hurt or unhealed trauma as it will be transmitted to your child as much as the mother would. It takes time and takes months or sometimes longer to clear yourself from any limiting belief, blame or criticism that creates feelings of doubt, failure or guilt. It is the father's task to recognize and acknowledge their children. So, if you have not received that kind of support from your dad, it might be difficult to give that kind of support to your child. Nevertheless, you can connect with other new fathers and learn from them.

On a physical level, life is transmitted through the sperm. Everything is recorded as memory in the cells and as such, also in the sperm.

"The father's seed contains a condensation of his quintessence. All that he has experienced in the past as well as his present life is expressed in his seed. And this means, therefore, that a man can give a seed of greater or lesser quality according to the kind of life he has lived in the past and is living now," says O.M. Aïvanhov[33].

The sperm is renewed regularly, but it takes two months to complete. So, take time out at least two months before conception so that you can start to prepare to physically detox. Give yourself the chance to let all alcohol, smoking or drugs to the side. Physical detoxing and nutritious food will give the highest potential to your sperm. Bring any negativity to awareness so you can release it and bring in a supportive energy.

Science tells us that the paternal effects of stress on gene expression are higher than those for the ovum. Paternal stress will cause the baby's brain to develop fewer synapses—fewer connections between the brain cells. It's time to relax as much as possible or pull back from workaholism!

Most of the time fathers feel involved by starting to remodel the house. But that turns out to be too stressful for the mother and baby. Even when the house is not perfect, the baby needs peace.

During pregnancy, your task is to be the sensitive gentleman around your wife, who respects and cares for her. How you deal with her will either create happiness or stress. So, leave the stress from work at the door and bring positive energy into the house. Otherwise, your stress will be brought over to your wife. If the mother is stressed, the gene expression will be altered in the baby, which has an effect on brain plasticity, which in turn can alter behaviour while growing up. A baby's brain is growing exponentially prenatally, and you can also positively affect his harmonious growth through your attitude.

You can make special moments of connection with your wife:

- Organize inspiring activities,

- Going on walks,

- Reading uplifting books together like poetry.

- You can also build in some sacred moments of meditation

- Listening to gentle music

- Watching inspiring movies

- Enable lots of bonding moments with her

- Bonding with your baby! The method of Haptonomy, founded by Franz Veldman teaches how you can connect and communicate with your baby in the womb through your hands on the belly.

Your presence is magic to your wife and baby during birth. The quality of your presence is more important than what you say. You can communicate, preferably by eye contact. Gestures without words will keep her in her cocoon, which is so important to let nature do its job. Next to the logistics, creating this sacred environment for her and the baby is a beautiful way to participate. All physical support during labour, all massages, touch, and gentle strokes can be your powerful collaboration.

And maybe you'll be the one who catches the baby at birth or who cuts the umbilical cord unless you choose to have a lotus birth, where the placenta stays attached until the umbilical cord falls off after a few days. Sunni Karll explains how to have this lotus birth in her book "Sacred Birthing."

Spiritual Connection

"It's never too late to be what you might have been"
- George Eliot

In this time and age, we can freely speak about the spiritual part of our being. Instead of hiding the idea to others, it is simply part of life. We feel the need to integrate again the sacredness of life, of nature, of relationships.

Life in society is a big distraction from our deepest essence. We try to find happiness in all sorts of outer attractions or material possessions that are supposed to give us fulfilment. But it can never do what our real being asks for: a connection to ourselves. We need to step off the hamster wheel.

If you are disconnected from yourself, from your soul, you are disconnected from Source, from God. This is a very vulnerable state in which you open yourself easily to discouragement, suffering, disempowerment, resentment, fear and anger. Everything in your life hits you up to blame the other, accuse him of your unhappiness, and maybe even to look for revenge. Violence – verbal, emotional, physical or sexual violence creeps in and destroys more and more your soul's integrity.

This continues until we realize that Love is always waiting for us. Forgiveness, letting go and moving on will bring you again to this inner field of peace, connection with the pure essence of the universe and this unconditional love that accepts all human beings in its open arms. Once again you are connected to your soul!

Every day, we can find that path again. Through seemingly minor adversities we can practice coming back to this soul connection. If we miss these opportunities to overcome setbacks, many toxic emotions accumulate until we're out of balance, and depression follows. This crisis state can finally be the opportunity to wake up and evolve. Finding your real essence again. It is not an easy path, but what counts is where you come out, renewed, finding your real self again, finding Source again. It is the only way to be fulfilled.

The divine shines through you even more if the road is clear. Real, lasting joy and connection to all that lives simply unfold. You created heaven on earth for yourself, for your partner, and now also for your future child.

The divine feminine is part of all creation. It is such an honour to represent this divine feminine as a woman. The divine masculine is the creator of life. The divine feminine gives it form. This connection with the principles we represent is ever- evolving through our efforts to play our role in the way it was foreseen.

Opening to this realm requires stillness, meditation, and inspiring music that brings you these higher frequencies. Prayer puts you on the wave of this other dimension that is there to help you, lift you up, and open the door to finding the answers coming from this higher point in us connected to the divine world.

Awakened souls have been looking out for this element in you. The more you can give attention to, respect, and develop this way of life, the more likely a higher-evolved soul will come to you. Opening into our deep spiritual roots is a natural result of the previous clearing and cleansing you went through.

CHAPTER 8

THE START OF A NEW LIFE

Women will become the architects of this planet because this magnificent work has been given to them.' - Natacha Kolesar, PhD

Conscious Conception

As we have seen till now, an optimal and conscious conception is dependent on the download of many elements:

- Each partner's essence

- The ancestor's influence

- The relationship itself

- The harmony of the moment

- The intention towards the creation of the child

- The influence of the environment

Conception is not just the start of a new life. It is the still point that separates the past from the future. It is the magical moment between two timelines of both the parents and the incoming soul. As we have seen, it is the moment that downloads lots of information into this first cell that is created.

A *conscious* conception is what is preferable for the wellbeing of the child. Can we speak about a conscious conception if the couple in the moment of intimacy is just conscious that they might be conceiving a child? Even if they can be on top of the sexual attraction and not be taken over by the power of the process, somewhere transcending the natural power into higher energy, we cannot fully speak about a conscious conception. If we know that this magical moment will give the synthesis of the parent's lives until then plus the dynamics of the moment to the first cell, it becomes obvious that the process needs a very special quality of consciousness.

The harmony or disharmony of the relationship will also be part of the blueprint of the incoming soul. We can just make the best of it: accept the challenges that are still ahead, knowing that the child will learn as we grow.

As we are also sensitive to the electromagnetic nature of our surroundings, a conception during a glorious morning of overflowing sunlight will interfere differently than during an electric thunderstorm or an eclipse. Here also comes the astrological influence on the moment of conception into account. Chinese astrology, opposite to Western astrology, takes into account the moment of conception rather than the moment of birth.

Parents, you can consciously invite the soul of your dreams by contacting this invisible soul, by explaining who you are, what you have to offer and what you wish for. You can write a prayer expressing your wishes or use a specific intention.

The power of intent is an important key to the start of a life during conception. "Intention is the seed that creates your future," says Jack Kornfield. Focusing on it during conception also creates your child's future. It will orient the energies it contains and attracts towards the realization of the intent. The vision of a well-balanced, generous and noble being will be the magnet that will attract such a life quality. It can even override genetic imprints that would be contrary to that intent. If this vision, intent or high ideal is nourished in the time before birth, it will be more present during the moment of intimacy. Focus on this intention in a high vibrational state to give it all the power to bring it into manifestation.

Of course, this intention needs to be nourished during gestation: the more you focus on it, the more you feel it and act on it, and the more it will grow and manifest later in your little one's life. Manifesting the values and qualities you wish to model will greatly enhance the intention you focus on.

To invite the soul you wish for, you can create an ambiance of selfless love and harmony during this magical moment. For the incoming soul, this will create the energetic blueprint of a healthy sense of self rooted in love, balance, and harmony.

Is there a greater moment of celebration than the intimate coming together in this serene harmony, in this sacred moment of connection with the soul and spirit of your partner, in unity with the soul you want to invite?

Consecrating this moment to the powers of light and love through meditation and prayer can be an inspiring build-up to that sacred moment. Allowing the purity of intention to guide all gestures and letting the magic play its part.

Wouldn't the moment of conception then become an enlightened point in time, a culminating point of all the work done before, into a point of eternity of selfless love toward the partner and the soul of the child? It would become a moment of participation in divine creation between the sacred masculine and the sacred feminine principle. The inheritance of such information will give the child the strongest possible roots even if later life events are difficult. Obstacles and eventual karmic patterns will be overcome more easily. This future human being would have the best chances to find and manifest its essence naturally.

Pregnancy, the Seed is Growing!

A pregnant woman is like an artist in full creativity,
living with her artwork, day and night, consciously
and unconsciously.
- Dr. Yves Moisan

In this book, I choose not to expand on the information you can find in so many books about pregnancy and birth: for example, good nutrition, healthy exercises, and what to avoid regarding alcohol, smoking, chemicals and toxins. There is a myriad of information to be found on the internet and in many books written on the topic. This is VERY important information and I hope you'll find your way to these resources. I wanted to focus on information you cannot find elsewhere: how to elevate your consciousness during this crucial time.

A baby is on the way! This news can immediately transform a man into a father, a woman into a mother, or a mother into a grandmother.

The coming of a baby has a power that goes far beyond it's simple existence. For the person who is willing to become conscious about this, a baby can throw the world upside down when one discovers the power of nature it brings with it. Pregnancy becomes a period of radical change: what we can learn and discover is mind-blowing.

Also, an incarnating soul going through this literal metamorphosis is forced to accept the requirements and expectations, the standards of the family, of the grandparents, of society. Embodiment is not an easy journey. A soul needs to adapt and fit in to be accepted and succeed.

As an incarnating soul, we easily forget our real nature, the goal of this coming life. A heavy blanket is thrown over the psyche of the fetus. The freedom of the soul cannot come through. Conscious parents can be there as a guide for the soul to embrace it in its struggle to adapt to this heavy overcoat it takes on and invite it to stay connected to the world of freedom, love and truth.

As a pregnant mother, you can stream your thoughts and feelings on beautiful inspiration and sounds of freedom: light and subtle, free of conditioning. Listen to the bird in your own heart that wants to fly freely, swimming in beauty, in the light and intensity of your heart and soul.

The baby will receive exquisite elements as nourishment for his emotional and mental bodies. These elements will become unit in the construction of a life that is more linked to his soul and his real self.

He will be more open to a higher source of inspiration to help him realize his soul's desires.

If you can reinforce your connection to this world of harmony, of Source, through meditation or prayer, you give the soul a feeling of trust. The soul doesn't need to let go of this connection to the divine world, where he comes from, as what happens in an unconscious pregnancy. He wouldn't need forty or fifty years to try to find this connection again. If the mother can feed that connection through these nine months, the soul will just continue to bath in these blessings of unconditional love, beauty and harmony. He will not forget it completely. He will be able to weave that connection in everything he will develop and grow up so that his being, talents, qualities and skills can be suffused with particles of this divine essence. Steadily growing, developing according to his soul plan.

It is only during these nine months that you have the opportunity to have such a deep impact on your baby. After birth, such massive influence is not possible anymore.

Keep a journal throughout the pregnancy. Use it to dialogue with yourself, see more clearly what you are experiencing, and meet your deeper self. This can help answer your questions or transform any tension or conflict.

But there is another reason to write in your journal regularly, to report what happens to you. Because it can be helpful after birth. This book shows how the prenatal period can affect life after birth. Ancient wisdom reports that here is a connection between the months of the pregnancy and the life's unfolding after birth. The last month of pregnancy is connected to the first ten years of life. The eighth month before birth is connected to the period between ten and twenty years of life. If something major happens in your child's life, you can always compare it to what happened before birth, thanks to your journal.

Honouring Your Child's Soul Plan

Wouldn't it be magnificent if you know what your child's soul is coming here to work out? What does he want to become more aware of? What does he want to develop, to master? Which qualities, virtues or skills does he bring with him or wants to develop more? What are the talents he has and wants to bring to the world? What are the challenges that he has planned in order to grow? How to accompany this soul as a parent? What are the pitfalls this soul has been falling in too many times and how can you help him to be more conscious this time?

That is the role of a parent. You are not only feeding or clothing this child, sending him to school, and watching him grow while you work hard to get the finances on board to support him. There is more...

Accompanying your child so he can find the path of his soul without having to deal first with healing trauma is so precious.

He will be guided in the right direction. Society's educational goals are to prepare children so they can be useful, productive participants in society. But what if that path goes against the grain of their soul? The commonly appreciated qualities are intellectual capacities, but in the process of developing them, the whole inner development, his character, his attitude, and his social engagement are left behind.

In this environment, the soul dries out and shrinks; it isn't nourished. The creative genius in the child is discouraged and even destroyed.

As people are now more in contact with their intuition, it might be possible to sense their child's soul purpose.

In meditation or dreams, the soul can talk to the mother or the father and tell them what it needs. During pregnancy, you can then focus your imagination on visualizing the qualities or virtues it would like to mature in.

Keep Your Vibrations High

Coming into the vibration
Of everything that sings
That loves creation
Everything that loves the Creator

Finding the exuberance
In the colours of flowers In the song of birds
In the freedom of fresh air
In the joyful flame of a candle

In the overwhelming power
Of a wave in the ocean

The food you eat, the music you listen to, the feelings and thoughts you cultivate create all a specific frequency.

Nature creates a range of different frequencies in the physical world. In the mineral world, a piece of coal will not have the same vibration or the same effect on its surroundings as a gemstone, which can heal.

There is a difference in frequency between a withered lettuce and a freshly harvested one. The first will be waste in your body, the second one will nourish you.

In the emotional realm, shame and guilt vibrate at a much lower frequency than unconditional love (see Dr. David Hawkins' Map of Consciousness below).

Name of Level	Energetic "Frequency"	Associated Emotional State	View of Life
Enlightenment	700-1000	Ineffable	Is
Peace	600	Blis	Perfect
Joy	540	Serenity	Complete
Love	500	Reverence	Benign
Reason	400	Understanding	Meaningful
Acceptance	350	Forgiveness	Harmonious
Willingness	310	Optimism	Hopeful
Neutrality	250	Trust	Satisfactory
Courage	200	Affirmation	Feasible
Pride	175	Scorn	Demanding
Anger	150	Hate	Antagonistic
Desire	125	Craving	Disappointing
Fear	100	Anxiety	Frightening
Grief	75	Regret	Tragic
Apathy	50	Despair	Hopeless
Guilt	30	Blame	Evil
Shame	20	Humiliation	Miserable

POWER VS. FORCE: The Hidden Determinants of Human Behavior by Dr. David R. Hawkins, M.D., PhD in Psychology. https://www.heartcom.org/SpiritualRevolution.htm

Self-serving thought has a lower vibration than a thought that wants to serve, help and support others.

We lower our vibrations when we are overwhelmed with

- sorrow,
- Anger
- Sadness
- Separation
- Division
- Fear
- Powerlessness
- Shame
- Guilt

The thoughts that bring vibrations down are suspicion, exploiting others, slick intentions, deception, lies, jealousy, judging, accusing, blaming, rejecting, projecting your own flaws onto others, negative beliefs about yourself, negative self-talk, being a victim…

On the level of emotions, we can slide down the ladder of vibrations with sadness, resentment, powerlessness, hate and anger. Shame and guilt have the lowest level of frequency, according to Steven Hawkins's chart. These negative emotions can happen at any time in life. But they are especially harmful if we keep them for a long time. We can cherish them and build our lives on them, so we'll fight off change as it feels very insecure to get rid of them. But at some time in our evolution, we'll be forced to let go of them and jump on the transformation train. Then we'll find a way back to the world that makes more sense.

It is of paramount importance The thoughts that bring your to orient yourself towards what is positive and harmonious in your choices of people to meet, places to visit and music to listen to. Avoid anything that drains your energy, that brings stress, tension, disagreement or discouragement. Listen to yourself and discern because negative energies are contagious and easily stick to your being. Neurological science has discovered the existence of mirror neurons in the brain. Unconsciously we mirror the behaviour, thoughts and feelings of others. Thus, look for uplifting people, even if it means temporarily avoiding family members who drain your energy easily.

The key is not to search for everything outside of us but to find it in ourselves and create the love we yearn for. It doesn't depend on others; it only depends on how we uncover our own resources to create the love, joy, and peace we would like to see in the world. Then, we can reach out to the world of the fetus.

He comes from a world of absolute harmony and indescribable beauty, an extremely precious atmosphere to the soul. He wishes to find that level of vibration here on earth.

The purpose of life is to bring that consciousness to the earth, to bring it with us, to incarnate this divine consciousness. That is why we must return so often, because it requires lots of learning and evolution. But the more we can keep the connection to this paradise world, the shorter the road.

This paradise world we have long forgotten, we only dream of. In fact, we all search for just this memory. Our whole lives are dedicated to reconnecting with this world. Separation became a big hurdle to overcome: separation from the divine, from ourselves, and from other human beings. Separation is at the origin of so many difficulties in life: disconnection, loneliness, sadness, depression, powerlessness, devaluation and even hate and violence.

Piercing through the veil of separation and reconnecting again to Source means working up the frequency ladder. After a long journey of suffering, searching, sacrifice, and letting go, we are finally determined to find this state of consciousness. When we have dropped all illusions, we can start elevating our feelings and thoughts to revolve toward this state of unity.

The transition to this world is not easy for the baby. Unconditional love is hard to find. It is a crushing experience for the baby to have fallen from the state of grace in which it was before. That is why babies cry at birth. It is such a difficult adjustment. But when the parents know this, they can turn that around and be aware and empathic for the baby's soul cry, offering him a gentler landing in the arms of your compassionate love.

Imagine if we can make that battle easier for this child. Mom is crucial to that. Without her collaboration it is impossible. Because what the mother feels, the baby receives also. She can create this column of light around her and inside of her. She can visualize that she has an intense, bright, shining sun in her heart. She can reach out to her child: "I understand where you come from. I'll be the link of light that you can hold on to. You don't need to lose this incredible consciousness of harmony." The dive will be easier for the baby. He will feel that he is still part of this divine world.

He will come into this world of struggle but with a window open to this higher world. He'll know that life can be difficult but that there is always a way to grow and transform. He receives vitamins for the heart that will stimulate him a whole life to overcome difficulties more easily. He'll be loaded with sparkles of light, of insight, of emotional strength and stability. Even more, he'll be a radiant messenger from this higher world, incarnating the beauty of a high ideal that his mom has deposited in him which she has condensed in him nine months long.

Every sublime thought is like a pearl or a precious stone that enriches the capital of his heart and mind. It will be the spark, the motor to incarnate this love and harmony he knew so well before. Every inspiring thought will be like a gold pellet that is embedded in his growing being. Every uplifting feeling of peace, love, forgiveness, solidarity, compassion, and beauty will be an indelible spark in his soul that will remind him of this world he came from, awaken the desire to bring it here and spin it in his activities, plans, and realizations.

You are the catapult of his life. You create his story of a hero who can fall but stand up again and learn, filling his treasure chest with precious stones of wisdom and strength.

This is a demanding undertaking because life is not that easy. Every event, small as it is, every conflict or happening in life is an invitation to grow. Yes, there are difficult circumstances in life, but how you cope with it is important. You are powerful: you can choose the way of suffering of a victim or be a winner. You can always grow through hardships.

If you are in a difficult emotional state, overwhelmed by sadness, anger or discouragement, just accept it. Life is unpredictable and you can't always control what happens. It is not a failure so don't feel shame or guilt. Just do what you need to do to work through it. But what is very important is to reach out to the baby and tell him that your inner state is not his fault. Babies, before and after birth, unconsciously take the emotional upsets of their mothers on them. They think they are the origin of their mom's problem. Of course, that is not true. Tell him that it is your luggage, not his. But especially he needs to hear that he is loved and cherished. That is the most important message he needs to hear and feel.

If this emotional upset is recurrent or stays for a long time – more than a few days – look for help from a friend or a professional because these inner states might create negative outcomes in the life of your child. Growing through this is an important life lesson for the baby. You can be unhappy at times, but you can find the way out of the maze and resolve the problem.

Your partner, your surrounding circle of friends, family, colleagues, and society as a whole are all invited to step up the ladder with you!

James Redfield in The Celestine Prophecy said it this way: *"We are designed to pop into a higher consciousness. Our brains are designed for it. It is built into the operation manual for planet Earth. So that lower consciousness happens to pop into higher consciousness."*

Loving Myself – the Umbilical Cord to My Soul

A friend lately told me, "I can finally honestly say 'I love myself.'" I saw her eyes speaking the truth. I was flabbergasted. Wow, this seems to be so essential. Can I say that about myself? Do I love myself? And lo and behold, I felt a timid, but subtle flow of warmth filling my being. I continued to ask this question to myself in the days and weeks after that moment. Even a few years ago, I wouldn't have been able to say that I love myself.

Loving yourself is the basis for loving anybody else. How can you really, sincerely and freely love somebody if you don't have that solid basis for loving yourself?

I don't mean that egotistical love of putting yourself *before* the other, being convinced that you deserve to be served first, having the biggest part of the cake etc.

It is that love in which you can feel that tender, subtle, warm love filling up in your heart. It diffuses in your whole body, everywhere. Love that encompasses all your skills, qualities, and virtues, as well as the ones you are still lacking. Love that extends to the space to be filled with new capacities and that nourishes everything still to be developed. Humbly accepting your errors, the dark spaces inside, flooding everything that lives in you with unconditional love.

Is there still space for rejection, which often echoes the rejection you received from your family or people in your life? Does that still belong to you?

Ask yourself: is there still space for judgment, blame or criticism towards myself? Or has that space been filled up with the knowing that there is nourishment to sprout the seeds of new capacities and develop what was not yet ripe? Maybe you are not always who you'd like to be, but you can love yourself where you are...

What are the limiting beliefs you still cultivate about yourself? If you struggle to undo yourself of the conviction that you are unworthy, small, insignificant, not important or to the contrary you're the only one who can save the world, the one who is always right, maybe it would be healthy to pierce the balloon of these inflating or deflating ideas about yourself. Replace them with healthy truths that support the unfolding of your being. Fundamentally accepting yourself in your real essence and growing it through mindful awareness.

This unconditional love for yourself gives you a foundation of strength, so you don't crave love or confirmation from another. Although this can be very comforting, you are no longer twisting yourself into being "the good girl" or "the good boy" to receive that love or confirmation. You are no longer depending on someone who loves you and believes in you to survive or feel that you deserve to live.

And if anybody doesn't accept you who you are, rejects you or criticizes you, you have this full-blown bumper of love in you that filters out what is useful in this criticism and what isn't. Before, you might have felt destroyed by criticism.

That love is the umbilical cord to your soul, who can only truly love you because it knows your deepest wishes, qualities and values, sprouting out of divine seeds.

Try looking at yourself as your higher self looks at you, like a mother connecting to her little one, knowing the truth of who you are. Something bigger than your small self loves you. What is that bigger you? Your soul, your higher self, the essence of life.

That's the love I invite you to and to nurture yourself so you can nurture this vulnerable incoming soul, building up its being with this essential nourishment of your love.

Connection and Relationships

"There are many tests wrapped in the package of love"
- Michael Newton

Connection is a bridge between two beings that dives deep into the soul of the other to understand the other and, in turn, feel understood and acknowledged.

Connection is the unspoken basic need of a human being. Connecting is cultivating the link with whoever is important to you, to feel supported, nourished, inspired and to support, nourish and inspire your partner. It is a necessity that has been trampled in the last few years with the health mandates that obliged people to stay home, disconnected from loved ones.

Connection is essential for the baby to thrive. It is embedded in the relationship between the parents. They create the nest of warm interconnectedness and harmony that a growing life needs.

Connection to yourself is hard to come by in this crazy world full of distractions from social media. The mindfulness of knowing how you are doing and what is happening in your inner world is not a habit that society supports that much. However, it is the key to conscious parenting. How do we know that we are on the right path if we can't check in with our heart and its needs?

Connecting to your partner beyond the superficial exchanges and building a solid love team for each other and the baby never will be as essential as in these nine months.

And what about connecting to the universe, the source of all energies building up your unborn child's being? Why not reach for the highest, most wonderful realms of the universe and receive daily blessings that will stay forever as indelible marks in his subtle labyrinth?

The baby's soul will settle in the cozy warmth of your heart, your stillness, the convincing YES from your being by connecting to him. Through you, he is connected to the essence: LOVE. Love from you, love from his dad—that is a translation for the love in the universe.

There the baby learns the most important lesson for his life: through the bonding with his mother, he creates the blueprint for a healthy relationship that he will be able to cultivate easily later in life.

Attachment is the natural outcome of this strong connection with your baby. Obstetrician Ikegawa, who has done research for twenty years into the revelations of the baby before and after birth, has discovered that the fetus himself is also actively trying to communicate with his mother! When Mom is upset, he frantically kicks or turns breach to tell her how he feels. Tune in to the baby, listen to him, and feel what he experiences.

Attachment and bonding do start long before birth. Mothers who have developed a deep connection with their unborn baby will have a safer and easier birth. If they have not been talking or connecting to the baby, delivery tends to get more complicated, according to Dr. Ikegawa. The mothers who invest their time and energy in connecting with their unborn baby will also be more able to understand their baby's needs after birth.

And you're not the only pregnant woman: connect with others who go through the same experiences as yourself. Knowing that everywhere in the world there are women expecting. You're part of the renovation team of humanity.

Couple relationships are the reflection of a sacred agreement between two people. There can be balance, and there can be imbalance. Love is the energy granted to us. How much can we receive it? How much can we manifest? How much do we shy away from it because we think we don't deserve it? How much can we immerse in it and discover the ladder to go higher up?

How much do we take it for granted?

In fact, relationships are the bridge between two parts of yourself: one is you, and the other is you, only in another body. He represents a part of you because we are all one.

We can discover ourselves through the other. What we admire in the other is what we have in ourselves. We have a sample in ourselves that matches what we see in the other. That is love: being attracted to the other through what lives in us. Seeing the beauty in the other can only be because we recognize in the other the beauty we have inside.

The same goes for ugly things. If we are touched by a devastating attitude or words of the other and get angry, we are, in fact, discovering ourselves in a way we didn't know ourselves. Can we feel the hurt? That is not difficult. But the real question is: What needs to be seen, developed, or let go? Can we forgive the other for showing a part of ourselves?

In my life, angry outbursts from others have diminished greatly since I discovered the load of anger I carried myself. Once I found the origin of it, transformed it, and healed it, it almost didn't happen anymore.

Relationships grow through resolving conflict.

- Every conflict comes to us, staged by our higher nature to be confronted with a topic that we are meant to focus on deeper. It invites us to look inside.

- Feel the pain and the emotions it wakes up in us. Do not focus on the other, what he shouldn't have said or done. But focus on the deep pain or trauma:

  - sadness

  - hurt

  - rejection

  - feeling judged

  - anger

  - not good enough

  - not understood

  - not heard

  - not valued

  - treason

Eleonor Roosevelt said once: "No one can make you feel inferior without your consent."

These emotions come from a weak point in our hearts that needs attention and healing. Once healed, it will not attract again the same pain. Our unresolved trauma opens the door to an arrow, an energy that can come in without warning. If we can see that the other who hurt us came to us because we 'invited' them unconsciously, we can even be grateful for the occasion to learn. Something needs to be understood and explored. Or maybe the reason our higher self has put us in that place, is to learn to let go, to pay for a transgression we did in a distant past. Humility is an invaluable virtue to be able to come to this. If we can see it like this, like courageous warriors, we can make big jumps in our evolution.

Reacting on the same wavelength as the other brings us into a war. Go to a frequency higher so you stay out of the lower level that urges you to defend yourself, reproach, accuse, judge, seek revenge, hate or reject the other. It can make us do or say the same ugly things as the other did, so we are as reproachable as them. It keeps the wheels of karma turning.

Buddhism teaches us to stay emotionally out of the game, towards the other: not reacting emotionally but observing ourselves and staying serene or coming back to it.

From this consciousness, we can come to forgiveness. Not condoning a negative behaviour but going straight to the soul of the other: forgiving him or her. Forgiving doesn't need to be done to free the other one. He or she will have to deal with their own consequences. The universe will take care of that. Forgiveness frees *us* in the first place so we can go on, liberated on our path. "To forgive is to set a prisoner free and discover that the prisoner was you," says Lewis Smedes. Forgiveness stops the wheels of karma.

Maybe in this struggle we can be curious about what brought the other to say or do what they did. When we discover the real background of the other compassion comes to your door. Understanding and compassion reveal the pain in the heart of the other one. Forgiveness is only possible if we can step into the shoes of the other one and see where he or she comes from and what they didn't have a chance to receive as a child. Then our heart opens to a small ray of sunlight and compassion pops up easily.

It is not easy not to focus on the regrettable behaviour of the one who has hurt us and reject or judge the other. We are who we are. Only, if we reject somebody's behaviour, we open the door for others to reject us in return.

If we could see the other through the eyes of Source, we would see a whole other panorama of qualities and vices. Why not try to see at least one quality, recognizing one strength, one virtue in the other? How would you feel if others could recognize one of your beautiful sides, next to experiencing one of your nasty sides? We would feel more whole. Why not do that for others? Anyway, it helps us not to focus only on the negative tendency of others.

You can send the other messages in silence, like "I wish we would come to a harmonious relationship," or "I love you." Visualize him or her surrounded by flowers or beautiful colours. This prepares for the possibility of opening to the other in all honesty in the future.

All this is not to withhold you from being mistreated without speaking up. Once the origin of the pain is dug up and healed you can find again your serenity. From that inner peace, the right words will come out without anger or revenge. You can choose to talk about what it did to you, to show the other about your state of mind without accusation or blame. Taking up all responsibility for yourself. The other can then engage in the same way of communication without violence and both can come to a better understanding of where the other comes from.

A criterion for a viable connection is having the same values and honouring them. When it comes to cultivating a healthy relationship, an authentic connection with the other, mutual respect and understanding are key. Trust should be the foundation of a thriving partnership.

The presence of reliability and integrity in your partner will only become clear after a while having been together but it will open the door to reciprocity and mutual support. As you are on a spiritual path, you can honour each other's choices that may even be different from yours. A relationship can only be alive if you have the space to grow and if you feel supported through the steps you take. It needs open exchanges and transparency and that cannot happen without vulnerability. If all these ingredients are there, you could say that your relationship can only be an harmonious one and a source of inspiration.

Living in Light

> *"We are in a moment in time where we have to ask ourselves: Are you able to take in the light, Hold the light AND cast the light?"*- Michael Swinwood

"Dar a Luz:" isn't it a beautiful expression in Spanish for giving birth? "Dar a luz" means literally, "give light!" What is in the word "light," and what does it mean to "give light?"

To be happy, healthy, and able to cope with life's demands, increasing your vibrations is the key to growing in intensity. It means growing towards the frequency of light.

O. M. Aïvanhov states: "The measure of the evolution of a being is the intensity of his life," and "He who lives an intense life maybe doesn't move at all but inside he vibrates as fast as the light and even faster."[34] Why is light such a powerhouse that it helps us evolve, harmonize, and be happy?

Light moves at 300.000 km per second, the highest frequency of what we know in the physical world. Genesis in the Bible states that Divine light created everything we know in this universe.

Light, what does it mean? When people talk about "Love and Light," what do they mean by light, working with the light? How can working with light be beneficial?

In everyday life, light is the element that makes you see in the dark. The expression 'Seeing the light at the end of the tunnel" or "A light bulb went on" or "Casting light on something" expresses the solution and insights it brings. In the world of darkness, ignorance, and lack of consciousness, the one who "sees" is the one who has discernment: he has the light to see and the **knowledge, insight and wisdom** to direct his life and keep him on his path.

Light is also what **protects us from harm**. Human beings have the tendency to be unsuspecting of negative influences or criminal behaviour in society. They have a basic goodness in them and don't expect otherwise in other people. If we were better at perceiving danger, we would have less criminal behaviour of some beings in our world; we would have the intuition to see, feel, and perceive that something is not right and do whatever is needed to avoid harm. **Intuition** is this form of inner light that warns us, informs us and keeps us safe.

Human beings are essentially **light beings**. In biophysics, light is made of photons, which are elementary particles of light. It has been scientifically proven that every cell in the body emits more than 100,000 light impulses or photons per second. These light emissions, which are not only emitted by humans but by all living things, are called biophotons and have been found to be the steering mechanism behind all biochemical reactions. The body uses biophotons as information packages to send signals from one point to another, like fiber-optic cables, which transmit signals using light. Biophotonics is one of the fastest-moving and most exciting fields in science today.

> *"We are still on the threshold of fully understanding*
> *the complex relationship between light and life, but*
> *we can now say emphatically, that the function of our*
> *entire metabolism is dependent on light."*
> - Dr. Fritz Albert Popp [35]

Science uses light in concentrated form, such as the laser, to heal, and it is used in surgery. It is also used in many practical applications, such as the exact cutting of diamonds.

Light is what **keeps us healthy:** Kirlian photography proves that the body radiates light. Aura pictures are possible now: the stronger the intensity of the colours around the body, the better protection it gives against influences from outside that can make us sick. Imagining light surrounding us can clear energetic disturbances we carry in us in the form of disharmonious emotions or thoughts.

Sunlight is a carrier of **life force**. Why do we feel such joy when the sun comes through the clouds? It brings the spirit of life that we so need. If there were no sun, we'd have no life on earth. But we take it for granted. The sunlight in spring wakes up all dormant seeds in nature through its life force, light, and warmth. How is it possible not to connect to that abundant source of life energy? The sun is the heart of the solar system and in this sense, it is the conduit for a divine energy that sustains all life in our solar system. Why not catch the first rays of the sun by its rising as they are charged with prana? You connect with this high energy and nourish it in yourself.

You can take a moment to visualize this living spirit of light with my visualization:

> *"Imagine yourself at the ocean at dawn.... A subtle coral pink has painted the sky at the horizon. It clears up little by little.... And then the first spark of light appears: the sun is born out of the ocean.... It traces its reflection on the moving water. As a sparkling pathway from where you are towards the sun..... The sun grows and invites you to join... You decide to step into the water and swim towards the sun. With every swimming movement of your arms, you come closer, immersed in the golden*

glow of its rays on the water…. Gradually the light becomes you: you become this shining ball of light…. Its warmth embraces you as a hug of recognition: yes, you became the sun, you ARE the sun. One with the light…. Light is everywhere: in you, around you…. You see all your organs bathed in light. And especially your baby: it shows itself as this condensed liquid light, murmuring a melody of happiness and joy…. That is its real essence: its' Soul Essence…. Anchor this soul essence in the baby's body… Everywhere your child will go in the future, it will keep the memory of this soul essence in the center of his being because you brought it into his biology, you lighted it up, you nourished it…. It will guide him, protect him and help him develop…. The seeds of his talents and gifts will grow because of this inner light that you nourished: the connection to his soul…. Later, he will find the Source of Life and Light more easily. He'll be able to nourish it himself…. And if difficulties show up on his path, he will be able to find a solution thanks to the connection to the light that is present everywhere."

Giving light - Dar a Luz - means building up your unborn baby with light! Surrounding it with light, drenching it with colours and light. Helping it to remember the world of light where it came from. Helping it remember that its essence is light. Reinforcing the continuation of light over the boundaries of dimensions. There is no separation between before conception, where the light was continuously present, and after birth: your work with the light guarantees the fulfilment of this essential need of the soul that the connection with the world of light also continues in the physical world. Dar a Luz is giving light - your baby - to the world.

Changing your vibrations towards the frequency of light is thinking thoughts that uplift, help you find solutions, and give you insights. It makes you feel connected to everything. It clears out all lower vibrations of struggle, anger or fear. It is that frequency that will make you feel happy and fulfilled.

The law of attraction states that what you feed in yourself— dark or light—you will attract. If you live in the most elevated energy, you'll attract the insights and solutions you need.

Visualize this life-giving light energy in and around your body and the baby's body daily. Fill it with the colours you feel are right at that moment. It is both an energetic protection against all that is disturbing and an uplift of your vibrations. Higher vibrations bring you into the feeling of love, trust, and happiness, which trigger the production of the love hormone oxytocin, which is the factor that stimulates growth, resilience, and the ability to connect with yourself and the baby.

Visualization, Imagination and Colours

"Energy follows thought"
- Albert Einstein

The focus on a certain thought or an image in deep relaxation or alpha state will manifest it, depending on the intensity with which you'll do that. Visualization means a conscious, directed focus on a specific thought. Imagination can be rather chaotic, swimming in a blurry nebulous cloud. It needs to be used in a conscious way. To realize your highest wishes, the most divine ones, you need to bring imagination and thought together in a conscious effort to direct your thoughts. It will create a vibrational energy that will condense itself in your life, in your qualities, capabilities and performances.

"Imagination is a messenger capable of reaching very high to register the splendours of heaven and provide them to you," says O.M. Aïvanhov.[36]

The power of visualization has been introduced at length: how it programs the subconscious and how it is used in healing. It is used also in sports to prepare for performances. Why not use it during pregnancy?

In fact, a pregnant woman, whether she knows it or not, is constantly programming the subconsciousness of her unborn baby through her thoughts, feelings, what she says, how she says it, and so on. It is left to chance how her baby is programmed for life. Why not take that into your own hands and use it consciously, as this book has been focused on all the way?

Take a few minutes of time in a busy day to relax and focus on this mini-human being daily. What values do you want it to develop? The qualities, virtues, and skills? You can visualize these qualities manifesting in your child after birth. You are birthing a baby, and you can imagine it as healthy and happy. But he or she will grow up, so visualize this grown-up child manifesting these qualities.

You can make a list, eventually pick some from the list in appendix 1 and with a background of music, you connect with your baby and tell him all you'd like to see him manifesting as attitudes about health and capacities. Especially visualizing these qualities and feeling how they make him and yourself happy and proud of him. You start his education already before birth. That is when it is powerful. After birth, the effects of education are so much smaller than before birth.

With your intuition, you can listen to the baby and receive the indications of the qualities it came here to develop. Take these specific choices of the baby into account in your visualization.

In Appendix 1, you'll find a list of qualities (for the mind), virtues (for the heart), and skills (for the body) that you can use to visualize your child. See him as a mature, balanced person radiating happiness, being smart and emotionally intelligent, loving, generous, and able to serve other people and humanity.

You can do so many things with it:

- write a poem about the quality you'd like him to manifest

- read a text about it

- search for examples in history

- focus on it in meditation or visualization

- breath them in

- work around it with creative materials

Here is an example of a visualization I conceived about willpower. You can make your own visualization about whatever quality, virtue or skill you prefer.

> *"See in your mind's eye your child grown up to be a young man/woman with a character that holds strength. Not necessarily a bodybuilder…But just a stable, balanced being…. Inspired by an idea that will bring a positive change to the world, fuelled by love for humanity…. Being able to stand in his/her energy. But especially having the willpower to act on his/her ideas. Materializing them… The inspiration, insights or ideas made visible or audible… Doing everything he or she can to think out all the steps in the realization process…. Overcoming self-doubts and withstanding criticism from others. He has the patience to look into the right moment to act. If needed he or she can take a step back to adjust to new incoming ideas…. So it is not stubborn willpower but sensitive willpower in service to consciousness, to a high ideal…"*

This is not an exercise in manipulating the baby, in wanting your child to compensate for the failures you had yourself. We don't want to focus on professions, like becoming a doctor or an attorney, but only working with moral qualities.

A beautiful subject for visualization is imagining the seven colours of the light spectrum, like when light passes through a prism and shows these pure primary colours. Each colour has a different frequency, stimulates a quality, and is linked to different parts of the body.

Red, the Spirit of Life, expresses dynamism, activity, and love for all creatures and is linked to the sexual organs and the muscular system.

Orange, the Spirit of Holiness, stimulates health and the desire for perfection and is linked to the spleen.

Yellow, the Spirit of Wisdom, stimulates intelligence and is linked to the nervous system.

Green, the Spirit of Eternity and Evolution, stimulates growth and development and is linked to the digestive system.

Blue, the Spirit of Truth is the colour of peace, religion and music and is linked to the lungs.

Indigo, the Spirit of Force, stimulates order and is linked to the bone system.

Violet, the Spirit of Divine Power and Sacrifice, stimulates mysticism and is linked to the glandular system and the chakras.

With these explanations, you can imagine the qualities you'd like your child to develop and stimulate the healthy formation of his body systems.

About Heart Coherence

Science has discovered that the heart is doing a lot more than pumping blood through the body.

The Institute of Heart-Math Science[37] has studied the relationship between the heart and the brain. Astonishing results came out of that study. We have always learned that the brain gives orders to the whole body. It was called "the Master Organ" in the body. Recent science discovered that the brain is not the only organ that has a nervous system: the heart also has one! It is called the fifth brain. With its 40.000 neurons, which add up to 65% of the heart's cells, it influences the function of higher brain centers involved in perception, cognition, and emotional processing. **Compared to the electromagnetic field produced by the brain, the electrical component of the heart's field is about 60 times greater in amplitude.** The magnetic component is approximately 5000 times stronger than the brain's magnetic field. There are more impulses coming from the heart to the brain than from the brain to the heart. The impulses the brain receives from the heart are then distributed throughout the body.[38]

Around the heart, a torus-shaped energy field - like a donut shape - covers about five feet (1.5 m). When the heart's energy is in harmony, it creates this state throughout your whole being, which is called **'Psychophysiological Coherence'**.

Feelings of gratitude and love are powerful creators of this state of coherence. Feeling these for two to three minutes stimulates the heart to produce anti-aging hormones such as DHEA (dehydroepiandrosterone), counteracting depression, for example. Furthermore, oxytocin or the love hormone can be created in the heart. Coherence is the optimal place to be when our body senses that all systems are synchronized: it is the state of being when we are at our best.

If we can be in this state of coherence we influence other people around us, as they adapt their internal state to a more harmonious one.

The four feelings that are the powerful instigators of this state of coherence are:

- gratitude
- appreciation
- care
- compassion

The ancient spiritual teachings have always known this. Science now has discovered the mechanism through which this takes place.

The recently discovered gamma waves that bring higher states of consciousness and problem-solving are generated by this state of coherence.

What interests us is the interaction between mother and baby. Mothers play a gigantic role in installing this coherent state in the growing baby, augmenting the chances of harmonious development a healthy emotional foundation and the capacity for self-organization. As a very young child is not able to regulate its emotions, he needs his mother or caregiver to do that with him. The baby learns to regulate his emotions through the way mother interacts and models that. Gregg Prescott, M.S. expresses:

"A body of ground-breaking work shows how the field of socio-emotional interaction between a mother and her infant is essential to brain development, the emergence of consciousness, and the formation of a healthy self-concept.

These interactions are organized along two relational dimensions—stimulation of the baby's emotions, and regulation of shared emotional energy. Together they form a socioemotional field through which enormous quantities of psychobiological and psychosocial information are exchanged.

Coherent organization of the mother-child relations that make up this field is critical. This occurs when interactions are charged, most importantly, with positive emotions (love, joy, happiness, excitement, appreciation), and are patterned as highly synchronized, reciprocal exchanges between these two individuals. These patterns are imprinted in the child's brain and thus influence psychosocial function throughout life.[39]

Solar Plexus

A special place in the body needs attention to bring harmony to the body, the mind, and the heart. It is the place people talk about when they say, "I carry a child under my heart." The real heart that looks after the baby is not the physical heart but rather the solar plexus, which is very close to where the unborn baby is situated. Why is it important?

The solar plexus is a nerve center in the sympathetic nervous system and is located behind the stomach. It regulates all the organs of digestion, circulation, respiration, nutrition, growth and execration. I'm sure you have noticed that you have a knot in the stomach when you feel stressed. It is not the stomach that contracts, but the nerve center behind it. When this solar plexus contracts because of stress, the stomach is not able to digest properly, and it feels as if a stone lies on the stomach. The brain has no conscious control over all these bodily systems. But the solar plexus does. Not only stress but also shock, or emotions like sadness, worry, disappointment, and anger, all emotions that have a lower vibration, destabilize and contract this nerve center, which influences circulation, respiration, etc. This nerve center is the reservoir of life force for the body. Disturbances can even totally empty it. You feel exhausted. Energetic and physiological blocks are created that, in the long run, are the origin of illnesses. That is how psychic disturbances affect the body.

The solar plexus is also this mysterious centre through which we feel connected to the universe and through which we feel nurtured by the immense sustaining energies that are brought to us all the time. The solar plexus is the principal door through which all subtle influences come: from the environment, from the cosmos, or meeting someone. It can be nourishing as well as disturbing. You could compare it with the principal door through which everybody has to go through to enter a building. You must learn to open and close it: opening to beneficial influences and closing when disruptive energies are coming in.

In this glorious state of pregnancy, your whole body needs to be able to work properly, because that is where the baby receives all its energy and material from to build its being. That is why consciously taking care of the solar plexus is, therefore, really important.

Being pregnant means also being very open to whatever surrounds you. The energies of the universe come in day and night to build your child. That is why your energy system is open. But sometimes, negative influences also come in easily while shopping, at work or in contact with people who don't have harmonious vibrations. You need to learn to close yourself, by closing the plexus when you perceive these disturbing, disharmonious people or events around you. You close it by putting your hand on the plexus and turning clockwise. And open again towards anything that is beautiful and sound.

But if you feel knocked out of balance, or discontent, fearful, angry or worried, it's time to restore it as quickly as possible so that the baby doesn't suffer from the negative effects of these disturbances. If we are conscious of what just happened, if we leave the door open to negative influences, we can transform the difficult emotions or the disturbances it has brought us.

Another great way to let go of the disruptions is to take a hot foot bath and you'll feel how your whole body can relax again and restore itself. That is because the feet and the solar plexus are connected. The stress is drained through the feet in the hot water. Take it as hot as you can bear.

If the solar plexus can be emptied, it can also be filled. One way to fill it is by observing a bubbling spring, a waterfall, or a fountain. Running water helps drain the negative elements and replenish the solar plexus. Also, the rays of the sun rising in the morning are very beneficial for filling up this powerful center. It can be harmonized again by putting your hand on the solar plexus and turning counterclockwise.

The solar plexus is also this mysterious center through which we feel connected to the universe and through which we feel nourished by the immense sustaining energies that are brought to us all the time. In this way, it is the solar plexus that supports and nourishes energetically the brain and not the other way around. This plexus is the place through which we feel. In contact with awkward people, it closes, but it opens when we are in contact with loving, magnetic people. In contact with nature, with beauty and harmony, it dilates; it simply feels good. But it can also feel what happens in the body and that's why it can restore balance again in the body.

To summarize the function of the solar plexus: by living a balanced life, you support this extraordinary life-giving center, and in turn, you are supported by the universe. Let yourself be carried by the waves of universal energy that wants to nurture you and your baby towards a future of magnificent development.

Creating Happiness

"There is no way to happiness – happiness is the way'
- Thich Nhat Hanh

Happiness is the ball we all run after, kicking it forward, never grasping it. Our whole life, we try to get to it, through all the meanders of life to find the perfect partner, the dream job, the long-wished-for mansion, or the absolute must-have of the latest iPhone. Did happiness finally fall in our lap? Maybe some fleeing moments. To land again inside, thirsting for happiness.

Happiness was lurking behind the flashing goal of pleasure.

"It is very simple to be happy, but it's very difficult to be simple," said Rabindranath Tagore.

In our body, the difference between pleasure and happiness is quite clear, as Laura Aboli states: "Pleasure releases dopamine; happiness releases serotonin. The more pleasure you seek and the more dopamine you release, the more neurons die. And the more dopamine you produce, the less serotonin you can produce because one down-regulates the other. It's almost like a joke from the universe. The more pleasure that you seek, the less happy you will be." – She goes on to say that serotonin brings a feeling of contentment, serenity, fulfilment or in fact, that elusive thing we call "happiness." [40]

Happiness is an inside job. It is more about how we perceive things than what life throws at us. It is not in "having" and "doing" but simply in "being." It is about becoming the one you really are, about living in harmony with the nature of your soul.

Marie-André Bertin, the former director of ANEP (Association for Prenatal Education) in France, stated that the only duty a pregnant woman has, is to be happy.

Being happy is the best way to walk through life, receiving whatever life makes us experience: connected inside and to your soul essence. It is so much easier to make sense of what happens to us, rather than always wanting things cleared up by outside situations.

What holds us back from happiness is wanting to control everything. Life is not controllable. You can plan events and try to make them happen in the best way possible. But life doesn't always listen to your wishes. It brings in whatever unwished-for situation you cannot control. You can only adapt to it by accepting what happens and learning or developing whatever it asks you to learn.

Whatever situation you encounter, you can ask yourself: What does it bring me, what does it ask of me? More resilience, more love, more patience? Things don't happen to us but *for* us—for us to learn, develop, and grow. Before you know it, you are evolving each moment toward the one you always wanted to be: becoming the real you. THAT is happiness.

What helps beautifully to come into that state of happiness is *gratitude.*

Mo Gawdat, expert in gratitude, stated: 'Gratitude is the ultimate solution to the happiness equation." Gratitude is receiving the bliss of the moment, even if it is far away from bliss. It is seeing that one flower in a dirty street. Hearing a bird sing in a noisy place. Did you catch these loving eyes of the person you just crossed? That is holding strong in your light essence in a world of chaos.

> *"Repeated complaining will attract more things to complain about. Repeated gratitude will attract things for you to be thankful about."* - Anonymous

Appreciating what happens to you and finding gratitude is equal to learning your lesson. So life says: "Lesson learned, we can move on." Things will improve at least inside of you, because gratitude lifts you up to a higher vibration. From there, the outlook changes, and your view on things improves. Insights begin to roll in and you begin to feel guided to the next interesting moment, attracting more to be grateful for.

"Real happiness is to be found in the expansion of consciousness, in the expansion, the sublimation, the divinization of love." - O.M.Aïvanhov [41]

Nourishing a High Ideal

We all have a special place inside ourselves, mostly unknown and well hidden, a little piece of paradise: consciousness in which everything is elevated, with perfect beauty and harmony. The baby wants to nourish himself with this energy because it is there that he finds the shape of the ideal, of perfection that orients him towards this new life to create it in himself. It's where our inner divinity lives that we are supposed to find to incarnate it in our thoughts, feelings and gestures, and thus create this paradise on earth.

As you, the baby's mom, cultivate this elevated vibration as much as you can, you weave into the unborn baby the energetic fabric of this High Ideal. It is an essence that pulls you up, towards a region of archetypes of harmony, nobility, purity, clarity, and truth, where reside the highest values we can cultivate as human beings. This archetype of perfection we all seek can become the blueprint for the incoming soul, who will unconsciously copy it.

When I was pregnant for the first time, which was only for a few weeks, a vision showed me this high ideal in the form of a cone. The top of the cone was filled with my High Ideal. I saw my little one, only a few weeks old, already pulling his energy into it: moulding in the same form for himself, modelling his high ideal after mine. His ideal and mine became the same.

How a high ideal helps you to realize it is explained by O.M. Aïvanhov like this:

> *"When you concentrate on the highest Ideal, God Himself, who is beauty, light, purity and absolute power, a magical phenomenon occurs: an entire network of energies is woven between the forces of your being and this ideal. This ideal activates hidden forces within our being; it awakens them up and draws them to itself. There is a polarisation between our being and the ideal, that not only*

serves as a means of comparison, a yardstick, a model, a sample, but it also serves as a magical element that activates the forces of consciousness, of self-consciousness. An ideal influences the mind, so that it learns to distinguish, discern, classify and recognize what is perfect. An ideal awakens warmth and love in the heart; and through an ideal, the will is stimulated and energized. Thus your high ideal attunes all your cells to God Himself[42]

By focusing on that bright ideal during pregnancy, you write a blueprint in his being that will attract and wake up the treasures hidden in him and put everything into action to realize it.

In fact, you're the writer of your child's story. Of course, this isn't literal; of course, you don't know which profession he or she will have, where he or she is going to live, or whom he or she will marry. But you can write a high ideal in his being. It will give him the emotional strength to overcome blocks on the road, or the capacity to find intelligent solutions for a problem. You'll be the one building the link with his higher self through this connection with a higher, subtler world. According to the quality of this ideal, he will attract all subtle energetic matter from the universe that will build up his body, heart and mind. It determines the resilience he will have on all these levels of being. His story can be one of a warrior for truth, a peace bringer or a talented artist who unveils the hidden world of harmony.

Clothing Your Baby with Beauty for Nine Months

"Beauty is the expression of the utmost perfection"

\- O.M.Aïvanhov

Beauty is a manifestation, the expression of a world of harmony, of a higher vibration. It is the subtle manifestation of a world of balance and of higher values. Beauty invites us into this world of harmony to absorb these higher vibrations and be uplifted. But the real beauty is not to be found in form. It is to be found in radiance, in emanations.

Ancient wisdom says that every object you contemplate tends to create in yourself the form, dimensions, and qualities of this object. Consciously or unconsciously, you begin to resemble the object that you look at. This is a natural, biological law. Use this law to bring in the energies of harmony so they can flow into your baby's being. Look at what is harmonious, beautiful, luminous, and perfect.

Goethe brought us an example of this phenomenon: A woman was pregnant. Her husband was the father, but this woman was secretly in love with another man who lived nearby. She thought of him all the time. When the baby was born, he had this man's eyes, not his father's.

Contemplating beauty, focusing on it, and absorbing it will make the unborn baby more sensitive to it. If you surround yourself with objects or pieces of art, even reproductions, and immerse yourself in them, it becomes like breathing that brings oxygen to the whole body. Harmony and beauty will imprint themselves in your baby's subtle meanders of his being.

If you are willing to look, you can find beauty in any prosaic activity of life, as R. Tagore expressed it: "Beauty is simply reality, seen with the eyes of love."

Even more so with art in all its forms: dance, poetry, literature, music, architecture, sculpture, paintings, movies, and theatre are all filaments in the immense fabric of beauty, depending on the level of perfection they express.

In this primal period, you are helping nature's forces to realize the plans of the architect of souls. He made the plan of a temple. An entrepreneur only needs to build it. You are the entrepreneur. Your work is to bring the right materials at the right time.

The materials you need for realizing the plan and growing the baby are, in addition to the physical, ultrafine, gossamer-fine materials, the finest materials for the heart: beautiful imagery, inspiring music, feelings coming from a bubbling source in your heart, of tenderness, compassion, joy, hope, and creation.

But the beauty institute that you are, by imprinting outer beauty, is also capable of instilling inner beauty. Imagining this inner beauty in your child as an expression of this higher world - inner beauty expressed in outer beauty. Both are connected and should be connected, as we, unfortunately, have lost that connection in society.

What can you do with this? As already mentioned, you can surround yourself with beauty and art in all its forms, you can visualize your baby with outer and inner beauty. And even better: you can create it.

Why not dance the miracle of creation, sing your wonder, and paint your enchantment? Find your creative side.

Increasing the presence of beauty in your life can be done in many ways:

- Flowers in and around the house

- Finding beauty in nature

- Decorating your house with clear colours straight from the rainbow. Accents on the walls, on the couch, or on your clothes.

- Surrounding yourself with beautiful objects that reflect a meaningful idea for you.

- An open book where every day another inspiring image is shown. You pick up some of its messages every time you come by it.

- Making art yourself.

- Listen to music that impregnates your soul with harmony, subtlety, tenderness and gentleness. Or making music yourself.

- Reading or writing poetry.

- Going to arts performances, museums and so on.

The Power of Sound, Music and Singing

The fetus bathes in a world of sound: the mother's heart rhythm, the bubbling of her intestines, and her voice are his daily sound environment.

Hearing becomes possible from the 24th week of gestation, but the fetus can perceive sound vibrations from the sixth week on through his sense of touch through the skin and bones.

We all know how the continuous passing of cars on the highway or on your street puts a strain on your nervous system, but the sound of waves at the ocean can calm us down. The power of music is used in movies where it paints the atmosphere on a subconscious level. The power of rhythm is used with drums by shamans to bring them to an altered state of consciousness: it brings them from beta over alpha to theta brain waves.

Speaking, sound, and music are ways of communicating and influencing a human being's emotional space. Communication is the transmission of information between the sender and the receiver. This communication is an essential part of our being: it brings us in contact with the other and nourishes us emotionally. The fetus in the womb is only the receiver of information. The sounds it receives are building blocks of his psyche.

Dvorak, an important 19th-century composer of classical music, also stated that music education starts in the womb. When his son told this statement to the principal of a music academy in Meise, Belgium, he was motivated to initiate music education with classes for pregnant women. That is how I was invited to bring my prenatal singing program to his academy in the 90s.

Sound also influences matter. The sound experiments of Ernst Chladni (1756-1827) and later Hans Jenny, a Swiss engineer, showed how sound organizes dust particles on a metal plate. Each square you see in the figure below is the effect of the dust particles by another hertz frequency: another geometrical figure is created by using a higher or lower tone. Fine sand was scattered all over the plate. The sound created this form by agglomerating the sand particles in a certain configuration. (see illustration below)

What is interesting is that the lines that are created are the lines of lower vibration. The black part is where you find the higher vibration: it vibrates so much that the sand is rejected to the places of a lower vibration. So, in nature the lower vibration tends to condense the physical particles. The higher vibration sheds them. We cannot see the energy lines with our eyes, but we can see how they condense matter.

(from www.are.na)

"The voice gives a rich image of a person's character," says Zeger Vandersteene, a Dutch tenor singer. He explains that there is no picture of a human being that can give as many details as the voice.

A fetus in the womb receives in this way a precise image of his mother: her intentions, her tenderness, her warmth, her hope, her fear, her tension, her love for him. He learns through her voice about his mother, himself, and the world. The sounds of his mother's language build the receptivity for these specific sounds. He is able to recognize his mother's language right after birth.

In his book "Pre-Parenting" Thomas Verny, PhD reported a tradition of how an East-African tribe prepares for the coming of a baby:

"In this tribe the birth date of the child is not the day of his or her physical birth, nor even the day of conception, as in other village cultures, but rather the first time the child appears in the thought of the mother's mind.

Aware of her intention to conceive a child with a particular father, the mother goes off to sit under a tree. There she sits and listens until she can hear the song of the child that she hopes to conceive. Once she has heard it, she returns to her village and teaches it to the future father so that they can sing it together as they make love, inviting the child to join them.

After the child is conceived, the mother sings this song to the baby in her womb. Then she teaches it to the old women and midwives of the village, so that through labor and the miraculous moment of birth itself, the child is greeted with his very own song. After the birth all the villagers learn the song of their new member and sing it to the child when he falls ill or is hurt. It is sung in times of triumph, and during rituals and initiations. The song becomes a part of the marriage ceremony when the child is grown, and at the end of life, his loved ones will gather around the deathbed and sing this song for the last time."[43]

Why not use this power of voice and music to bring an explicit message of love, of a plethora of emotions through sound images? The bonding process can be hugely enhanced by singing for the baby by both parents. Three people coming closer together in a musical experience.

A composer said once: "Music is love searching for words." The vibrations of the singing voice are sensory stimuli for the fetus that have an effect on all organs and systems of his growing body. In a way it enhances its intelligence by stimulating the nervous system that is growing at a super speed.

Singing releases oxytocin, the love hormone in the body, which stimulates growth in the baby and has healing capacities.

The womb is the first classroom where sensitivity to music, rhythm, and sound can start before birth. Several well-known musicians, such as Rubinstein, Olivier Messiaen, and Yehudi Menuhin, have testified that their prenatal experiences have woken up their interest in music.

The fetus can have its own preferences for music: according to a study by Dr. Michèle Clement, music from Mozart or Vivaldi enhanced the heart rhythm of the fetus and made it kick less with its feet. All forms of rock music and certain music of Beethoven and Brahms, on the contrary, made the fetus more restless.

You can choose to listen to music that brings you closer to your inner source of love and inspires and enhances your connection to yourself, your partner, or your unborn child. Music can talk about a world of unseen subtle beauty and touch the strings of your soul in remembering where you came from, where your baby came from. It gives a glimpse of paradise on earth.

And why not sing yourself? Love songs, sacred songs, joyous songs, learning lullabies already? It helps to release tension, to fill up again with life energy. The stream of energy does miracles in transforming life from stress, weariness, and powerlessness to relief, calmness, harmony, and the power to be you.

In my prenatal classes in Belgium, I used to dedicate the second part of the class to singing with the future parents. It was a great way to bring them together and fill them again with love and joy, which is nourishment for the fetus.

Nourishing Your Soul

Optimal pregnancy is all about living in a higher vibrational state, absorbing beauty and harmony, because these are living elements that nourish your soul and your baby's soul. It releases the purest inspiration and connects you to the soul of the world: the Universal Soul that permeates everything in nature, makes it grow and enriches it.

But how to get to that feeling of being nourished, bathed in the Soul of nature? Going out in nature is sure a start. Only, you can be in nature and still be in your head, thinking about all the problems to resolve. You see everything as if *outside* of you. It doesn't really touch you. It calms you down, yes. You'll have had your 10,000 steps for the day maybe, but did you really *see* the trees, the flowers, the sky, the creek? Did you feel the energetic load, *the soul* of the blossoms, the soul of the rock?

Here is how it works:

The best exercise is to do this exercise in nature or in your garden. Look for a tree or something in nature you love or you feel attracted to and come closer to it. Look at the tree's outside form. Observe the colour, the bark, the form it creates.

Observe how you feel by just looking at it…

> *"Now close your eyes and breathe a few times deeply…. Come inside your body and feel your body from inside… Connect to your heart and visualize a gigantic sun in it…. It is glowing with warmth and love. Your love…. It is your essence, your soul essence… Look how this light can expand and retract…in and out… By expanding it now embraces the tree or the other element you have before you…as if you put your energetic arms around it…not your physical arms though… it feels like hugging the tree from a distance. This warm hug opens the perception of the essence of the tree, its emanations…it is as if you can feel inside the tree. The hardness of the wood under the bark, the sap streaming to the top…you feel how the tree radiates energy…how it wants to connect with you…and give you from its essence…how you become one with the tree…observe what you feel through this*

deep empathic connection…how your soul is enriched by the revelation of this beautiful energy…how is it different from just looking at the outside form of the tree…

Now you know the tree from the inside out, you have created a bridge to the soul of the tree."

This way of connecting is also what you can do with your partner. This deep connection interlocks both your souls in a huge embrace. The sum of these two energies is a lot bigger than two separate souls. It will nourish deeply all three of you and connect to the enormous forces of life. The baby will just be happy and thriving in this rich nourishment of love.

Meeting the soul of your baby has the same recipe: extend your heart around the uterus. Discover there your unborn baby in a new way. Detecting the jewel in him.

With ultrasound, we discover the reality of the presence of the baby's body. You finally know: 'There is really a physical baby in my belly! It is real!' Yes, it's true, but it is only the physical body we see there in the ultrasound picture. It is very moving, especially the first time. But by looking at the picture, have you connected to the *soul* of the baby. Have you *met* your baby? You can only do that from the inside out. Knowing him in the most subtle energy, his own quintessence: only your heart can discover that. You find the face of his soul. Then you really meet your child, knowing him from the inside out. It will feel more like a mystery inside of you. A felt mystery that is very intriguing. A sacred mystery. That mystery was erased by the use of ultrasound pictures.

Preparing for Birth

The preparation for birth extends over many topics:

- being in good shape physically

- learning to relax deeply

- learning breath work

- learning to program your subconscious, focusing on opening, strength, letting go…

- the emotional part is as important as the physical preparation: mastering fear and cultivating trust.

- clearing your own birth experiences: mom AND dad!

- clearing all negative experiences regarding childbirth in the family tree

- you need to know enough about the physiology and possible interventions, mainstream as well as alternative possibilities. Be realistic as well as idealistic!

It is of capital importance that you undo yourself from the belief that birth is dangerous. Because you have heard so many stories about the cascade of interventions. Maybe in your family history, there were some unwished-for outcomes. Neutralize this fear because it can be precisely the cause of interventions. Fear is counterproductive for the hormones like oxytocin that is needed for a natural birth. It stops the labour process.

Obstetric and Pediatric Nurse and Prenatal Psychology Educator Anna Verwaal has often experienced in the maternity ward that the mother reactivates how she was born herself. The same can happen for the fathers who can come up with reactions from his birth process. If we don't want to go that path of reactivating, it is unavoidable to revisit our own birth process and release all the negative aspects before the birth of your baby.

Conscious Birthing

> *"Learn to respect this sacred moment of birth, as*
> *fragile,*
> *as fleeting, as elusive as dawn."*
> – Frederick Leboyer, OB-GYN

Having cleared so many aspects of yourself, in your prenatal period, your childhood, your relationship, your connection to yourself and a higher world, a conscious birth is only a result of all that hard work. You have learned to live on a higher frequency, connected to Source, so the next step will be in the same line: birthing your baby consciously.

If nature can have its way and love is present instead of fear, the birthing process will start with the production of the love hormone **oxytocin,** which is crucial to creating the 'snowball of labour' as Dr. Sarah Buckley coined it. The secretion of oxytocin creates contractions that in turn stimulate the brain to release even more oxytocin in a feedback loop. The absolute conditions are an uninterrupted calm environment, dimmed lights, no words and lots of tactile support. The oxytocin will continue its effects after birth to help mother and baby deeply connect and help the start of breastfeeding. The presence of oxytocin also later in life triggers connection and social behavior. Give nature a chance to operate in full trust of your body!

Another kind of birth is needed for a conscious, fearless birth. That doesn't mean disrespecting the professionalism of medical staff. It can mean paying attention to the expansive world of the one who is born: he is more than a tiny body. He carries an impressive spirit and soul that is very wise and conscious. He needs to feel supported emotionally.

"The soul of birth is missing," says Anna Verwaal. The medical paradigm is invited to orient itself towards a profound consideration of all aspects of a human being, especially the awareness and vulnerability of the baby being born.

Even if you choose to give birth in a hospital, the possibilities are present there also, to connect to the baby and what he experiences. You will have to be assertive and install your priorities during birth, but it is not impossible. Now you know how birth can affect the baby, you can offer him an accompaniment that makes him feel understood and recognized in his struggle. All along the contractions, the pushing stages and the birth itself, you can encourage him and let him know that he is listened to, that he is not alone. If there are blocks on the way, you can help him over it through your intuition. He would experience a whole other birth in this way. He would make his entrance into the world in a much freer way. There would be less or no traumas, an easier adaptation. He would stay more connected to the invisible world and adapt easier to life in a physical body.

Keiko Kishimoto, a Japanese midwife and founder of the Kishimoto Midwifery Center, said: "It doesn't really matter if you give birth in the hospital or in a Birthing Center. The difference is made by the connection to the baby during pregnancy." [44]

Sunni Karll, a midwife in the US, intuitively connected to the baby during birth. If there were blockages, she was able to release them through this compassionate contact and by reassuring and guiding the baby, asking it to move if needed. She had a very low intervention rate.

You can tell baby you're not perfect but that your love is what is essential. The deep connection with his soul will be so powerful that he will feel guided by your respect and listening ear.

Birth is a sacred moment: heaven comes to Earth through a physical door. The opening to this higher world is the baby's reality and going through birth can bring the sacredness of life to our consciousness. Wanting to open to this reality will also benefit the mother because she will feel helped through the labour and pushing stages. Letting herself be helped by higher powers that can work through her on a physical level.

As the moment of birth itself is the culmination of this sacred journey onto this earth, you can choose to honour the baby by welcoming him in dimmed light and silence. The first sounds he hears are deep imprints, so you can choose to welcome him while speaking out a specific intention or a prayer.

If the umbilical cord is not cut immediately, the baby still receives vital blood from the mother until the cord is no longer pulsating. A lotus birth, where the umbilical cord is not cut, gives the most stream of blood and energy to the recovering baby after birth. The cord will fall off naturally after a few days, and in the meanwhile, the baby will have had a continuous energetic connection to the organ that gave him life, and he'll recover quicker. More about how to do this can be found in Sunny Karl's book: "Sacred Birthing."

Many parents have been able to witness how the baby can move itself up to the breast immediately after birth.

The first hour after birth, the baby is extremely aware, and this is the best time to continue the deep bonding you have built up before birth, but now through skin-to-skin contact. Now the father can finally build up this precious contact too.

Birth is a very sacred moment, and we have turned away from that reverence in the medical world. It is necessary that we reconnect with this sacred essence also during birth. And if people present at birth could reach into that higher consciousness of divine presence, they could maybe feel this essence of the divine sacred feminine in the form of the Divine Mother, present at birth. Even if you don't feel this presence, you know She is there. She can help to support the intensity of labour if you want to connect with Her.

If the baby can be accompanied through birth with this conscious connection to his experience, the baby as a new human being *might* close his eyes and install a kind of screen to see less, as described in the part about Bernard Montaud (p. 117). The physical world is still so much different from where he came from, but the screen will be thinner, and he'll still be able to perceive some light from the other world and to pierce through his screen earlier and with less effort, because the repeat cycle of traumas will not be present or less present. He'll want to look for what he left out. As an adult, the yearning for his soul will be sharp enough to look for what was left out and have him discover his essence.

If there have been difficult circumstances during birth, it is possible to alleviate the burden on the baby that could become a trauma by empathically telling the story of the birth from the total beginning of labour to the moment of birth. Tell it while giving attention to the reactions of the baby and acknowledge his reactions in which he remembers the difficulties he went through. He might sway his arms and legs or make sounds, or cry as a reaction. Empathically sense where it was difficult and make him feel acknowledged and understood. In this way, he can let go of the pain.

Breastfeeding is, of course, the natural extension of what you did before. The baby needs his mother's milk to be able to develop harmoniously. While nursing, she can concentrate on the baby and imagine love, light or peace streaming through the milk. Here also, the inner state of the mother is very important. Be aware that when she is troubled, upside down, angry or sad, these negative states turn the breastmilk into a substance that can make the child unwell. Even when breastmilk is not an option, giving a bottle needs to be done with the same attention, warmth and connection so the baby feels equally emotionally supported as if he was drinking on the breast.

Educating Your Child

In the best scenario, you started this gigantic project long before conception and created optimal circumstances during pregnancy and birth. After birth, this conscious effort continues, but in another way.

Love will still be the primordial energy the baby and the growing child need. Lack of it will bring in seven behaviours of adults unloved as children:

- lack of trust

- poor emotional intelligence

- fear of failure

- toxic relationships

- insecurity and attachment

- depression and anxiety

- oversensitivity

Your interactions with him are still building up his self-image, self-worth, and resilience. Your way of being and your communication are imprinted in your child's subconscious and express themselves later in his behaviour and attitude in life.

Your words plant seeds in your children's hearts.
From those seeds spring up either confidence or
uncertainty,
Dignity or dishonour, worth or worthlessness.
Your words create the beginning of their life stories
And they will carry this story
with them always.'
- Rebecca Eanes

It is in the parent's hands how much time, energy, love and attention they can invest to guarantee the optimal development of their child. How they interact with their child will expand or block this development, as explained by Dr. Land in a longitudinal study.

Dr. George Land and Beth Jarman studied the creative genius of school-aged children. Using a longitudinal study model, Land and Jarman studied 1,600 children at ages 5, 10, and 15. When the children were given a problem with which they had to come up with an imaginative, and innovative solution,

- **98 percent of five-year-old's tested at the "genius" level: they brought up brilliant, original solutions.**

- At age 10, the percentage of genius-level imaginative and innovative thinkers fell to an unthinkable **30 percent.**

- At age 15, the percentage of genius-level students had dropped to an abysmal **12 percent.**

- **Only 2 percent of adults (Age 31) still retain their ability to think imaginatively, with creativity and innovation.**[45]

The researchers linked this phenomenon to three aspects of education: judgment, criticism, and censorship. When met with criticism, children stop expressing their innate capacity for thinking for themselves and coming up with helpful solutions; they just follow the masses, dumbing themselves down. The fear of not conforming holds them back.

Dr. Land explains that the brain has two opposing functions: one that is divergent: creative, innovative, and inspirational. The other is convergent: judging, criticizing, testing, and evaluating. The first one accelerates, and the other is like a brake. It is devastating to their potential to censor and cancel out ideas that would be brilliant solutions.

We can support the development of this divergent function, when judgement, rejection and fear are absent, even as an adult. Possibilities for development are unlimited; we just must believe in it.

Examples of Prenatal Learning

Throughout this book, we have seen how the fetus is learning tremendously about life, the world, connection and relationships, music and rhythm, and his mother tongue. He takes over his mother's beliefs about herself. He takes it all in and makes it his own. This becomes his modus operandum.

Parents who have invested themselves in this prenatal education have children that, compared to their peers, are

- are happier

- calmer

- they have a more respectful attitude

- they are more mature

- more conscious

Throughout history this prenatal learning has been transmitted in stories from around the world.

The Mahabharata is a well-known Indian epic story about a war that took place thousands of years ago. It tells about Abhimanyu, the son of Arjuna. He was a warrior who was confronted with a very ingenious war formation that was almost impossible to break through if you hadn't been instructed. He was not taught the very specific formula of how to defy the formation, but he was able to break through it. How did he do that? He was not taught the formula while he was growing up, but his father had taught him while he was still in the womb, and he somehow remembered the formula right at the dreadful moment and saved himself.

In the bible, the story of Genesis (Ch 30; V 37-42) tells about the arrangement between Jacob and his father-in-law Laban. Jacob had served Laban by herding his flock of sheep and goats for many years. In the meanwhile, his family had been expanding, and he wanted to prepare for the future once he left Laban to install his own tribe. Jacob and Laban made a deal which was that Jacob would take with him all the spotted, speckled and streaked animals and leave the white ones with Laban. Laban asked his sons to take care of the spotted, speckled and streaked ones, leaving three days of walking distance between this flock and Jacob's white animals that he herded for Laban. Jacob then started to take green poplar and chestnut rods and pilled white strakes in them. And made the white appear, which was in the rods He put these rods in front of the white-coated animals where they would mate. Their offspring was speckled, spotted and streaked. He had found a way to enhance tremendously the size of the herd that would belong to him by using the ancient knowledge that the animals would copy in their skins the pattern of the image they perceived during the reproduction cycle.

But also in recent times, there are many examples of how prenatal learning happens:

Jehudi Menhuin, a musician of the previous century told his story of how his mother was aware of the importance of her experiences during pregnancy. During every pregnancy, she made sure she went to concerts, more frequently than normal, because she knew that these experiences for the unborn baby would somehow give him a first music teaching. He became a world-famous violin player, and he attributes this, among other things, to his imprinted musical perceptions in utero.

One of the major composers of the 20th century, Olivier Messiaen, talks about his mother, the poet Cecile Sauvage, who wrote a bundle of poems during pregnancy: 'L'âme en bourgeon' (The Budding Soul) in which she expressed her rich feelings for her growing unborn child. Olivier connects this work with his love for music with the following words: *'In the poetry of my mother and especially in*

'L'Ame en Bourgeon' a taste for observation of nature and a wealth of images is present from which I retained my love for the brilliance of sound and my love for the songs of birds.' Olivier became an ornithologist, building the song of birds in his musical work.

What do you think about the four-year-old son of the well- known violin player Leonid Kogan? When the boy had a violin in his hands for the first time and without any previous music lessons, he was able to play melodic phrases from a piece that his father had played often during the pregnancy.

During my pregnancy, I regularly watched a video series in which each episode started with the same music intro. After birth, I continued to watch and saw that my son Omael, while breastfeeding, turned his head away from the breast towards the source of the sound that he recognized: he remembered the intro of the video after birth.

Omael, at three months old, had a stuffy nose and woke up crying at night because he couldn't breathe through his nose. It continued for more than two weeks. Then I saw the correlation between the hour he always woke up which was around four am. I remembered the time that his dad drowned which was four pm. The brain doesn't make a difference between am and pm. Four o'clock was when the memory came up of not being able to breathe. When I told him that, he healed immediately.

A mom in Belgium who, during pregnancy, often spent time in nature, meditating, and connecting to the elementals—the gnomes and fairies—observed that her child, at three-four years old, always wanted to put goodies and indications for the gnomes everywhere.

A toddler remembered the place in the house at the staircase where his mom fell while pregnant, and screamed on top of the staircase, refusing to go down.

A mom reflects on the character of her children and sees the difference between them, especially the boy who seems rather stuck. She carried him while there were difficulties in the relationship, which was not the case with the other four children she had.

Joanna Mari, a previous Judge at the Supreme Court in Greece, reported the following stories from more or less recent times: [46]

"Father Porfyrios, a monk who lived a few decades ago was attached to a large hospital in Athens when some doctors asked him why an infant who had just been born with a cheek deformed by a black swelling resembling an eggplant. The father meets the mother of this child, and he learns from her that in the city block where she lived, she frequently came across a young man with a black cheek deformed like an eggplant and that she had pity for the guy. But when she became pregnant, to view this man became a nightmare. She was filled with terror and often thought: "How terrible it must be for a mother to have such a child". If I were in her place, would I support that?" Father Porfyrios felt certain that the repeated image of the cheek, accompanied by a great fear had been able to interfere with the development programme of the child. The mother and the doctors could agree to that.

The Dutch doctor Van Sweten, when he noticed a caterpillar on the neck of a young woman, made a gesture to remove it. But the woman told him laughingly: "Let the caterpillar be. I am obliged to keep it for the rest of my life." It wasn't any real caterpillar at all, but a fleshy swelling that closely resembled it. "When my mother was pregnant," the woman continued, "a caterpillar fell on my mother's neck and caused her great fear. I was born with this caterpillar on the same spot of the neck."

In the eighties, a British judge had to treat a remarkable case. An English couple having only white forefathers gave birth to a black child. The husband accused his wife of adultery and demanded a divorce. His wife denied the accusation firmly and gave the following explanation: in the sleeping room of the couple a portrait was hanging of a young black man which she found beautiful. During the pregnancy, she contemplated the portrait often, her heart filled with joy and admiration. The English judge was convinced deep inside of the formative power of the imagination of pregnant women, accepted the explanation and a divorce was avoided."

Little baby
First I saw your head
Then came your warm body
You slipped through my hands
In the arms of your mother
Your scream of revulsion became whining
Your whining became silence
Your silence brought peace
You laid there
Very intense

One moment you were my master
And me
I was allowed to be your disciple
You taught me
That gentleness
Gives the chance to awaken
You showed me that simplicity
Is the key to life
You gave me the confidence
That patience
Is the right way
You taught me
What I didn't know
Being there
In silence
For you

- Ann Somers, midwife

CHAPTER 9

NEW GROUNDS

*"If you take time for silence,
the sacred will unfold"* - Rod Stryker

Sacredness

Sacredness has gathered dust in our prosaic lives that immerses us in the outer core of life. Looking to the origin of humanity, where people felt connected to higher sources of life, they felt vulnerable and dependent on this connection to the divine. They attributed their happiness to giving time, attention, and worship to these higher energies, call it God, Source, or the Divine, as you wish.

Modern life has created the illusion that we can live without that connection. If you have money, you are fine, you're safe. And on top of that a family that loves you, even better. We don't feel the need to find something deeper. We think we can live without knowing the laws of nature, without knowing the real origin of life. Some people suffer from emptiness, loneliness or hopelessness. Well, there are drugs or alcohol to cover up the suffering.

We are at the lowest end of this cycle of disconnection.

*"Awareness of the sacred in life is what holds our world together, and the lack of awareness of the sacred
is what is tearing it apart."*
- J.D. Chittister

The soul can only breathe in reconnection with its essence. It revives through gratefulness or forgiveness. Gautama Buddha said, "To understand everything is to forgive everything."

Gratefulness is the key to coming into this higher vibration of love and appreciation of everyday aspects of life we take for granted... It's the first step towards connecting with the sacredness of life.

Religion helps to rebuild this awareness of the sacredness of life. But sacred life flourishes everywhere in nature. It's a gigantic temple where love finds its myriad of forms through the nourishment of sacredness.

Why would a relationship not be based on this sacredness? Bringing a baby to this world is nothing less. It is collaborating with sacred energies, building up all the physical and subtle organs of his being. A pregnant woman is literally surrounded by these light builders from the universe; she is *impregnated* by their essence. Would that be the real meaning of the word 'pregnant'?

How can we bring sacredness back in our lives? Eckhart Tolle expresses it like this: "To do everything in a sacred manner is to do everything in a state of presence."

Divine Masculine and Divine Feminine

Once we have found sacredness in nature, in the food we eat, in the breath we take in, we might be able to find it in our partner. The sacred dance of life… in the world between two poles: a man and a woman. Two opposite poles chasing each other, spiraling up towards the Divine Masculine and the Divine Feminine. Huge undiscovered worlds…

Everything in life can be brought back to one of these two polarities. Are they fighting? Or creating? They balance life. And it is up to us to use this balance by letting them play out inside and outside of us. We are ever-learning, ever-growing.

The masculine and the feminine are both in each of us. One is exteriorized, and the other is inside. We find the two poles equally in the two sides of the brain: the left side is more logical, analytic and related to language. The right hemisphere speaks to us about emotions, creativity and art, synthesis and sensing.

The characteristics of masculine manifestations are reason, logic, action, strength, courage, decisiveness, and firmness: doing.

The principle of the feminine energy is love, feeling, magnetism, gentleness, caring, compassion, receptivity and intuition: being.

These aspects we encounter everywhere in nature and through the men and women we encounter daily. But what we are really looking for in this eternal attraction between two poles is the Divine, unpolluted essence of the other principle: what a man looks for in a woman and a woman in a man.

So, what is the *Divine* Masculine about? It is about connecting masculinity to a higher level: the Spirit. The All-Powerful Invisible Intelligence that created the Light. From reason to Divine Wisdom, from strength to Divine Power. This invisible essence is radiating more or less through all men: providing, protecting and guiding. Through them, we can connect to this quintessence that connects us with Spirit or the Divine Father.

And the *Divine* Feminine? It is about spreading its wings into the Universal Soul. It is the principle of Universal Love that has given form to everything that lives. From the limited love of the heart to pure, unconditional love. Through women emanates in various intensity and infinite forms this divine feminine essence of subtle, ethereal, enchanting, intuitive, compassionate and inspiring energy that connects us with the Divine Mother.

Before we can get to that higher connection inside of us and in the other, men need to heal the wounded masculine: domination, absence of emotion and violence. Women need to grow out of the wounded feminine: neediness, powerlessness, manipulation, unworthiness.

Changing the essence of the role one fulfills—man or woman—is crucial in re-establishing harmony in the world. Men have exterminated women, and women have exterminated men, each in their own way. Imagine how the world would be if each of these poles could reconnect again with their sacred principle and manifest itself fully!

The Laws of Nature

> *"There is a real world independent of our senses. The laws of nature were not invented by man but forced on him by the natural world. They are the expression of a natural world order."* - Max Plank

A pregnant woman grows a baby based on natural laws, which are mostly unconscious. In our current times, we are asked to become more aware of these laws and use them consciously.

We know about *laws in society:* they are there to organize life in an orderly way. If you don't respect them, you must pay a ticket or go to jail.

The laws that nature created organize life on all levels and everything created obeys these laws. In school, we all learned about the *laws of physics,* like the law of gravity, the law of polarity and the law of inertia. Nature obliges us to obey the laws that are embedded in life: when it is cold, you need to dress warm. Otherwise, you freeze.

There are other laws active in life that are not described in physics laws but that are also weaving the fabric of life. The more we know about these laws, the more we can stay in tune with the evolutionary program of the universe.

The Law of Humans

In the animal kingdom, the reigning law is the survival of the fittest. The life form that is the best adapted or the strongest will survive. Humans have identified quite a bit with this law of the strongest, which has brought us many complications and dragged down our value as human beings. Eternal wars, violence, domination, oppression, and extortion have been the face of this law that doesn't fit in with humanity's real purpose.

In fact, the law that reigns in humanity is the **law of service**: How to serve the other, how to serve that higher part in us. Your work as a mother or a father is part of this law of service, service to a seedling of humanity.

The Law of Recording

All through life, everything we think, feel and do is recorded in our body. We have looked into the existence of cell memory and how it is possible to retrieve this information. Pregnancy is THE important moment to remember this law and being mindful about your state of mind. What you go through as a pregnant mother will be recorded also in your unborn baby.

The Law of Attraction

What you focus on, what you contemplate, you will attract, or you will become. If you focus on all the violence, treason, or injustice in the world, you attract very low vibrations that only take away your energy and your love for life and, slowly but surely, create the same circumstances in your life.

If you focus on the light, on the sun, you attract elements of a very subtle nature that will gradually build up your life, and you will start to shine with light and love!

Also, you, as a mother, attract the subtle elements from the etheric world to build up your baby. These elements correspond to the quality of your emotions and thoughts, to your ideal. Projecting a clear vision of what you would like to see as qualities and virtues in your baby will already attract the subtle material. The function of the three-dimensional world in which we live is to condense this subtle matter in the mental, astral and physical bodies of the baby. It all depends on what you focus on and the intensity, desire, wish and concentration if this law will manifest in your life in a positive way.

The Law of Causes and Consequences

Nature is very clear about this law: if you plant seeds of pumpkins, you will grow pumpkins. No cucumbers. The action you take will have its result in good or bad consequences. What you send out will come back: if you reject or judge somebody, you open the door to be judged.

If you kill another person, you will be killed one day.

If you give love, in one way or another, love will come back to you.

You might be living through consequences from past actions that can be challenging. But you can also prepare for a bright future by consciously planting seeds of happiness now: by creating uplifting thoughts and sending them to the whole world.

What you invest in your child now regarding presence and loving attention will have endless beautiful consequences for the life of your child, and it will surely come back to you in some way.

The Law of Resonance

The law of resonance comes up when you have two perfectly attuned pianos. When you play a note on one piano, the other one resonates with the same tone. The same is true when you go into nature and open yourself up to the harmony in nature: it will awaken harmony in you.

We see the same phenomenon between two people: the state of mind of one spills easily over into the other, who unconsciously tunes in to his way of thinking, feeling, speaking, or acting.

Through the mirror cells in the brain, we often imitate unconsciously what another person does. From there, choosing who we connect with is important, especially during pregnancy.

But it is also important in spiritual practice: connecting to a higher invisible power or Source makes us vibrate in tune with this essence and the qualities it carries, and in this way, we gradually receive and integrate some of these qualities.

The Law of Sacrifice

We see this law in our lives every day: if we want to have something from a store, we will receive it, in return for money. We must sacrifice to give something so something else can come back. As a mom it is included in the package: your life will never be the same. You'll not sleep as you did before being pregnant. But your reward is there in the baby.

Sacrifice is a word that is not very welcome in our culture. Every time you pass on the next step of evolution you leave the old behind to receive a new energy. Letting go of the old brings in the new. Like the wooden branches that we have to put in the stove in order to be burned, in order to be warm.

Ever Evolving

Becoming the person we would like to become is, of course, the path of a lifetime. Many lifetimes. It is a never-ending ascension towards our own essence, our summit, our soul. Observation of any meander in your heart, any ripple, strong through very subtle means: tensions in the body, pains, and illnesses are one way. Being aware of where our feelings and emotions lead us is another. But observing our thoughts and looking from a distance at our monkey mind, which is jumping from one superficial thought to another, is the hardest.

If we can create an atmosphere of looking inside all the time while we are acting to the outside world there is hope. Take the habit of stepping away from what drives us, what feels through us, what thinks through us. It brings clarity, step by step. We must undress from so many layers of programming, traumas big and small before we can enter the temple of our soul, naked, symbolically speaking.

Our thoughts and emotions are like little children that need to be educated, one at a time.

Don't be disappointed if it takes a long time. Anyway, this is the program I have taken on, and it is still ongoing. Again and again, how did that feel? Where does it come from? Where does it lead me if I continue in that direction? How do I get out? What does it want to teach me? What should I let go of? We have a sample inside that tells us if this or that emotion, thought or action is good or bad. We can just compare it to that sample.

Inside you, there is a fountain of knowledge, of learning the essence of life. In every experience is a seed planted. Something your soul wants to teach you, or to develop, to let go of or to learn. Increasing the awareness of this will bring you such a rich treasure of insights, of power over yourself.

It will push away all limits and blocks in the way. It means not to be wallowing in victim mode. Poor me! Why? Why did he do that to me?

Make friends with the truth. It cuts right through your ego, which is painful, but it is not the pain of the soul. The soul laughs about it; it is not touched by it; on the contrary, it encourages you to go on.

A small family unit is what life has been about for eons. The new wave of energies that are coming in are asking us to see also a broader connection and collaboration. We need completely new ways to organize society, based on spiritual values and principles of collaboration and natural law.

Conclusion about the soul

We have touched on so many aspects of the soul: Let's synthesize the five poles that show the importance of the concept of the soul.

1. We are all souls, but we walk through life without realizing it. If we were aware of this and connected consciously with this expansive world that is at the basis of creation, we could make gigantic steps forward. We would feel guided, nourished, and inspired.

2. Through the transformative power of the soul connection, we can heal in the most efficient way. Looking upon our painful experiences and traumas from the level of the soul is the most rewarding and fulfilling way to alleviate them. The soul represents Source in us and has the power to heal thoroughly the heart and the mind and is a huge support in the healing of the body.

3. Our essence is immortal and we come back in cycles as a soul to learn another step in our evolution toward perfection. It may or may not be your conviction but in many spiritual traditions in human history reincarnation is seen as the mechanism of our evolution as we cannot become a perfect manifestation of the divine in one lifetime. I can help us to understand that what we experience is the school program we have determined ourselves before coming here. It helps us to make sense of our experiences and the need to transmute them, to learn, develop and lift more and more the veil of the illusion and become one with Source.

4. The child we want to invite into our lives comes here also for *his or her* school program. Knowing how difficult it is to transition from this higher world of unconditional love to

this 3D world, we can accompany this soul and be motivated and inspired to be the best parents we can be to it.

In our growth process through the connection with the soul and the spirit, we learn the divine laws that we are supposed to respect to manifest a society based on respect, harmony and love.

Afterword

Becoming the one your soul has intended to be is the most outstanding present you can give yourself. In turn, it is a tremendous gift to help your child to develop and manifest its' real essence. Listen to the call.

Opening to the other reality we have forgotten is a never- ending discovery. The soul and spirit world is gigantic, but every revelation and transformation puts a jewel in your heart. It requires constant adaptation and adjustment of your thoughts, feelings, and actions to live accordingly. Untangling from the false reality we thought was right, all awareness and dedication are needed. Nobody has been perfect in one go. Success and failure will be the meanders of life through which to navigate. But steadily coming back to the light that beckons you will grow the channels of connection.

The downward spiral of illusion and separation is getting exhausted. The dense physical world where we seek everything outside of us is worn out. We are turning the spiral upwards now towards the exploration of the best-hidden secret: the love, peace, power and the light inside of us.

We will bring the best of ourselves to the world through the children we bring into it to create harmony and peace. They will be the natural extensions of our attempts to continue to rescue what is true: humanity based on the highest values of love and connection to the divine world.

The world needs the assistance of the dimension of the soul in order to find true love and truth.

David Chamberlain, PhD, said, "As a psychotherapist, I am especially aware of the need to create mentally and physically healthy babies to have a healthy and peaceful world. Babies are the key to the future of the world."[47]

Let's be part of that gigantic undertaking, together with all the awakened souls on earth and the help from the invisible light beings who only need our invitation to reinforce our efforts.

> *"In the world, the number of enlightened spirits*
> *depends on the number of enlightened mothers."-*
> Peter Deunov

LIST OF VIRTUES, QUALITIES AND SKILLS

Qualities of the heart: Virtues

Love

Moderation

tact

harmony

modesty

courtesy

selflessness

sacrifice

temperance

care

harmony

service

compassion

flexibility in

detachment

tolerance

emotions

equanimity

affection

adaptability

magnificence

nurturing

humour

confidence

gratitude

safe

self-confidence

joy

secure

goodness

nobility

steadfastness

goodwill

dignity

stability

resilience

honour

self-regulation

trust

kindness

charity

trustworthy

goodness

dedication

reliability

gentleness

devotion

vulnerability

tenderness

fidelity

justice/fairness

mercy

prudence

creativity

humility

openness

purity

spontaneity

empathy

solidarity

commitment

inclusiveness

involvement

openness

morality

spontaneity

perseverance

solidarity

faith

inclusiveness

hope

assertiveness

forgiveness

co-operation

gratefulness

loyalty

reverence

peacefulness

generosity

grace

helpfulness

respect

Qualities of the Mind: Qualities

intelligence

attentiveness

mindfulness

consciousness

focus

awareness

self-awareness

understanding

comprehension

insight

critical thinking

competence

clarity

concentration

perception

sensitivity

idealism

nonjudgement

impartiality

discernment

perspective

appreciation

responsibility

reconciliation

communicative
honesty
sincerity
genuine
authenticity
integrity

analysis/synthesis
logic
determination
leadership
unity

Qualities of the Body: Skills

will power
courage/bravery
strength
endurance
discipline
orderliness
cleanliness
flexibility of the body
self-control
precision
accuracy
excellence

diligence
coherence (heart math)
equilibrium
powerful
delicacy
energetic
dynamic
expressive
beauty
harmony in gestures
nonviolence

Spiritual qualities

truth
intuition
wisdom
healing
capacities
transformation
transmutation
contemplation
identification

APPENDIX 2

STRESS EFFECTS ON PREGNANCY

Stimulus	Definition	Physiological effect and consequences
Acute psycho-emotional stress	Chronic distress associated with important tensions (severe marital difficulties, prolonged disagreements with family members or neighbors – permanent stress (impossible to resolve through action or resignation) (M.H. Stott). Recent consequence of miscarriage or pregnancy interruption [1], Strong guilt. Unwanted and regretted pregnancy. Paroxysmal emotion	Acute fetal suffering (AFS): bradycardia, arterial hypotension, respiratory acidosis, hypoxy, probably linked to a circulatory uterine- placenta vasoconstriction affected by the catecholamines. Late Intra-Uterine development. Morphological anomaly of the placenta vascularization. Gravidic hypertension [2]. At 8 months, inferior neuro-motor development. For unwanted pregnancies, inferior academic performance, language difficulties, more excitable and irritable [3]. Twice slower mental development / precarious health [4] Primary insomnia, diarrhea, paroxysmal screams.

	Same, but at the end of pregnancy	Same + increase of uterine contractions [5]. In the long run, basic fetal activity multiplied by 10, irritable & hyperactive newborns with eating difficulties [6]. Regurgitation, vomiting, stenosis of pyloris in the infant due to excess gastrine overcoming the placental barrier and creating a hypertrophic pyloric muscle [7].
	Maternal psycho-social stress in second third of pregnancy	Critical and important period in the massive migration of neurons towards the cortex. Establishment of the thalamus, centre of emotions, between the 3rd and 5th month of gestation [8]. Asymmetry of dermatoglyphs between right and left hands, higher perinatal mortality, but no effect on weight or prematurity [9]. Schizophrenia [10].
	Death of a twin in the uterus, associated to unexplained metroragies. Massive distress of the mother.	Severe behavioral troubles, resolvable through recollection and post-natal analysis of the serious events that occurred in the uterus [11].
	Severely depressed mothers,	Severe neonatal anorexia

	without distress, with anticipated certainty of their child's death.	[12]
	Death of the father between 3rd and 5th month of pregnancy. Father's death during year following birth	Suspicion of anomaly in the formation of the hypothalamus, centre of behavior. Can result in criminal tendencies and severe psychiatric pathologies in the adult [13].
Chronic or sub-acute stress	Abnormal or exaggerated anxiety because repressed, or contact with a handicapped child, women who had a miscarriage or interrupted pregnancy. Indifference or apathy. Pregnancies disturbed by slight but continuous conflicts.	Chronic abnormal secretion of catecholamine affecting the physical and behavioral development towards the mother, and uterine problems – Sympathicotonia, convulsions, hyper osteo-tendinous reflectivity, hyper sensitivity to noise, difficulty sleeping & eating, difficult
		personality, digestive troubles, of rhino-pharyngites, repeated earaches, bronchitis. Possible accidents between 18 months and 3 years, becoming obesity or thinness, lateness growing, fevers, malformations, behavioral troubles and nausea, headaches, diarrhea and asthma at six years old [14]. Maternal anxiety lasts beyond birth, leading to

		emotional conflictual investment (hostility, authoritarianism, dissatisfaction of role as mother)[15]
Epiphe-nomenal environ-mental stress	Result of a few stressful events during pregnancy	Variable result depending on coincidence with a sensitive period of fetal development
Mother's protective role in severe stress situation	Pregnancies during war time	Child born on time and normal [16]
Permanent harmonious stimulation	Love cultivated in father-mother-fetus relationship. Psychic and physical communication with the unborn child	Influx of endorphins. Huge organizational value of the interaction between mother and child observed during 6th postnatal month [17]. Child is healthier and blossoming [18]

[1] E.R. Grimm, *Psychological investigations of habitual abortion,* 1962, 24, pp. 369-378

[2] R.E. Meyers, *Acta Endocrin, Suppl,* 1972, 166, pp. 221-257 et Organisation Gestosis Press, 1975.

[3] A. Davids, R.H. Holden, G.B. Gray, *Child Development,* 1963, 34, pp. 993, 1002 et Z. Matejcek, Z. Dytrych, V. Schuller, Int. J. Behav. Dev., 1980, 3, p. 243-251.

[4] D.H. Stott, M.A. Camb, Ph.D. Lond, Lancet, 1957, 18, pp. 1006- 1012.

[5] R.E. Myers, *Am. J. Obstet. Gynecol.,* 1975, 122, p. 47-59 et H.O.

[6] Morishima, *Am. J. Obstet. Gynecol.,* 1978, 131, p. 286-290.

[7] L.W. Sontag, *Ann. N.Y. Acad. Sci.,* 1965, 134, pp. 782-786

[8] S. Wolkind, *Pregnancy: a psychological and social study,* 1981.

[9] C. Trevarten, 3e Journées Européennes "naissance et avenir", 1994.

[10] L.L. Newell-Morris, C.E. Fahrenbruck, G.S. Sackett, *Biol Neonate,* 1989, 56, pp. 61-75.

[11] H.S. Bracha, E.F. Torrey, I.I. Gottesman, L.B. Bigelow, C. Cunnif, *Am J Psychiatry,* 1992, 149, pp. 1355-1356.

[12] B. Martino, *Le Bébé est une personne,* 1985 / F. Dolto, *Tout est langage,* 1988 / T. Verny, *La Vie Secrète de l'Enfant avant sa Naissance,* 1982

[13] L. Kreisler, *La dynamique du nourrisson,* 1983, p. 84-101 / M. et J.M. Porte, *Psychiatr. Enf.,* 1982, 25, pp. 261-294.

[13] R.O. Huttunen, P. Niskanen, *Arch Gen Psychiatry,* 1978, 35, pp. 429-431.

[14] M. Choquet, S. Ledoux, *Arch F Pédiatr,* 1985, 42, p. 541-546 et

D.H. Stott, *Develop Med Child Neurol,* 1973, 15, p. 770-787.

[15] S. Richard, *Progrès en néonatalogie,* no 10, 1990, pp. 202-223.

[16] A.N. Antonov, *J Ped,* 1947, 30, pp. 250-259.

[17] C. Amiel-Tison, *La Surveillance neurologique au cours de la première année de la vie,* 1985.

[18] First World Congress on Prenatal Education, 1996.

REFERENCES

1 Next Level Soul Podcast. (2023, November 14). Yale Doctor uncovers New Evidence Connecting Mystical Spirituality & Science!   [Video] YouTube. https://www.youtube.com/watch?v=FJp91sEmNtQ

2 Weiss, Brian. Many Lives, Many Masters: The True Story of a Prominent Psychiatrist, His Young Patient, and the Past-Life Therapy That Changed Both Their Lives. Touchstone, 1988.

3 Renée, Lisa. (2016 June). Soul Psychology. Energetic Synthesis. https://energeticsynthesis.com/resource-tools/2776- soul-psychology?highlight=WyJzb3VsIiwiYW5pbWFscyJd

4 Newton, Michael. Destiny of Souls, New Case Studies of Life Between Lives. Llewellyn Publications, MN, 2000

5 Ibid.

6 Aïvanhov, O.M, The Key to the Problems of Existence, Complete Works, Book 11, Prosveta.

7 Kolesar, Natacha. [IDEAL Society]. L'Homme est composé de quatre Courants par lesquels l'Âme se manifeste. [Video]. YouTube. https://www.youtube.com/watch?v=oL5eP2Q7Gbo

8 Newton, Michael. Destiny of Souls, New Case Studies of Life Between Lives. Llewellyn Publications, MN, 2000, p.386.

9 Schore, Allan. The Effects of a Secure Attachment Relationship on Right Brain Development, Affect Regulation, & Infant Mental Health – Infant Mental Health Journal, 2001, 22, 7-66.

10 Lipton, B. (1998). Nature, Nurture and the Power of Love. Journal o Prenatal and Perinatal Psychology and Health, 13(1), 3-10

11 Lipton, B. [The Journey – Brandon Bays & Kevin Billet]. (2017, June 14). Cellular memory and the power of beliefs with Bruce Lipton. [Video]. Facebook. https://fb.watch/rn0Y1Q_JuT/

20 Bassbex. (2013) Biology of Transformation - The Field. [Video]. YouTube. https://www.youtube.com/watch?v=Ns5sLo59Kak

13 IONS Communications Team. (2023, October 26). Doctor Explores What Near-Death Experiences Reveal About Life and Beyond. www.Noetic.org https://noetic.org/blog/near-death-experience

14 Lipton, B. [The Journey – Brandon Bays & Kevin Billet]. (2017, June 14). Cellular memory and the power of beliefs with Bruce Lipton. [Video]. Facebook. https://fb.watch/rn0Y1Q_JuT/

15 Linn, D. Emerson, W. Linn, S. Linn, M. Remembering Our Home, Healing Hurts & Receiving Gifts from Conception to Birth, New Jersey: Paulist Press, 1999.

16 Terry, K. Implantation Journey – The original Human Myth. https://ktbabytherapy.com

17 Ibid., p65

[18] Terry, K. (2004). Observations in the treatment of children conceived by in vitro fertilization. In: Janus, L. (ed.). Pränatale Psychologie und Psychotherapie (Prenatal Psychology and Psychotherapy). Heidelberg: Mattes Verlag.

[19] Verdult, R. (2021). The psychotherapeutic treatment of IVF/ICSI babies. A Clinical Report. Handbook of Prenatal and Perinatal Psychology, Switzerland, Springer.

[20] Athias, G. Boos, I. (2018), Tarot et Trame énergétique – Les 22 Souffles et l'Empreinte universelle, Édition Pictorus, France.

[21] Montaud, B. (1997), L'Accompagnement de la Naissance, Édition EDIT'AS, France.

[22] Todeshi, K. (2012) Edgar Cayce on the Akashic Records, VA, A.R.E. Press.

[23] Ibid., p.xii

[24] Barnett, L. (2023) Your Soul has a Plan, Awaken to Your Life Purpose through Your Akashic Records, FL: Haniel Press, p.130

[25] Pert, C. (1999) Molecules of Emotion: The Science Behind Mind-Body, N.Y: Simon & Schuster.

[26] Lipton, B. (2016) The Biology of Belief 10th Anniversary Edition: Unleashing the Power of Consciousness, Matter & Miracles, Hay House.

27 Lipton, B. H. 2001 Nature, Nurture and Human Development. Journal of Prenatal and Perinatal Psychology and Health 16:167-180

28 Meacock, R. (2022) Wave Genetics as Developed by the Late Professor Peter Gariaev, DNA Gene Expression, Issue 281, Sept. 2022

29 ThisIs432. (2013) Water Experiments, Aerospace Center Stuttgart. [Video]. YouTube https://www.youtube.com/watch?v=cWLPFK3sXdw

30 Emoto, A. (2005) Hidden Messages in Water, Atria31

31 McCarty, W.A. (2012) Welcoming Consciousness, Supporting Babies' Wholeness From the Beginning of Life, Wondrous Beginnings Publishing, p.103

32 Brébion, J-P. (2004) L'Empreinte de Naissance, 27 Mois pour une Vie, Ed. Quintessence

33 Aïvanhov, O.M, (1982) Education begins before birth, Collection Izvor n.203, Editions Prosveta, p21.

34 Aïvanhov, O.M, (1980) Life and Work in an Initiatic School, OC XXX, Editions Prosveta, p. 192

35 Swanson, C. The Light Body: Biophotons & Biology. www.subtle.energy.com https://subtle.energy/the-light-body-biophotons-biology

[36]Aïvanhov, O.M, (2000) Creation: Artistic and Spiritual. Izvor 223, Editions Prosveta, p43

[37] H M Embeds (2021) The HeartMath Experience (Full length 90 min) [Video] YouTube. https://www.youtube.com/watch?v=ifonDyhv-XI

[38] McCraty, R. Bradley, R. Tomasino, D. (2015, January 10). The Heart has its' Own 'Brain' and Consciousness, IN5D, Esoteric, Metaphysical, Spiritual Database. https://in5d.com/the-heart-has-its-own-brain-and-consciousness/

[39] Schore, A. (2015) Affect Regulation and the Origin of the Self, The Neurobiology of Emotional Development, NY: Routledge

[40] Aboli, L. (2020, November 13) Happiness vs Pleasure, https://www.lauraaboli.com/post/happiness-vs-pleasure

[41]Aïvanhov, O.M. (2008) Love and Sexuality, part 2, Complete Works 15, Editions Prosveta, p 231

[42]Aïvanhov, O.M. (2022) Daily Meditations June 17 2023, Editions Prosveta

[43] Verny, T, M.D, Weintraub Pamela (2003) Pre-Parenting. Nurturing your child from conception, Simon & Schuster, p217-218.

[44] Kishimoto, K. (2024, March 25) Reviving the Spirit of San- Ba: A Global Movement For Maternal Well-Being? Prenatal Online Summit, Pregnancy Alliance

[45] Skillikorn, N. (2016, Aug. 5) Evidence that Children Become Less Creative Over Time (and how to fix it), idea to value. Youtube.

[46] Mari J. (1994) La Mère: une Puissance Formatrice de Vie, Sa Reconnaissance, de la Grèce Antique à nos jours, L'Éducation Prénatale de la Grèce Antique au XXIiéme Siècle, Deuxième Congrès Mondial sur l'Éducation Prénatale, Athens, p54-57.

[47] Chamberlain, D (2013) Windows to the Womb, Revealing the Conscious Baby from Conception to Birth, Calif.: North Atlantic Books

BIBLIOGRAPHY

~313~

Emotional Healing – Self-Healing

Athias Gérard, *Racines Familiales de la 'Mal a Dit'*, Paris : Pictorus, 2002.

Aïvanhov Omraam Mikhaël, *Hope for the World: Spiritual Galvanoplasty*, Izvor Collection 214, Ed. Prosveta, 2000.

Bays Brandon, Billet Kevin, *Light In the Heart of Darkness, The Surprising Truth About Depression & How to Free Yourself Completely from its Grips,* Calif.: Best Selling Publishing, 2018.

Bays Brandon, *The Journey, A Practical Guide to Healing Your Life and Setting Yourself Free,* N.Y.: Simon & Schuster, 2012.

Brebion, Jean Philippe, *L'Empreinte de Naissance, 27 Mois pour une Vie,* Ed. Quintessence, 2004.

Imbert Claude, MD, *Faites Vous-Même Votre Psychothérapie, d'Aujourd'hui à votre Enfance, Vol 1,* Paris: Ed. Visualisation Holistique, 2002.

Imbert Claude, MD, *Faites Vous-Même Votre Psychothérapie, d'Aujourd'hui à votre Enfance, Vol 2,* Paris: Ed. Visualisation Holistique, 2001.

Imbert Claude, MD, *Un Seul Etre vous Manque, Auriez-vous eu un Jumeau,* Paris : Ed. Visualisation Holistique, 2004.

Levine Peter, *In an Unspoken Voice, How the Body Releases trauma and Restores Goodness,* North Atlantic Books, 2010.

Martinez Mario, T*he Mind Body Code: How to Change the Beliefs that Limit Your Health, Longevity and Success*, Co: Sounds True, 2016.

Myss Caroline, *Anatomy of the Spirit, The seven Stages of Power and Healing*, N.Y.: Harmony Books, 2017.

Noble Elisabeth, Primal Connections, *How our experiences from conception to Birth influence Our Emotions, Behavior, and Health*, N.Y.: Simon & Schuster, 1993.

Rialland Chantal, *Cette Famille qui vit en Nous, Guide Pratique de Généalogie*, Paris: Ed. Robert Lafond, 1994.

Rosenberg Marshall, Chopra Deepak, *Non-Violent Communication, A Language of Life: Life-Changing Tools for Healthy Relationships*, Puddle-Dancer Press, 2015.

Preconception - Prenatal Preparation and Health

Agin Dan, *More than Genes, What Science Can Tell us About Toxic Chemicals, Development and the Risk to Our Children*, N.Y. Oxford University Press, 2010.

Axness Marcy, PhD. *Parenting for Peace, Raising the Next Generation of Peacemakers* Sentient Publications, 2012.

Aïvanhov Omraam Mikhaël, *Education begins before Birth*, Ed. Prosveta, 1982.

Chamberlain David, *Windows To The Womb,* North Atlantic Books, 2013.

Chamberlain David, *The Mind of Your Newborn Baby*, North Atlantic Books, 1998.

Chopra Deepak, M.D., *Magical Beginnings, Enchanted Lives. A Holistic Guide to Pregnancy and Chidbirth,* N.Y.: Three Rivers Press, 2005.

Chopra Malika, *100 Promises to My Baby,* N.Y. Rodale, 2005. Emerson William, Linn Dennis, Linn Matthew, Fabricant Linn Sheila, *Remembering Our Home: Healing Hurts & Receiving Gifts from Conception to Birth,* Paulist Press 1999.

Evertz Klaus, Janus Ludwig, Linder Rupert, *Handbook of Prenatal and Perinatal Psychology, Integrating Research and Practice,* Switzerland: Springer, 2021.

Grof Stanislav, *Les Nouvelles Dimensions de la Conscience,* Ed. Du Rocher, 1989.

Imbert Claude, MD, *L'Avenir se joue avant la Naissance, La Thérapie de la Vie Intra-Utérine,* Paris: Ed. Visualisation Holistique, 1998.

Janov Ludwig, Imprints, *The Lifelong Effect of the Birth Experience,* N.Y.: Coward McCann, Inc, 1982.

Janov Ludwig, *The Biology of Love,* N.Y.: Prometheus Books, 2000.

Janov Ludwig, *The Feeling Child,* N.Y. Simon & Schuster, 1973.

Kalef Mia, DC, *The Secret Life of Babies, How our Prebirth and Birth Experiences Shape our World,* Calif.: North Atlantic Books, 2014.

Karll Sunni, *Conceiving Souls of Magnificence,* Sunni Karll, 2017.

Kolesar Natacha, *Prenatal Education. Brochure in the series of "Know Thyself",* I.D.E.A.L. Society, 2004.

Kolesar Natacha, *Qu'est-ce que l'Âme, Conference, Ideal Society.*

Linn Sheila Fabricant. *Emerson William. Linn, Dennis, Linn Matthew, Remembering Our Home, Healing Hurts & Receiving Gifts from Conception to Birth,* New Jersey: Paulist Press, 1999.

Luminare-Rosen Carista, Ph.D, *Parenting Begins Before Conception, A guide to preparing body, mind, and spirit for you and your future child.* Healing Art Press, 2000.

McCarthy Wendy Anne, PhD, RN, *Welcoming Consciousness, Supporting Babies' Wholeness From The Beginning of Life,* Calif.: Wondrous Beginnings Publ, 2012.

Menzam-Sills Cherionna, *Spirit into Form, Exploring Embryological Potential & Prenatal Psychology,* Cosmoanelixis, 2021.

Nathanielsz Peter, MD, PhD, *Life in the Womb, the Origin of Health and Disease,* N.Y. Promethean Press, 1999.

Odent Michel, *Primal Health: Understanding the Critical Period Between Conception and the First Birthday,* London: Clearview Books, 2007.

Paul Annie Murphy, *Origins, How the Nine Months Before Birth Shape the Rest of Our Lives,* N.Y. Free Press, 2010.

Romm Aviva Jill, *The Natural Pregnancy Book. Herbs, Nutrition and other Holistic Choices,* Canada: Celestial Arts, 2003.

Tomatis A.A., *La Nuit Utérine,* Ed. Stock, 1993.

Verny Thomas, Kelly John, *The Secret Life of the Unborn Child,* New York: Dell, 1986.

Verny Thomas, M.D, *Weintraub Pamela. Pre-Parenting. Nurturing your child from conception,* N.Y.: Simon & Schuster, 2003.

Weed, Susan, *The Wisewoman Herbal for the Childbearing Year,* N.Y.: Ash Tree Publishing, 1986.

Weinstein Ann Diamond, *Prenatal Development and Parent's Lived Experiences, How Early Events Shape our Psychophysiology and Relationships,* NY: W.W. Norton & Co, 2016.

Metaphysical Approach and the Soul

Barnett Lisa, *Your Soul Has a Plan, Awaken to Your Life Purpose through Your Akashic Records,* FL: Haniel Press, 2023.

Braden Gregg, *The Divine Matrix: Bridging Time, Space, Miracles and Belief,* USA: Hay House Inc., 2008.

Carman Elizabeth and Carman Neil, Cosmic Cradle, *Spiritual Dimensions of Life Before Birth,* Calif: North Atlantic Books, 2013.

Chang Penny, *Conversations from the Womb, Communicating with Your Baby During Pregnancy and Before Conception,* VA: Healing Heart Press, 2012.

Hallett Elisabeth, *Stories Of the Unborn Soul, the Mystery and Delight of Pre-Birth Communication,* N.Y. Writers Club Press, 2002.

Head Joseph, Cranston S.L., *Reincarnation, the Phoenix Fire Mystery,* N.Y.: Julian Press/Crown Publishers, 1977.

Hodson Geoffrey, *The Miracle of Birth,* The Theosophical Publishing House, 1981.

Lipton Bruce, *Biology of Belief, Unleashing the Power of Consciousness, Matter and Miracles,* Hay House Inc, 2016. Lipton, Bruce, *The wisdom of your cells: How your Beliefs Control your Biology,* Boulder: Sounds True, 2006.

Makichen Walter, *Spirit Babies, How to Communicate with the Child You're Meant to Have,* Delta Trade Paperbacks, 2005.

McTaggart Lynne, *The Field, The Quest for the Secret Force of The Universe,* N.Y.: HarperCollins Publishers, 2008.

Newton Michael PhD, *Destiny of Souls, New Case Studies of Life Between Lives,* MN: Llewellyn Publications, 2000.

Ouellet Sylvie, *Bienvenue sur Terre!, Accueillir, Comprendre et Accompagner l'Âme dans le Processus d'Incarnation, Québec,* Le Dauphin Blanc, 2008.

Pert, Candace. *Molecules Of Emotion: The Science Behind Mind-Body,* N.Y: Simon & Schuster. 1999.

Powell A. E., *Le Double Éthérique,* Paris: Ed. Adyar, 1993. Powell A. E., *Le Corps Astral,* Paris: Ed. Adyar, 1994.

Powell A. E., *Le Corps Mental,* Paris: Ed. Adyar, 1993. Powell A. E., *Le Corps Causal,* Paris: Ed. Adyar, 1990.

Rinpoche Namghyal, *The Womb, Karma and Transcendence, A Journey Towards Liberation,* Ont: Bodhi Publishing, 1996.

Schwartz Robert, *Courageous Souls, Do We Plan Our Life Challenges Before Birth?* USA: Whispering Winds Press, 2007

Todeschi Kevin, *Edgar Cayce on the Akashic Records, The Book of Life,* Virginia, A.R.E. Press, 2012.

Wise Anna, M.D., *Awakening the Mind, A Guide to Mastering the Power of Your Brainwaves,* N.Y. Jeremy P. Tarcher/Putnam, 2002.

Zukav Gary, *The Seat of the Soul,* N.Y. Simon & Schuster Paperbacks, 2014.

Birth and Early Parenting

Brott Armin, *The New Father, A Dad's Guide to the First Year,* N.Y.: Abbeville Press, 1997.

Buckley Sarah, MD, *Gentle Birth, Gentle Mothering, A Doctor's Guide to Natural Childbirth and Gentle Early Parenting Choices,* Calif.: Celestial Arts, 2009.

Cozolino Louis, *The Neuroscience of Human Relationships, Attachment and the Developing Brain,* N.Y. W.W. Norton & Co, 2006.

Davis Elisabeth, *Pascali Bonaro Debra, Orgasmic Birth, Your Guide to a Safe, Satisfying, and Pleasurable Birth Experience,* PA: Rodale, 2010.

Davis-Floyd Robbie, *Barclay Lesley, Daviss Betty-Anne, Tritten Jan, Birth Models That Work,* University of California Press, 2009.

Davis-Floyd Robbie, *Birth as an American Rite of Passage,* University of California Press, 2003.

England Pam, *Ancient Map for Modern Birth, Preparation, Passage and Personal Growth during Your Childbearing Year,* NM: Seven Gates Media, 2017.

England Pam, Horowitz Rob, *Birthing From Within, An Extra- Ordinary Guide to Childbirth Preparation,* AU: Partera Press, 1998.

Gabriel Cynthia, *Natural Hospital Birth, The Best of Both Worlds,* MA: The Harvard Common Press, 2011.

Gaskin Ina May, *Ina May's Guide to Childbirth,* N.Y.: Bantam Dell, 2003.

Gaskin Ina May, *Spiritual Midwifery,* LA: The Book Publishing Company, 1990.

Goer Henci, *The Thinking Woman's Guide to a Better Birth,* N.Y.: The Berkely Publishing Group, 1999.

Grille Robin, *Parenting for a Peaceful World,* AU: Longueville Media, 2015.

Karll Sunni, *Sacred Birthing, Birthing a New Humanity,* Canada: Trafford Publishing, 2003.

Montaud Bernard, *L'Accompagnement de la Naissance,* FR : Ed. EDIT'AS, 1997.

Odent Michel, *Birth and Breastfeeding,* US: Greenwood Publishing Group, 2012.

Odent Michel, *Birth Reborn,* AR: Birth Works, 1994.

Odent Michel, *Childbirth and the Evolution of Homo Sapiens,* London: Pinter & Martin, 2014.

Odent Michel, *Childbirth and the Future of Homo Sapiens,* London: Pinter & Martin, 2013.

Odent Michel, *The Scientification of Love,* London: Free Association Books, 2001.

Placksin Sally, *Mothering the New Mother, Women's Feelings and Needs after Childbirth,* N.Y.: New Market Press, 2000.

ACKNOWLEDGEMENTS

The writing of this book is a result of abundant life teachings and life experiences, although many words came not from me but through me. These insights came into being because I was helped by several accomplished teachers on the level of health, psychology, and spirituality.

I would like to express my gratitude for the ever-revealing truths coming from the source of their wisdom and insights. I want to thank wholeheartedly all of them, but especially Omraam Mikhaël Aïvanhov, Natacha Kolesar and many other wisdom keepers like dr. Claude Imbert, Pam England, Brandon Bays and Lisa Barnett who have been the bringers of transformation and insight in my life, along with many more.

I have lots of gratitude for all my clients who have accepted to contribute to this book through the stories of their transformation.

I give thanks to the people who helped me through the publication of this book, through their encouragement or direct support.

For more information on my work:

www.christinawarmenbol.com

www.lightstepsforyou.com

www.akashicsoulwisdom.net

More Websites Resources:

www.idealsociety.org/wellness

www.seedsofhappiness.ca

www.prenatalalliance.org/

www.facebook.com/OMAEPong

www.APPPAH.com

www.ISPPM.ngo

www.ingramcontent.com/pod-product-compliance
Lightning Source LLC
Chambersburg PA
CBHW050457160726
48003CB00001B/57